$IX-
FIGURE
FREELANCING

The Writer's Guide
to Making More Money

Kelly James-Enger

Random House Reference

New York Toronto London Sydney Auckland

Six-Figure Freelancing: The Writer's Guide to Making More Money

Please address inquiries about electronic licensing of reference products for use on a network, in software, or on CD-ROM to the Subsidiary Rights Department, Random House Reference, fax 212-572-6003.

This book is available for special discounts for bulk purchases for sales promotions or premiums. Special editions, including personalized covers, excerpts of existing books, and corporate imprints, can be created in large quantities for special needs. For more information, write to Random House, Inc., Special Markets/Premium Sales, 1745 Broadway, MD 6-2, New York, NY 10019, or e-mail specialmarkets@randomhouse.com.

Visit the Random House Web site: *www.randomhouse.com*

Library of Congress Cataloging-in-Publication Data is available.

First Edition

0 9 8 7 6 5 4 3

ISBN: 0-375-72095-2

To Erik, my true companion

Contents

Acknowledgments vii
Introduction ix

Section 1: Mind-Set 1

1 You're in Business Now, Baby:
   Getting Your Head Straight 2

2 The Full-Time Freelancer:
   Are You Determined Enough to Take the Leap? 15

3 Laying the Groundwork:
   Your Office Needs, At a Minimum 45

4 Boosting Your Bottom Line:
   Planning—and Negotiating—for More Money 69

5 Think Business, Not Hobby:
   The Armchair Accountant 95

Section 2: Efficiency 107

6 No Need to Re-create the Wheel:
   Designing Effective Writing Templates 108

7 No More One-Story Sales:
   Getting More out of Everything You Write 152

8 Watching the Clock:
   Time Management Techniques for Every Writer 180

Section 3: Connections 215

9 The Low-Maintenance Writer:
   Make Editors and Clients Love You 216

10 The Members of Your Team:
    Working with Agents, Experts, and Other Writers 237

11 Where Do You Want to Go?
    Your Writing Career Now—and in the Future 265

Get in Touch 289
Appendix 290
Index 297

Acknowledgments

Freelancers may work alone, but if they're lucky, they have a number of people supporting them behind the scenes. I thank my agent, Laurie Harper, and my editor, Jena Pincott, both of whom helped bring this book into existence.

Thanks also to my fellow six-figure freelancers who graciously gave me their time and enriched this book with their experiences, advice, and strategies: Beverly Bachel, Peter Bowerman, Andrea King Collier, Lisa Collier Cool, Sondra Forsyth, Karen Frankel, Sam Greengard, Tim Harper, Leah Ingram, Jennifer Lawler, Margaret Littman, Robert McGarvey, Victoria Moran, Jim Morrison, Brian O'Connell, Jennifer Pirtle, Erik Sherman, Jim Thornton, Sarah Wernick, and Terry Whalin. Thanks also to freelancers/tax experts Joe Anthony and Julian Block for the insights they shared that appear in chapter 5.

My sincere appreciation to the wonderful staff at the Downers Grove Public Library, who have made my job easier dozens of times, and to my friends and family, especially Cindy, Abby, my parents, Andrew, Mark, and my Solid Gold Sister, Steph. And finally, thanks to Erik, who was here at the beginning of my freelance career and to whom I owe much of my professional success, as well as my happiness. I couldn't have done it—and couldn't do it—without you.

Introduction

Last year I was asked to speak on a panel on six-figure free-lancing at the 2004 American Society of Journalists and Authors Writers Conference. I agreed, and then discovered I had a mere twelve minutes to compress more than six years' of full-time writing experience into simple, practical tips that attendees could use in their own writing careers to work more efficiently—and more lucratively. How could I possibly cram everything into my speech? Fortunately, I realized that the strategies I had employed over the years to grow my business from $17,000 my first year to more than $100,000 my sixth came down to three simple ideas: having a business mind-set, working as efficiently as possible, and making and sustaining all-important connections with editors, clients, experts, agents, and other writers.

Mind-set. Efficiency. Connections. That's how I've built my freelance business. I started with no journalism background, no connections in the publishing world, and no experience. I learned along the way and began employing strategies that help me maximize my time and fatten my wallet in the meantime. When I began teaching writing classes and speaking at writers' conferences throughout the country, I discovered that many freelancers were unaware of these kinds of techniques. They knew plenty about how to write, how to overcome writer's anxiety, and maybe even how to pitch their work. But they didn't grasp the importance of taking a businesslike approach to their writing, identifying ways that they could produce more work in less time, and creating and maintaining relationships with clients and colleagues.

That's why I wrote this book. I know what it takes to start

and operate a successful freelancing business, and in the pages that follow, you'll learn the secrets I and other writers have had to figure out the hard way. Take your writing business from so-so to six-figure by employing the mind-set, efficiency, and connections strategies set forth in the pages that follow.

Section 1
Mind-Set

CHAPTER 1
You're in Business Now, Baby: Getting Your Head Straight

I believe all writers fall into two categories: writers who simply want to write and those who want to make money doing it.

There's nothing wrong if you claim membership in the former group. I wrote for years because I felt compelled to, churning out a lot of bad poetry and so-so short stories. Writing gave me a satisfaction nothing else did. But when I decided to quit my full-time job as a lawyer and try to make a go of freelancing full time, I knew that meant changing my attitude as well as the type of writing I did. I'd already discovered that the markets for short fiction were few and far between. All magazines published lots of nonfiction articles, however, so I decided to take my writing career in a (hopefully) more lucrative direction.

During my first few months as a full-time freelancer, I read every book on writing, self-employment, and marketing I could get my hands on. With the help of my techie boyfriend's advice, I outfitted my office, created letterhead, and began publicizing my services. I learned which business-related expenses were legitimate tax deductions, how to track income and expenses by categories, and how to manage my workload.

Sure, I'd been writing short stories for years (that, strangely enough, usually featured unhappy female lawyers), but I had little practical experience when it came to nonfiction articles. I had to learn how to write features, profiles, roundups, and service articles for magazines. I wrote short front-of-book articles, 2,500-word features, and everything in between. I learned how to analyze markets, pitch attention-getting queries, and set myself apart from other writers. I expanded into writing for businesses and worked for corporations, nonprofit organizations, ad agencies, and small companies. And along the way, I learned how to write ad copy, brochures, press releases, newsletters, annual reports, and even books.

I was amazed to discover that I could in fact make a decent living as a freelancer. Within three years, I was making as much as I did as a lawyer—admittedly an underpaid one. By my sixth year, I made more than twice as much as I ever did as an attorney—with no need for suits, pumps, and pantyhose. Yet, today I work less than I did eight years ago, when I started freelancing, and still produce a comfortable living.

I'm not a genius. I'm not a workaholic and, truth be told, I'm not even an exceptional writer. There are probably millions of writers out there who are more talented, more creative, and more gifted than me. But unlike many of them, I've figured out how to run my writing business—and it is a business. It wasn't talent that transformed me into a six-figure freelancer. It was my attitude, my approach to my writing career, and my drive to succeed.

The Business Mind-Set

If you want to make money as a freelancer, stop thinking of yourself as a writer first. Instead, consider yourself a self-employed businessperson—whose business happens to be writing. That means you're no longer writing purely for satisfaction. Now you're writing for money. That simple fact is a major mind-set change for most freelancers.

But every writer is different. Only *you* know your motivations for turning what has primarily been a pleasurable activity into a moneymaking venture. Maybe you think that writing for money will make you a "real" writer. Or you'd like the satisfaction of seeing checks for your hard work. Or you'd like to produce additional income from your writing. Or maybe you're freelancing full time already but you'd like to make more from your writing (and who wouldn't?).

So, take a few moments and think about money. How important is it to you? Are you happy with the amount you make from your writing? (My guess is no, since you're reading this book.) How much do you want to make? How much do you *need* to make? Why? What are your expenses? Are you living within your means, or do you scrabble by, paycheck to paycheck?

I know we don't talk openly about money in our culture, but you don't have to share these thoughts with anyone. Thinking about money is simply a way to help you start thinking of your writing not only as something that you enjoy doing, but also as something that produces income. This doesn't mean you can't continue to write for yourself or for causes you believe in for free. It does mean embracing the fact that your writing has value.

If you want to make more as a freelancer, you first have to determine where you are now—and then decide on the direction in which to take your writing career. Take a few minutes to answer the following questions—I've given you room to make plenty of notes.

Your Money Mind-Set

What are the reasons you write? (list all that apply—these could be anything from creative satisfaction, to producing income, to the delight of seeing your name in print)

_____

_____

_____

What types of writing are you doing? (e.g., articles, books, copywriting)

_____

_____

_____

What subjects are you writing about?

_____

_____

What markets/clients are you writing for?

_____

_____

What subjects/topics do you have specialized knowledge of/experience with?

_____

_____

_____

The $64,000 question: Are you making money freelancing?

_____

How much? (shhh . . . I won't tell)

_____

Is this more or less than you've made from your writing in the past?

_____

If the amount has changed, why is that? (e.g., you've lost markets or you're spending more time pitching than you have in the past)

_____

_____

_____

Where does most of your income come from? Is it from many clients or just a few?

_____

_____

_____

How much do you *want* to make?

_____

Let me say something about the last question—how much you want to make. It's fine to say you *want* to make $300,000 a year, but is that realistic if you're making $15,000 a year now? Probably not. But you should have a goal to shoot for—a realistic but attainable goal.

When I started freelancing full time in 1997, I never dreamed I'd be able to make a six-figure income as a writer. In fact, my financial goal that first year was modest: to make $10,000 a year. To date, I can't remember just why I picked $10,000. It seemed like a nice, neat, round number. I had no experience and no idea of what to expect during my first year of freelancing, but simply setting this goal helped remind me that I was now writing as a living, not as a hobby. Every assignment I took should be moving me closer toward that goal of $10,000—meaning that every assignment should pay, even if only a little.

The first year was definitely the roughest. But by the beginning of my second, I had a couple of steady clients—a trade publication and a local hospital—and was starting to get more magazine work. I set a new annual financial goal of $30,000. My third year, I considered what I'd made the year before and the amount of work I thought I could handle, and readjusted my goals upward to reflect that. Over the years, that process continued—at the end of each year, I'd revisit my current income and financial status, set my writing goals for the coming year, and choose a financial goal that reflected those priorities.

You may have set goals for yourself as a writer—to be published in a major magazine or to finish your novel—but have you set financial goals as well? Consider the work you're currently doing and how much time you spend writing, and pick a dollar amount to aim for—and then break this amount down into monthly, weekly, and daily goals.

For example, during my fourth year of freelancing, my goal was to make $60,000 freelancing full time. At first blush, this number might seem daunting, but when I broke it down (assuming that I'd work 240 days out of the year—that's Mondays through Fridays, with four weeks off for holidays and vacations), it came to $5,000 a month, or $250 a day. Instead of trying to make $60,000, I focused on producing $250 worth of work each day—and then I tracked my progress. As long as I met my daily goals, I'd achieve my annual income goal as well. I'll show you how to apply this strategy to your own writing career in chapter 3.

Making the Most of Your Background

When you approach your writing as a business, one of the first illusions to fall by the wayside is that you're only going to write about:

1. Topics that interest you
2. Topics you care about

3. Topics that make a difference in the world
4. All of the above

This is a common misconception I encounter when I tell people that I'm a freelancer. I hear things like, "How wonderful! So you can just write about whatever you feel like and get paid for it!"

Um, no. Sure, I occasionally write articles about subjects I find fascinating—like hypnosis, for example. I've been fortunate to pen work that may actually have a positive impact on readers' lives, like a story I did for *Redbook* a few years ago on the health benefits of taking oral contraceptives continuously. And sometimes I get to take assignments that are just plain fun or that pay off in other ways. I did a big feature on "chick lit" (books aimed at young women, like *Bridget Jones' Diary* and *The Devil Wears Prada*) last year that gave me the opportunity to interview some top agents and editors—and I just happen to write chick lit on the side myself.

But the majority of the time, I'm working on projects I don't necessarily find fascinating—like writing the copy for an advertisement about which HMOs a local hospital accepted. But that's part of the gig when you write full time. I was doing a lot of work for this client—a small rural hospital—and I wasn't about to say, "Thanks, but this assignment sounds a little too boring for me to take on."

I'm not saying you must take on work you detest. But if you're going to make a living as a freelancer, you need to accept that plenty of what you write isn't going to thrill you the way working on your novel or screenplay or personal essay will.

With this no-nonsense, businesslike approach in mind, take a look at where you are now in your freelance career. What kinds of subjects do you already know about? What industries are you familiar with? What hobbies or interests do you enjoy? What types of personal connections do you have?

Every writer has a unique background, life experience, and set of skills. Start figuring out what yours are and how to maximize them.

In my case, I started writing for women's magazines because there were a lot of them, they paid well, and I am a woman. I'd been a runner for years, and was interested in nutrition and women's health issues as well, so it's not surprising many of my early articles covered these kinds of topics. I used my legal background to pitch business stories early on, and I wrote a lot of bridal stories early in my writing career because I was planning a wedding. If I'd been a parent, a scuba diver, or an engineer, I'd no doubt have pitched stories that grew out of those experiences. You don't have to start out writing about subjects you're already familiar with, but probing your life experience and knowledge for potential ideas—and markets—saves you time pitching and researching articles. I've also found that having firsthand experience with a subject makes it more likely for an editor to give you an assignment, which is critical when you're starting out.

The Importance of Your Mind-Set

If you're new to the writing business, let me help you overcome the stereotype about freelance writers. Many people think of self-employed writers as:

- Disorganized
- Unprofessional
- Creative
- Unconcerned about money
- Difficult
- Angst-ridden
- Naive
- Distracted

- Sexy, wonderful, charming, intelligent people (Oops! That's what *I* think of self-employed writers.)

You, on the other hand, will shatter the stereotype. You will present yourself as a smart, savvy, business-oriented professional. Yes, you can still be creative. Yes, you can still be deep. You can even still work in your pajamas. But starting with your perception of yourself—and just as importantly, to the world at large—you're going to embrace the mind-set of success.

One of my favorite benefits of freelancing is that you can forget about dress codes. Now you wear pretty much anything you want to. When I practiced law, I was in court nearly every day, and I usually wore a suit. I hated it. As soon I walked in the door at home, I peeled off my jacket, blouse, skirt, pantyhose, and heels, and slipped into sweats, an old T-shirt, and thick fluffy socks.

Now that I freelance full time, pantyhose are a thing of the past. I usually wear overalls, jeans, or yes, pajamas when I work. If I'm on deadline, I may not even take a shower and get dressed until late afternoon . . . or not at all. It's a luxury I appreciate.

But when I have a meeting with a client out of the office, or attend a writers' conference, I dig in my closet and pull out my "grown-up clothes." For me, that usually means tailored pants, a nice blouse, and possibly a jacket. I wear makeup and take my hair out of its usual messy ponytail. Why bother? Because my professional image is an important part of selling my skills whether I'm pitching a project or speaking about how to succeed as a freelancer.

Writers often focus on the words they sell and don't worry about how they come off to clients. I think that's a huge mistake. Your demeanor and attitude can mean the difference between scraping by as a freelancer and making a good living. That fact was drummed into my head as I spent several months interviewing other successful six-figure freelancers for this book. Some had only been writing full time for a few years; others have weathered more than twenty years in a highly competitive business—and continue to thrive. Some write for corporations; some focus on writing books; others make the majority of their income from magazine articles. They write about subjects ranging from biotechnology, to investing, to golf, to dog-friendly businesses, to martial arts. Some maintain speaking and consulting careers in addition to freelancing; others are more comfortable behind their desks. But despite their differences, they have many things in common.

Although racked with self-doubt at times, they have all learned to project confidence. When facing a changing business environment, they were able—and willing—to adapt, to grow, to learn new skills and pursue new opportunities. While they didn't toil for clients who refused to pay them what their work was worth, they were committed to working long hours if that's what was necessary to launch and maintain their businesses.

Erik Sherman, who's been freelancing full time since February 1996, believes his willingness to work harder than most writers is the key to his success as a six-figure freelancer. "I have an extremely strong work ethic. I do not roll my eyes if I have to work fifty hours [a week]," says Sherman, who's based in Marshfield, Massachusetts. "I will work seventy or eighty hours a week. I'm the sole support for a family of four. Look at freelancing as a business. If you own a small business, you're going to be working a lot of hours to really make it. . . . In my view, if you're coming in and you don't have connections, you have to work your rear off [to succeed]."

Sherman makes an important point that many would-be writers would choose to ignore. Yes, your attitude is important, as is having the essential tools at hand to run your writing business. (We'll cover what you need in chapter 3.) But don't forget your mind-set and office setup can only take you so far. It's your work habits (or, sadly, lack of same) that will largely determine your success as a freelancer. Consider this: one of my first clients was an editor at *Fit* magazine. When assigning my fourth piece, she commented on the fact that she knew I'd make my deadline. "That's so great!" she said. "You're one of the only writers I know who always turns stuff in on time."

To me, that's a no-brainer. But many writers don't treat deadlines seriously—if they meet one, fine; if not, no big deal. If you're a big-name writer, you can get away with blowing a few deadlines. If not, you can't. Start researching a story as soon as it's assigned; if you can tell that you're going to need more time to finish a piece (say, one of your critical sources is unavailable until after the piece is due), talk to your editor immediately. Ask for an extension so she can plan for the late story. The *worst* thing you can do is simply not turn it in, and then dodge your editor who's wondering where the story is.

Good writing skills are not enough to be successful in this competitive business. To get and keep clients, you must also think of yourself not only as a writer, but also as a self-employed business owner who will make your customers happy. We'll talk more about that in chapter 9, but at a minimum, that means:

- Being pleasant to work with. If an editor asks for last-minute revisions, I don't complain about the short notice—I do them immediately to help make her job easier. An editor trying to close an issue has plenty on her mind already; she wants to work with writers she knows won't give her a hard time.
- Being able to argue without getting nasty. There will be instances in which you disagree with your editor or client about how to word something, or argue over a contractual provision. You don't have to be a jellyfish, but you can disagree respectfully and thus maintain your relationship.

- Delivering what you promise. This goes beyond meeting the deadline. It means that you turn in a story that meets your client's specifications as closely as you can. If she wants 1,500 words and two sidebars, that's what you write—not 2,000 words, figuring that she can cut it down.
- Honoring your commitments. If you've arranged an interview with a source at 4:30 P.M., call at 4:30, not at 5:00 P.M. If someone asks you to let him know when a story runs, do it. This enhances not only your reputation, but also that of the client you're working for. If you're on assignment for *Woman's Day*, for example, you're also representing that magazine to the people you come into contact with.

Unfortunately, writers sometimes have the reputation of being disorganized, distracted creative types who can't be counted on in a pinch. You can overcome that impression by always presenting yourself as a professional. Treat your writing as serious business and others will, too.

Remember that you can be professional and personable at the same time. Nearly all of the successful writers I interviewed for this book mentioned the importance of developing and maintaining cordial relationships with clients. Yet, they're businesslike when it comes to issues like negotiating contracts, asking for more money, and standing up for themselves. They're resilient. They're smart. And they're extremely motivating to speak to. When asked about their strategies for success, nearly every one mentioned that you have to be confident. You have to believe that you can do this. You have to have faith in yourself and your abilities.

When I started freelancing, I wouldn't have dreamed of making $100,000 a year. I really didn't even believe that I could make $10,000. I was unprepared, inexperienced, and full of doubt. But I did have a lot of energy, enthusiasm, and hope, and I knew I could learn what I didn't know. Over the months and years, I improved my marketing and writing skills and developed confidence in my abilities. Every obstacle I encountered and overcame helped build my faith in myself as a self-employed writer. I became successful because I *believed* I could become successful.

You can, too. *Believing* that you can is the first step.

CHAPTER 2
The Full-Time Freelancer: Are You Determined Enough to Take the Leap?

I f you're currently freelancing part time, you've probably considered—or fantasized about—ditching your day job and going full time. What stops many writers from taking the leap is the fear that they won't succeed as full-time freelancers. After all, the statistics can be disheartening—at least the ones you can find. There aren't many numbers floating around about what writers make, but according to a survey conducted by the National Writers Union in 1995, a mere 16 percent of full-time freelancers make more than $30,000 a year.

Before you toss this book in disgust, realize that this depressing figure belies your potential income as a freelancer. Plenty of writers make $50,000 annually, and a smaller percentage make six-figure incomes. In fact, according to a 2003 survey of 369 members of the American Society of Journalists and Authors, 41 percent make more than $50,000 a year, including 12 percent who make more than $100,000 annually.

If you're not making this kind of money, take heart. The writers who make a good living—say, $50,000 a year and up—may not be better writers than you. But I'm willing to bet they're more efficient writers than you are. They may have better marketing skills than you do. They may be able to develop and maintain relationships with clients more effectively than you do. But these are skills that can be learned. Master them and you too can make a six-figure living as a full-time freelancer.

That being said, freelancing full time isn't for the faint-hearted or easily distracted. If you're already employed, you give up the security of regular paychecks, paid benefits, pension plans, vacations, and sick days for the feast-or-famine lifestyle of a freelancer. If you're a stay-at-home parent trying to juggle freelancing and your family, you may have to reduce the time you spend with your children to focus on building and maintaining your writing career.

The majority of freelancers start out as part-time writers, building their portfolios, amassing clips, and gaining experience before they take the leap to freelancing full time. But making that decision—to cut all ties with your "real" job—can be a harrowing one. How do you know when you're ready to do it? How can you even be sure that freelancing is right for you? How can you prepare for this transition—and ensure that it goes as smoothly as possible?

First, you'll need some kind of financial bumper. When I quit my job as a lawyer to freelance full time, I had saved enough money to cover six months of living expenses. I'd also paid off my credit card debt and reduced my living expenses as much as possible, although I still had a car payment and student loans to keep up on. While I did realize it would take some time before I had steady income rolling in, I underestimated how long it would take me to get paid—and consequently the amount of savings I needed.

Consider this scenario: You send a query out in January. The editor likes the idea and calls to assign it in March with an April deadline. You turn in the story on time and then wait a couple of weeks to hear from her. She asks for some revisions to the piece; you comply and turn in the final version in May. She e-mails you a week later to tell you that the story has been accepted and that she's putting payment through. Great! Now you only have to wait another four to six weeks before you receive your check. In the meantime, you still have to pay your rent, your car insurance, your mounting phone bills, and the pizza delivery boy.

Keep in mind this scenario assumes that your idea sold on the first try rather than the second, third, or fourth. Early in your freelance career, you're likely to spend more time *marketing* yourself than actually writing—and that marketing time doesn't pay off until you actually get an assignment. That's one of the reasons why, if you're considering freelancing full time and are wholly or partially responsible for supporting yourself or anyone else, you need to have enough money saved to cover expenses while you build your business.

The amount I'd saved before I ditched my legal career—six months' worth of living expenses—may seem like a lot. In reality, it may not be enough for you. I know that in retrospect, I would have saved more money. As it was, my savings had dwindled to $111 by the time checks started trickling in . . . and I was applying for part-time jobs to pay the bills when I finally received a check for $3,000 for a big project that saved my full-time freelance career. I could have avoided a lot of stress and anxiety if I had saved a little more money *before* I quit my day job. We'll cover how to figure out how much to save later in this chapter.

The Loneliness of the Full-Time Freelancer

While fantasizing about it may be common, freelancing full time isn't for every writer. Many writers love the freedom and the ability to set their own hours, but others find the constant marketing most freelancers must do to be a draining experience—and wind up back on staff in a year or two. The unpredictability and isolation of freelancing can depress even the most go-getting of writers.

My prior career as a lawyer meant that my days had been filled with phone calls, court appearances, depositions, meetings, and conferences. I could count on human contact—sometimes more than I wanted—every day. And I was never alone. If I was having a problem with a client or struggling to write a brief, I could walk down the hall and stop in a fellow lawyer's office for a brainstorming session. When I was ready for a break, I had an office full of lunch mates and after-work-drinks-and-darts buddies to choose from. I took this all for granted.

I hadn't realized the extent of the social contact I enjoyed through my job until I started freelancing full time. Sure, there were days when it was great not to have to interact with anyone. No more meaningless meetings. No more command-performance office parties or sucking up to the partners. But most of the time, I felt isolated in the extreme.

Part of this was due to the unique circumstances I was in. After having a long-distance relationship, I'd recently relocated to move in with my boyfriend, Erik. We lived in a small town, and other than the lawyers I'd worked with and a friend who lived thirty minutes away, I knew no one else locally except my boyfriend's family. It could have been worse; I did have a fuzzy golden retriever puppy who was delighted I was home to play with her all day, and she would cock her head when I spoke to her, giving me at least the illusion of two-way conversation.

I took to falling on Erik as soon as he walked in the door at night like a blood-hungry tick, starved for news of the outside world. "How was your day? Did anything exciting happen? Who'd you talk to? Hear any new jokes? What was work like?" After eight or ten hours of dealing with computer network problems, the last thing Erik wanted was to have to amuse me with entertaining stories from his job. After a few weeks, we both realized that I needed to incorporate some human contact into my regular schedule or neither my freelance career—nor our relationship—would survive.

For me, the solution took several forms. I joined writing-related e-mail lists and newsgroups and began to correspond with other freelancers online. I attended a local writers' conference, where I made several new friends. And I started teaching magazine-writing classes, where I met other local writers. Today, I have a network of in-person and online writing buddies that has made a huge impact on both my job satisfaction and my personal happiness. As an extrovert in an introvert's job, I look for ways that I can add more social and professional contact into my week—the stimulation is always worth the time away from my desk.

As a full-time freelancer, you'll be spending the majority of your time alone. When I'm busy, that doesn't bother me. But the bad days seem magnified when you work alone. Most days, I love my job, but there are some (happily, not many) days when freelancing, quite simply, sucks. I'm trying to get in touch with an expert I need to interview for a story and he's unavailable. I find out an editor wants significant revisions on an article I turned in two months ago—by tomorrow. I have to write about a subject that I don't find interesting, and the words just aren't flowing the way they sometimes do. I'm bored or lonely or craving outside stimulation, but am trapped in my nine-by-ten-foot office with no opportunity for human contact unless you count the UPS man.

The Successful Freelancer's Mind-Set

But despite these occasional challenges, I enjoy my work. Freelancing full time has spoiled me—I can't imagine anything I'd rather do more. Sure, to succeed as a self-employed writer you have to approach your work as a business. But don't overlook the emotional aspects of freelancing. Over the years, I've met hundreds of successful freelancers—including many who make six-figure incomes—and have found that they have a number of personality characteristics in common. I'm generalizing, of course, but nearly all share the same traits:

- Ability to prioritize tasks and manage their time
- Self-direction—meaning they don't need a "boss" standing over their shoulders to make them work
- Businesslike approach to their writing careers
- An interest in the world (if you're not interested, how will you make a living researching and writing about subjects you may not care to know anything about?)
- An aggressive nature when it comes to marketing themselves
- Commitment to producing work that will please editors and clients
- Flexibility and ability to learn new skills and adapt to changes in the market
- Ability to develop relationships with editors and other clients
- Confidence in their abilities and a positive attitude toward their writing careers

What am I forgetting? Oh, *and* they all have decent writing skills. Some are good writers, some are great writers. But despite what you may believe, exceptional writing ability isn't a requirement for successful freelancing—even six-figure freelancing. Being able to motivate yourself, to manage your time, to develop a sense for what an editor wants, and then be able to deliver it by deadline are all more important than outstanding writing skills.

Besides, you can always improve your writing skills just as you can become a more aggressive marketer and a faster researcher. Your personality, however, is less likely to change, and it will influence your chances of enjoying—and succeeding at—a full-time freelance career to a large degree. If you're an extrovert who can't stand being alone, you're going to find it more difficult to freelance than if you cherish the opportunity to be by yourself most of the day. If you get frustrated easily waiting for people to get back to you, slow responses from editors may drive you bonkers. And if you stress easily about money, waiting for checks may only add to the pressure you feel.

As a magazine writer, I've written slews of quizzes ranging from "What's your workout personality?" to "What's the right birth control for you?" If you're thinking about/considering/ruminating over/dreaming of full-time freelancing, take a closer look at whether it's a good fit for you by answering (honestly) these questions:

1. In your ideal job, you'd work:
   a. alone.
   b. alone part of the time and with others part of the time.
   c. with groups of people.

2. You slaved for months over a profile that just appeared in a national magazine. How likely are you to let people know about your latest clips?
   a. Very likely—you're proud of your work.
   b. Somewhat likely—depending on whom you're talking to.
   c. Not very likely—you don't like to toot your own horn.

3. How would you describe your organizational skills?
   a. There's a place for everything and everything is in its place.
   b. I know where important documents are, but tend to make piles to be sorted through later.
   c. Organizational skills? What are those?

4. You're working for an editor for the first time, and it looks like you may not meet your deadline. You:

    a. sacrifice sleep to finish the story and turn it in on time.
    b. call the editor a week before the deadline and ask for an extension.
    c. figure it's no big deal and turn in the story a few days late.

5. In general, you'd describe your spending habits as:
    a. fairly frugal.
    b. average—you spend money when you have it, but cut back when you need to.
    c. expensive—you like to have the best.

6. The current state of your savings account is:
    a. secure—you have an emergency fund set aside to cover unforeseen expenses.
    b. like most people, you live paycheck to paycheck.
    c. savings? You'll have to pay off your credit card debt before you even think of saving money.

7. How often do you like to socialize with friends and coworkers?
    a. Occasionally—I like spending time alone, too.
    b. It depends on how busy I am, but I enjoy the interaction.
    c. Frequently—I'm happiest in a group.

8. Which phrase best describes your emotional and physical health?
    a. Fit, strong, and healthy.
    b. I could get more exercise (hey, who couldn't?), but in general I'm in decent shape.
    c. I have chronic health problems.

9. What is your attitude toward stress?
    a. It's part of daily life, but I've developed ways of coping with it.
    b. It sometimes takes a toll on my emotional and physical health.
    c. It's often a real problem for me mentally or physically.

10. The idea of being your own boss makes you feel:
    a. excited about the chance to control my time and future.
    b. somewhat apprehensive.
    c. scared—I don't know if I'd be able to force myself to work on my own.

11. Which sentence best sums up your approach to selling your writing?
    a. I enjoy the pursuit of a potential new client.
    b. I accept it as a necessary part of freelancing, but I'd rather not have to do it.
    c. I have to force myself to do it. Why can't editors just come to me?

12. How stringent are you in maintaining records for your writing business?
    a. I have a system in place for tracking income, expenses, submissions, and current assignments.
    b. I keep records, but I'm not that faithful about keeping them up to date.
    c. Not at all—I hate paperwork.

How'd you do? While this isn't the Myers-Briggs of free-lancing, these questions address some of the issues full-time freelancers face. Reading and answering them should give you some clue about your marketing and organizational tendencies, your financial stability (or lack of same), your overall health, and your personality. There aren't any right or wrong answers here, but if you answered mostly As, you may be more well-suited to freelancing full time than if you mostly answered Cs. A lot of B answers, on the other hand, mean you could go either way. Think about it. I'd say that a driven, time-oriented, healthy writer who prefers working alone is a better fit for full-time freelancing than a chronically disorganized, easily distracted person who prefers the interaction and stimulation of an office environment.

Successful freelancers must be able to market themselves

and find clients, mange their time effectively, work on multiple projects simultaneously, and handle their business finances and paperwork (or hire someone to do it for them). Most are also self-directed, motivated, deadline-driven, and goal-oriented—probably not the mental picture most people have when they envision a writer at work. The perception persists that full-time writers lounge about in their sweatpants, take an hour or two to read the paper, and then jot down a few well-crafted sentences before settling in for a leisurely lunch. The reality is that freelancing full time is hard work.

Looking *Before* You Leap

Freelancing on the side while you pursue another career is a great way to produce additional income, build your portfolio, and indulge your creativity. If you're considering doing it full time, though, you have to take a businesslike approach to the decision. There's a big difference between freelancing part time because you *want* to, and freelancing full time when it's your sole source of income and you *have* to.

Before you leave behind a steady paycheck, toss aside your freelance fantasies and ask yourself some tough questions: When it comes down to it, are you self-motivated? Have you had trouble meeting deadlines at work in the past? If so, will you be able to set your own hours and work when no one's around? Does the idea of giving up a regular paycheck and the intrinsic support and human interaction a "real" job provides make you uncomfortable?

I suggest that before you make the leap, you read as much as you can about full-time freelancing (see the appendix for more resources on this subject). Seek out full-time freelancers and ask them what their days are like, how they manage their time, and the types of work they do. Joining writers' organizations and participating in online discussion lists or newsgroups can provide you with additional information to help you make the decision.

Many successful writers freelance part time for years before taking the leap to full time. Andrea King Collier had dabbled as a writer for years, but began freelancing full time in 1992 so that she could care for her mother, who had been diagnosed with ovarian cancer. "When she died, I figured out that I never wanted to go back to the grind of nine to five," says Collier, an author, freelancer, and health-care consultant based in Lansing, Michigan. Rather than focusing on one particular area, she decided at the outset of her career to keep her options open. "I decided I would be flexible and diverse," she says. "I threw a lot of spaghetti against the wall to see what would stick. I knew my income would have to come from a lot of different freelance sources."

Other writers decide to focus on a particular niche or specialty when they leave behind a corporate career in favor of one that offers more flexibility. Freelancer Brian O'Connell had worked for a trade publisher in Boston and a computer technology magazine before he began working for a professor at Harvard and freelancing on the side, writing case studies, white papers, and other pieces for corporate clients. After one more full-time gig working for a financial publisher, he opted to freelance full time beginning in January 1995.

"It was like I was walking down Fifth Avenue, and it was really crowded and hectic and that was my corporate life," says O'Connell, who's based in Doylestown, Pennsylvania. "And then I turned this corner and there was this wide-open road. There was nobody there, but there was a lot of freedom, flexibility, and fulfillment."

Other freelancers start out in publishing on the editor's side of the desk. Sondra Forsyth has been writing since she was in her twenties, as both a staffer and a freelancer. Over the years, she's worked at magazines including *Bride's*, *Cosmopolitan*, and *Ladies Home Journal*. In 1992, Forsyth decided to pursue a full-time freelance career. "I left the *Journal* because I love to write," says Forsyth, who lives in Manhattan. "I always wrote when I was on staff and I felt at that point, I was doing so much administrative work I wasn't really being creative."

While she was fueled by the desire to spend more time writing, she took a pragmatic approach to being self-employed. "I started off as a businessperson. Right off, I got disability insurance and health insurance," says Forsyth. "I thought of myself as an entrepreneur, not as a person who likes to write. I was a businesswoman as an executive editor, and now I'm a businesswoman as a writer."

Show Me the (Saved) Money

If you want to freelance full time and make a living doing it, you can't just quit your job, start looking for assignments, and hope that enough money will roll in to make your mortgage. I assume you wouldn't dream of opening a restaurant or starting your own company without doing some market research. While you can launch a freelance writing business with a minimum of equipment and investment (more about that in chapter 3), don't shortchange yourself on the necessary emotional—and financial—preparation you should make beforehand.

Question number one: How much money do you want to make? Six figures, you say? That's why you're reading this book? Fine. But the next question you should ask yourself is how much money do you *need* to make? Track your current income and expenses and determine what you'll need to live on at the beginning of your freelance career. You know what you're making now, but how much are you spending and on what? If you haven't budgeted your income and expenses, I suggest you take some time to do it now. Doing this will give you an idea of what you'll have to make as a full-time writer.

Monthly Expenses	Current	Expected
TAXES		
Federal	_____	_____
State	_____	_____
Social security	_____	_____
Local	_____	_____
Other	_____	_____
HOUSING		
Rent or mortgage/ real estate taxes	_____	_____
Renter's or homeowner's insurance	_____	_____
Utilities	_____	_____
Gas/electric	_____	_____
Water/sewer	_____	_____
Telephone	_____	_____
Repairs/ maintenance	_____	_____
Assessment	_____	_____
Other	_____	_____
AUTOMOTIVE/TRANSPORTATION		
Car payment/lease	_____	_____
Car insurance	_____	_____
Train/bus passes	_____	_____
Parking	_____	_____
Gas	_____	_____

Maintenance/repair   _____   _____

Other   _____   _____

FOOD

Groceries   _____   _____

Takeout food   _____   _____

Eating out   _____   _____

Toiletries/household
supplies   _____   _____

FAMILY

Child care   _____   _____

Children's clothing   _____   _____

Children's
entertainment/
games/toys   _____   _____

Other   _____   _____

PERSONAL

Clothing   _____   _____

Laundry/
dry cleaning   _____   _____

Movies/
theater tickets/
other entertainment   _____   _____

Other   _____   _____

INSURANCE

Health   _____   _____

Dental   _____   _____

Vision/other   _____   _____

Life _____　　　　　_____

Disability _____　　　　　_____

Other _____　　　　　_____

SAVINGS/DEBT PAYMENTS

Student loans _____　　　_____

Credit cards _____　　　_____

Personal loans _____　　　_____

Child support/
alimony _____　　　_____

Savings _____　　　_____

Support of nonprofit
organizations _____　　　_____

Other _____　　　_____

How'd you do? You may be surprised at the amount you're spending—or you may see some ways to reduce your average monthly expenses. After you've tracked your current expenses, pay special attention to the categories that will change when you begin freelancing full time. For example, if your employer currently pays your health insurance, you'll have to add that to the amount you need to make. As a freelancer, you're responsible for paying both the employer and employee portions of the tax that pays for Social Security and Medicare, which comes to 15.3 percent of your net freelance income. On the other hand, you're likely to save on commuting costs, clothing, and away-from-home food costs when you freelance from home.

However, your business expenses will increase once you start writing full time. If you've been freelancing part-time, you presumably already have the basic equipment you need, but you're probably going to spend more on office expenses like long-distance charges, postage, printer cartridges, and paper. When I was freelancing on the side, I didn't pay attention to what I spent on these things. When I started keeping track of it, I was amazed at how much I was spending to simply run my office. I hadn't anticipated these kinds of expenses—or that our utility bills and even grocery costs would be higher now that I was working at home and, yes, snacking frequently.

While I only saved six months' worth of expenses to live on when I started freelancing, I had several things going for me. Number one, I was living with my then-boyfriend in his townhouse, and he'd agreed to pay the entire mortgage while we shared the phone bill, groceries, and other expenses. In other words, I knew I'd have a roof over my head if my writing career didn't pan out.

Second, I was only responsible for myself. I was worried about failing as a full-time writer, but I wasn't supporting a child or other family members. If I couldn't make a decent living as a freelancer, I would have to take another full-time job I hated or give up on takeout pizza for a while, but I wasn't going to lose my home or go to bed hungry. If you are supporting a family, however, you need to have a safety net in place, or a spouse or partner who can pitch in if necessary.

Financially, I could have been in much worse shape. I'd managed to pay off my credit cards in the months before, and I could make small, regular payments on my student loans. My car payment was less than two hundred dollars a month. However, I was worried about health insurance—at my old job, my employer had covered me as a benefit. Because the cost of health insurance was so high, I skimped and bought a cheap policy with a huge deductible—$5,000—so I'd be covered in the case of a catastrophic accident or illness.

I figured the odds of that were slim, though. I was in good health and highly motivated. I knew that I'd be putting in long hours to get my writing business off the ground. But I was used to working at least forty to fifty hours a week as a lawyer and freelancing on the side. Five-and-a-half years as a lawyer had taught me how to juggle multiple deadlines, work with different kinds of clients, and manage my time efficiently. Even then, I had no idea of how tough the first eighteen months or so would be.

Sure, some writers launch writing careers to maximize their incomes, but your primary goals as a full-time freelancer may not be exclusively financial. Victoria Moran, a freelancer and author based in Manhattan, had lost her husband and wanted to spend more time with her young daughter when she quit her job to freelance full time. Lisa Collier Cool of Pelham, New York, also had small children when she left her previous career as a literary agent to write full time.

"My goal when I started my freelancing career was to get enough work to make a viable business of it," says Cool, who has written hundreds of magazine articles and books including the classic for magazine writers, *How to Write Irresistible Query Letters*. "I had twins who were eighteen months old and I'd previously been a literary agent. My idea was to leave the nine-to-five life and find a business I could run at home while also raising children. I wasn't looking for a big income as much as a reasonable income."

But within a few years, Cool adjusted her expectations upward. "First, after previously writing about whatever topic I thought I could sell, I did choose to specialize in primarily writing about health," says Cool. "I found after a few articles about that, I could see that there was a steady market for that type of story, and the more I did it, the more I became known for that kind of story, so people sought me out and gave me assignments. That definitely enhanced my income."

I suggest that you assume that the first few months of your freelance career will be the toughest from an income standpoint, and plan accordingly. Imagine you'll have nothing com-

ing in, at least at first. If you have a financial safety net, you'll
be able to focus more on developing relationships, building
your portfolio, and getting work, rather than on worrying
about your dwindling bank balance.

Grow Your Portfolio

When I left the law firm to freelance full time, I had two—
count 'em, two—clips. That was it. (By the way, here's a tip:
When querying magazines during that time, I would always
include the phrase "I have included two *recent* clips." Were
they recent clips? Sure. Were they also my *only* clips? That's
right—but why advertise that fact to an editor? By referring to
them as recent clips, it made it sound like I had dozens of
others but had chosen to send these two. I was a contract
lawyer in my previous life. Sometimes the way you word
something makes a big difference in the way it's perceived.)

I only had two clips to my name. I also had no journalism
background, no connections in the publishing industry, no
experience, no regular clients, and, alas, no trust fund. I had to
create my career literally from scratch, which took months—
lean months where I struggled to pay my bills while I learned
how to pitch editors, conduct research, write compelling articles, and run a writing business.

The smarter approach? Build your portfolio while you're
writing part time and develop relationships with clients who
you can work for once you're freelancing full time. Erik Sherman was a marketing consultant who'd written for newspapers and produced a weekly food column for fun in the past.
Early in 1996, he began publishing articles in technology magazines like *MacWeek* to enhance his authority as a consultant.
Using his extensive background in technology and education,
he quickly parlayed his part-time assignments into a full-time
freelance writing career. "I placed my first magazine piece in

February, and by August, I was doing it full time," says Sherman. "I started moving up pretty quickly." With little professional writing experience, Sherman hit the six-figure mark his second year as a freelancer.

Brian O'Connell had been freelancing for several years before he went full time. He was also able to do some writing work for his former employer when he first began freelancing. In the meantime, he quickly built up a stable of regular clients by using his work background and experience on Wall Street. "I'm a former Wall Street bond trader, and I started gravitating back toward that as a full-time freelancer," says O'Connell. "I worked for New England Funds, a big mutual funds company in Boston, and was writing a lot for the *Boston Herald* and *Globe*, and *Boston Business Journal*. I built my practice, for lack of a better word, on the financial side. I think that's one of the things people should focus on to be a six-figure freelancer—specializing."

Early in your freelance career, it's natural to want to approach as many markets and clients as possible. It's more effective, however, to look for a smaller stable of clients—but those who will give you steady work. This was another lesson I learned the hard way. When I started freelancing, my focus was on writing for national magazines. With little writing experience, my query success percentage was dismally low. I wrote dozens of queries, but few were accepted.

I persisted in sending them out and would occasionally get lucky. I picked up a short assignment for *Good Housekeeping*. I got an assignment from *Bridal Guide*. I eventually landed an assignment with *Shape*. But for every assignment I received, I got at least ten rejections, what I call "bongs." I was spending a lot of time pitching magazines and writing queries, and much less time actually writing the articles, which paid money. Even when I got an assignment and turned in a piece, it was usually a month or two before I saw my check.

About six months into my freelance career, I decided I

needed to diversify. I would continue pitching to magazines, but I would look for other work in addition to magazine article assignments. I offered to write articles for the local newspaper. The pay wasn't great—usually between $35 and $75 a story—but it gave me some work and made me more visible in the community. While working on newspaper stories, I often came up with ideas for magazine articles as well and pitched them to appropriate markets.

I knew from reading books on freelancing that working for business and corporate clients could be very lucrative, but I had no marketing background. To get up to speed, I read books on copywriting like Robert W. Bly's *Secrets of a Freelance Writer: How to Make $85,000 a Year* and learned how to write "you-oriented" copy that focuses on the customer, not the company, and why describing the benefits of a product or service rather than its features is a more effective selling technique. I joined the local chamber of commerce, where I had the distinction of being the only writer in town. That simple step led to three new writing gigs in a month's time.

A local advertising agency hired me to write the copy for a brochure, a project that led to other work. Another company that sold technology modules to schools hired me to write a series of profiles about its customers that it could use for marketing purposes. Each story took a few hours to research and write. The owner was pleased with my work and would send me a new list of schools to profile every few months. That gig continued for several years.

Finally, the local hospital hired me to do some freelance writing work. What began with a simple press release led to me writing dozens of ads, newsletters, letters for the hospital CEO, and even a video script. Remember, I had no experience with any of these kinds of writing projects, but I was willing to learn how to do them. Best of all, the hospital turned into a steady client. I could count on about $1,000 worth of work each month, often more. Another advantage of working with these local businesses was that I knew when I sent an invoice, I could expect a check in a week's time, rather than the four to six weeks I'd come to expect from national magazines.

In addition, I began writing regularly for *Chamber Executive*, a monthly association magazine for members of the American Chamber of Commerce Executives. I'd sent the editor a query on community leadership schools the year before, and the editor called to offer me another assignment. The work was straightforward—I wrote business articles and profiles of successful programs being implemented by chambers throughout the country. After my first two articles, the editor asked me to write for the magazine every month. Some issues, I wrote two stories; other times, I wrote three or four. In all, it produced between $400 and $700 each month. Not a lot, but I could count on the income—and I didn't have to query the editor with ideas. She simply sent me an e-mail each month with the subjects she wanted me to cover and contact information for suggested sources. I then researched and wrote the stories.

While I continued pitching national magazines, I also began focusing on developing relationships with editors. After my first assignment at *Fitness* was accepted, I immediately followed up with another idea, which was assigned. I then wrote three more articles for my editor there. I used the same approach with *Fit*, *Bridal Guide*, and *Woman's Day*. Rather than pitching several dozen magazines (which was time-consuming as I tried to keep up with the current issues and topics they were covering), I chose to focus on magazines that I *could write for more than once*. That change in focus—and opting to specialize in health, fitness, nutrition, and bridal subjects—paid off.

I still maintain that kind of focus. I'm not interested in writing for a publication or a client once. Instead, I look for magazines and clients I can develop ongoing relationships with. It's much easier to do a lot of work for a handful of clients than to write one-shot stories for several dozen different publications. Most six-figure freelancers have developed a similar stable of clients for whom they work. When you don't have to spend as much time pitching to new markets, you have more time to work on your paying assignments. And as you develop these relationships, clients are more likely to come to *you*.

The Importance of PMA

When I was a competitive swimmer in high school, our coach talked to us about the importance of having a positive mental attitude (PMA). In our teenage arrogance we mocked him for this idea, but the fact is if you're going to freelance full time, PMA is critical. That means believing in yourself and your abilities.

It's normal to have days where you doubt your writing abilities or worry that you won't have enough work coming in to make it as a freelancer. Every self-employed writer—even a six-figure freelancer—experiences that. That *doesn't* mean you're going to share these feelings with the people you work for or let them waylay you. With editors and other clients, you're going to present yourself as a self-assured, well-qualified professional who can give them what they want. That kind of confidence—even if you have to fake it occasionally—can help you succeed when the glass-half-empty types are scurrying back to the security of the corporate world.

Jim Thornton has been freelancing full time for more than twenty years and has ridden the ups and downs of the economy during that time. "When I first started writing, it was in a flush time, but probably around the time my first son was born in 1988, there was a bit of a pullback. I had all these hospital bills and it became a real struggle," says Thornton, who's based in Sewickley, Pennsylvania. "Basically, the magazine economy seems to go through various cycles. There will be times when there are a ton of magazines and work to be had by every hack in the world and then there will be times, which usually have something to do with the general economy, where ad revenues shrivel up and it becomes much more cutthroat." Thornton's solution? To take on other types of work when necessary. While he's primarily a magazine journalist, his confidence in his ability led to other types of work including speech writing, television scripts, and corporate writing.

"I was writing for a company doing custom publications for Fortune 500 companies, and it wasn't . . . too big of a step from doing feature articles on their products to an occasional speech for an executive in their company," says Thornton. "I'd never written a speech before and I was sort of nervous but I acted as if I could do it, and it went over great. . . . [You have to] feign confidence. Even if you don't feel particularly adept at a particular kind of writing, just act as if you can do it. If you're a good magazine writer, you can do pretty much any kind of paid writing work."

Confidence and a positive attitude can give you a leg up on other writers as well. Focus on what you *can* do—sending out queries, calling new potential clients, and scouting for regular gigs—rather than on what you can't control. No, you can't force an editor to give you an assignment or turn a $20,000 advance into $200,000 by snapping your fingers. But you can choose to be positive as you pursue your career. Setbacks are normal. It's how writers cope with them that makes a difference.

"There are so many writers who do nothing but complain. Life is frustrating. Business is frustrating," says Erik Sherman. "Get used to it and move on. If you want to gripe, go find a friend you can gripe to. But when you're composing that message and feeling embittered, think of how much time it would have taken you to write a query and get it out to another market. You have to stay focused on getting stuff done."

Finally, if you're debating whether to make the full-time leap, Brian O'Connell believes that it's mentally easier to freelance full time than to juggle part-time writing with another career. "You can't serve two masters. You can't work for an employer and yourself—you can't get any traction," he says. "If you really want to do this you have to cut the cord and jump in, make a big splash and work like hell, and make something of it. . . . Clear the decks and be committed to being a full-time freelancer."

The Feast-or-Famine Syndrome

Ask any full-time freelancer about one of his or her biggest struggles, and chances are that one of the answers will be the ups and downs of both the workload and the income—the "feast-or-famine" syndrome. You're either swamped with work to the point that you're spending nights and weekends at the computer to make your deadlines—or you have so little to do that you're overcome with simultaneous boredom, malaise, and hand-wringing anxiety. As a freelancer, you're constantly proving yourself. There's an almost constant fear that every assignment may be your last. The most difficult times for me are the slow periods, when I have too little work to do and too much time on my hands. And I'm not the only writer who feels this way.

"I like being busy. I prefer to be busy and fully engaged in work," agrees freelancer Sam Greengard of Burbank, California, who specializes in business and technology writing. "If I have more time, I find that I slow down. . . . It's like I feel better about myself and my work, and I tend to be more organized and more focused when I'm busy."

Constantly marketing himself helps Brian O'Connell maintain a steady stream of work and stay positive, especially during slow times. He sent out hundreds of queries during the first few months he launched his full-time freelance career, and he continues to market himself aggressively. "You have to be upbeat and optimistic. You're going to have weeks and months where the income isn't where you want it to be," he says. "I think the best antidote to that is staying busy, whether it's sending out 100 queries or 10 queries or networking or finding new ways to sell stories."

You don't always have power over the amount of work you have coming in, but you do dictate the amount of time you spend pitching ideas and marketing yourself. The tricky thing is that when you're swamped with assignments, it's all too easy to stop querying . . . only to find that a month later, you're completely caught up on your work and have no new stories coming your way. (Even as I write this, I'm living this first-hand. After a couple of crazy months of deadlines, I now only have three current magazine assignments on my desk, which means it's time to query.)

One of the techniques I've used to help ensure a steady stream of work is mentally dividing assignments into three categories: work that's been completed and accepted (and for which I'm awaiting payment), work that's been turned in but hasn't been approved by the editor or client yet, and work that's "on my desk" that still has to be researched and written. I then try to maintain a certain amount—say, $5,000—in each category at any given time. (The more you want to make, the more that amount should be.) If I'm looking at $6,000 worth of work in my accounts payables, and another $5,000 that's awaiting approval, that's great—but if I only have a $2,000 assignment "on my desk," I know I need to get cracking to line up some more assignments or my checkbook will look pretty thin a couple of months from now.

Sondra Forsyth maintains query and cash-flow charts and makes sure she has at least three to five queries circulating at any given time. From time to time, she has also secured exclusive writing contracts with magazines including *Mademoiselle*, where she produces a set number of pieces for a retainer. She recently took on a contributing editor position with *Ladies Home Journal*, her former employer. The trade-off is that she can't write for the magazine's competitors, but often the steady nature of the gig is worth it.

"The noncompete clause isn't all that restrictive in this case, and the deal was sweet. I can still write for *More*, *AARP*, *Reader's Digest*, and all the younger women's mags such as *Glamour* and *Cosmopolitan*, and I get to write the new 'Can This Friendship Be Saved?' column every month along with my share of 'Can This Marriage Be Saved?' and 'Was This Marriage Saved?'" she says. "Also, I get paid extra for any other articles I write for *LHJ* . . . taking an exclusive contract is not the kiss of death if you have other things going on."

Benefits? What Are Those?

Along with juggling cash flow, as a full-time freelancer you also have to consider how you'll pay for traditional job benefits like health insurance and retirement savings. If you're married to someone who can include you on his or her health insurance plan, take advantage of it. If not, you'll have to find affordable insurance that meets your needs, which can be a tall order. Some organizations like the Author's Guild offer health insurance to members. Or look for an independent agent who specializes in policies for small businesses and the self-employed. It may be that you're better off choosing a less-expensive, high-deductible policy like I did early on and paying for regular checkups out of pocket.

Since they don't have 401(k) or pension plans, freelancers must also create their own retirement savings programs. Many have Simplified Employee Pension (SEP) plans or Solo 401(k) savings plans—ask your accountant or financial advisor about setting one up. As of 2003, you can put up to 25 percent of your income or $40,000, whichever is less, in an SEP or Solo 401(k) plan.

During my twenties, I didn't even consider saving for

retirement—that was for old people. But I changed my attitude when I became self-employed. My first year of freelancing, I netted a whopping $11,000, but I did open an SEP plan with $1,000 as an investment in my future. In the years since then, I've deposited at least 10 percent of my net income into it, sometimes more. If I want to freelance the rest of my life, I realize that I have to set money aside for the future as well. Even if you have to start small, open a retirement savings account the first year you freelance full time.

Sam Greengard set up an SEP plan within a year or two of launching his freelance career; he's since then switched to a Keogh plan, which allows him to put more money into it each year. "I realized how important it was," he says. "I personally think you're a fool as a writer or any self-employed person if you don't have some kind of retirement account. This is a way you can reduce the amount you pay to the government and build up your savings for future retirement, too."

Too Much Work, Too Little Fun

Finally, if you're freelancing full time, don't forget to plan for time off. I've learned that some days, I can sit at the computer and write for several hours. I get in that flow state, and the work is effortless. However, not every day is like that. Okay, most aren't. And some afternoons, I reach a point where the words won't come, my thought process feels stalled, and I start getting antsy. There's a moment when I know I'm done for the day. I'm not going to get any more quality writing done.

I used to force myself to stay at the computer in an attempt to overcome my mental inertia, but it never worked. Instead, I wound up writing rambling e-mails, surfing the net, or generally wasting time. Now, when I need a break, I take one—a real one, away from the computer. I might play with my dog, read fiction for a while, run some errands, or even go to the gym. If

I have to knock off for the day, I will. Sometimes, I'll put in another hour or two at night, but by then, I've had the mental break I needed and the work comes much easier.

I'm amazed when I read of writers who say that they write eight or ten hours a day. That just isn't possible for me. I might *work* that amount of time, but a good chunk of it isn't writing per se. I may be reading research studies, transcribing interview notes, making phone calls, working on query ideas, or looking for new markets. The problem is that I have a difficult time not working at all. I tend to read magazines or skim books while the TV is on, and I'm compelled by some outside force to check my e-mail every morning, even on weekends. What can I say? I'm a bit of a workaholic. But I'm learning to set some boundaries for myself. For example, I won't work at all one weekend day each week or I'll take Friday afternoons off during the summer. If I don't plan that time and commit to taking time off by writing it in my calendar the way I would any other appointment, I wind up at my desk. The fact that I do take time off makes me more productive when I am working.

"I think in any professional pursuit, you can't keep going full speed ahead without ever taking time off," says Greengard. "You've got to recharge your batteries. Downtime is extremely important." Schedule some time off into every week. If you can't afford a week's vacation, at least get away for the weekend—or visit friends and family for an inexpensive writing reprieve. Hit the library or bookstore to browse the latest magazines. Make a lunch date with a friend. Head to Starbucks for a latte. But do get out of your office occasionally. Being able to set your own hours and create your own schedule are two of the biggest conveniences of freelancing. Make sure you take advantage of them. Your career and your attitude will both benefit.

Finally, I'd like to suggest that as you commit to full-time freelancing, you also commit to a regular exercise program. (No groans, please!) Writing is a sedentary business, and working out will reduce stress and help you maintain a healthy weight. Working from home, it's all too easy to head to the refrigerator for a distraction—and those little snacks can add up.

Exercise has proven mood-boosting benefits, and while I can't cite a study, I'm sure that regular exercise makes you more productive in your writing as well. Many of the six-figure writers I know are also athletes as well. Jennifer Lawler is a black-belt martial artist. Sam Greengard runs. Sondra Forsyth dances. Brian O'Connell runs, lifts weights, and plays golf. Yes, exercise—even a quick walk around the block—takes time out of your day. But it more than pays for itself with increased productivity, better mood, and, I'd say, more creativity as well.

Remember, the biggest asset you have as a writer, besides your time, is your good health. When you feel good, it's all too easy to take it for granted, but when you feel lousy, it can drag your productivity to a halt. I was reminded of this last month. Usually, I'm vigilant about working out, but I'd been lazy over the holidays, and several weeks of inactivity caught up with me. After a vigorous round of snow shoveling, I strained my back. For three days, I was doped up on muscle relaxants and analgesics, but even with the drugs, my back hurt too much to sit at my desk. I was able to do some work from bed, but I had to reschedule some interviews until I felt better. That experience was the impetus I needed to get back into my regular weight-lifting and running routine. When I'm exercising regularly, my aches and pains are minimal, and I'm able to cope with daily stressors much better. I think you'll find the same is true as well.

While this chapter is meant to get you thinking about whether full-time freelancing is for you, don't let it dissuade you from making it your goal, either now or in the future. Remember what O'Connell says: You can't serve two masters. I meet a lot of writers who are freelancing on the side, but who can't seem to make the jump to doing it full time. They seem to be waiting for the "perfect" time—when they have their house paid off, when their kids are out of school, or when they have enough experience that they're sure they'll be able to succeed at writing full time. While these are all valid considerations, sometimes you just need to be willing to take the leap and go for it.

CHAPTER 3
Laying the Groundwork:
Your Office Needs, At a
Minimum

O ne of the attractive things about launching a freelance writing business is that you need a minimum of investment and equipment to get started. You don't have to write a business plan, invest in a lot of inventory, or plunk down a chunk of change to buy into a franchise. You can start your freelance career with as little as a computer, e-mail access, and some ability to string words together in a pleasing fashion.

Yes, you can begin your freelance career with a minimal office setup, but that doesn't mean you can work efficiently with it. If you want to make a good living as a writer, you need the tools in place that will help you do so. That means outfitting your office for success.

When you're writing for the sheer pleasure of it, any old location may work for you. If you're freelancing as a business, however, you need an office. If you can set aside a separate room as your office, that's great. Remember, if you use it solely and exclusively for operating your writing business, you can take a home office deduction as well. (More about that in chapter 5.) But at a minimum, you need a place to make phone calls and conduct interviews, maintain files and other documents, take care of paperwork, and write. I've had a separate office since I started freelancing full time in 1997.

If you're limited space-wise at home, or find it impossible to focus while working at home, consider renting office space. Minneapolis-based freelancer Bev Bachel started freelancing in 1986, when she was in her midtwenties. She thought it would look more professional to have a separate office. "I had a small apartment, and in order to be credible, I decided to have an office outside my home," says Bachel, who works for a variety of corporate clients. "I didn't want to justify spending the money on rent, so I managed to talk a friend at an ad agency which had extra space into a relationship. They gave me an office and I did five hours of PR and agency work for them every month. I got downtown office space, and a relationship with them and their clients."

Bachel found that having an office outside her home improved her visibility, provided her with some initial work, and kept her from being too isolated. But for new freelancers, an outside office may not be worth the expense. Consider these factors when deciding whether to opt for a separate office:

- What type of work will you be doing?
- Will you have to meet with clients at your office, or can you visit them at other locations? If you do a lot of work for magazine or book publishers, face-to-face meetings may be rare, and a home office may be a smarter bet.
- How much are you currently making? One of the biggest advantages of a home office is that you don't have to pay additional rent—you're already forking out money to live there. Depending on the size of the office and the area in which you live, rent for a small office can run from $400 to more than $1,000 a month—and that may not include utilities, phone lines, and other expenses. That can make for a high overhead when you're starting out.
- What are your work habits like? Are you able to work at home and ignore distractions, or would you be more pro-

ductive if every morning you got up and "went to work"?

- Are you juggling other responsibilities during the day? It's not surprising that many writers and editors with young children choose to freelance so they can work *and* parent—but this plan is often better on paper than in reality. Forget your best intentions. The bottom line is that if your children are young and you're responsible for them, your freelance career will be part time unless you find outside care for your kids—or are willing to work when your children are sleeping. "You do need some kind of child care when you're freelancing, especially if you're trying to make a living at it," says Jennifer Lawler, who is a single parent with a young daughter who has health problems. "I had a lot of trouble at first getting help. Sitters would not bother showing up or they'd have car trouble or whatever and I'd be stuck with a deadline and no clear idea how I was going to meet it! I tried child care centers, but because Jessica had so many medical problems, it never worked very well— usually the child care providers were well intentioned, but they just couldn't cope." Lawler's initial solution was to work at night after her daughter was in bed, and on weekends when Jessica visited her father. (See the end of this chapter for her suggestions for combining parenting and freelancing.)
- Would an office outside your home lead to more busi- ness? Bachel's arrangement guaranteed her work for the advertising agency she leased space from. An office in a downtown building or a business suite provides more visibility than working out of your home, which can lead to a higher profile and more clients.

Finally, it's worthwhile to check with your local governing agencies to make sure that there are no local restrictions on operating a home office. Some municipalities require free-lancers to register their businesses; for example, the city of Chicago requires anyone who runs a business from home to register with the city for $125, and registration must be renewed annually.

The Basic Tools

So, you've got your office either in your home or at an outside location. What's next? Fitting it with the basics, which include designated workspace, a telephone, a computer, ample hard drive space, and appropriate software. If the latter subjects make you woozy, take heart—I'm a technophobe to the extreme. When I started freelancing full time, my computer knowledge was sketchy. I'd only used word-processing soft-ware at work and didn't even know how to install it. I was for-tunate to be living with my now-husband, a techie to the extreme.

The Christmas before I left my legal career to freelance full time, Erik gave me six months' worth of Web access and my own e-mail account as a gift. I was somewhat nonplussed. He means well, I thought, but I'm never going to use the Internet *that* much.

I still preferred the print world: books, magazines, and newspapers. I wrote most queries and articles in longhand before typing them up on the computer. Sure, I was impressed by the amount of information online, but I had no idea of the role it would play in my fledgling writing career. Under Erik's tutelage, I learned how to "surf" and use search engines like *www.altavista.com*. I wasn't going to wholeheartedly embrace technology the way he did, but I was willing to be dragged into the twentieth century.

Good thing—in 1997, most of my articles were submitted via fax, regular mail, or by disc. Today, all of my articles are submitted via e-mail, and I send most article queries via e-mail as well. (The exception is when an editor has said she prefers snail-mail queries—then I comply with her wishes.) I use e-mail every day, and I rely on the Internet almost as frequently to conduct background research, locate statistics, and track down sources. (See chapter 8 for more on research techniques.)

In the years since then, I've upgraded from dialup to a DSL connection, which means I spend less time online finding the information I'm looking for. It also means I don't have to tie up a phone line to get online (although there are tools that allow you to receive telephone calls while you're online if you do have dialup). Remember, at the minimum, you need a decent computer (I'm a PC person, but many freelancers swear by Macs), Web access, and an e-mail account. The following are some factors to consider when shelling out for the foundation of your office.

The Computer

Your first, and probably biggest, purchase for your freelance business will be your computer if you don't already have one. If you need to buy one, consider whether you'd benefit from a laptop. Yes, they're more expensive than desktops, but their portability may make one worthwhile. If the smaller keyboards bother your fingers, add a regular-sized keyboard or buy a docking station so you can use your laptop with a regular monitor and keyboard. After years of using a desktop and borrowing a laptop for travel, I switched to a laptop/docking station, which has been much more convenient. If this seems like a lot of clutter, connections, and cables to deal with, many of the newer laptops rival desktops by offering larger screens and keyboards and may be a better option if you don't mind lugging the extra pounds across town or the country.

Once you've decided on a standard desktop or laptop, check some basic things before you make the purchase. The amount of RAM (memory) you should consider depends on your budget and what applications you will run on your computer. If you stick to basic word processing, 256MB should be sufficient, but if you have to do graphics editing or presentations (using software like Adobe, Publisher, or PowerPoint), 512MB may be more appropriate.

One critical piece of hardware and software you'll need in your technology center is a computer backup system. This can be as simple as a keychain USB drive, ZIP drive, CD-RW drive, or DVD-RW drive, or as complex as a setup involving backup software, tape drives, or other removable media. You can also choose a one-touch USB or FireWire drive that can back up your system automatically at the press of a button.

The Operating System

Once you've decided on the hardware platform, choose what operating system (OS) will run on the hardware you've chosen. The most popular are Microsoft Windows and Macintosh. Many hardware vendors "bundle" OS and application software together to make it easier for consumers to pick what's right for them. As of today, Windows XP Professional is the latest offering from Microsoft that can run all of your applications, and it's compatible with both PCs and Macs.

Application Software

With Microsoft enjoying more than 90 percent market share in the office suite arena, it's a safe bet that the clients you will be working for will be using Microsoft operating system Microsoft Office. If, however, you use a non-Microsoft product suite such as the Macintosh and Linux operating systems, make sure it has export or conversion tools built in that allow you to save documents in many popular word-processing formats. While you may want to consider adding accounting software like QuickBooks to help run your writing business, Microsoft Office provides the basic software you'll need to get started.

Accessing the Internet

With the plethora of choices now available to allow you to connect to the Internet, you'll probably find several that suit your office needs. Options include basic dialup, Integrated Services Digital Network (ISDN), cable modem, Digital Subscriber Line (DSL), digital satellite, and dedicated leased line. While dialup is available nearly everywhere, the other, higher-speed options, commonly referred to as "broadband," may not be available in your geographic area yet. Costs range from $15 to $100 or more per month, depending on the type and speed of the connection. You may also have to pay for initial setup costs for additional wiring or necessary equipment.

Dialup is still quite popular with occasional Internet users, but I recommend a higher-speed connection for full-time freelancers. The equipment you'll need to connect your PC to the Internet can vary from a simple modem using your home phone line to more complex systems requiring network cables, hubs, and routers. This isn't as complicated as it sounds—with the numerous advancements in wireless technology, there are several easy-to-install wireless devices for older homes that aren't wired for data cabling.

When determining what type of connection to choose, cost is a factor. So are the number and types of features offered by the provider or Internet Service Provider (ISP). There are many companies offering perks like free e-mail and free Web sites, but consider the business implications of choosing a provider. How much is it worth to you to have nearly 100 percent uptime for Internet and e-mail access and for your Web site? "Free" may be fine for the occasional user, but generally companies offering these free features do so at the expense of other features that may contribute to the professional image you want to present.

If you have a Web site, research your chosen ISP's offerings before signing up for Web hosting as well. Some professional hosting companies may provide you with more options than does your ISP, so be sure to fully evaluate the providers before you choose one. Sites like *www.dslreports.com* have unbiased reports about DSL providers from current and previous subscribers, along with a DSL-provider locator feature with pricing and ranking to make it easier for you to make an informed decision. To find a suitable ISP and hosting company, you can do some research ahead of time at a local library. For example, a Google search (*www.google.com*) for "hosting companies" provides several sites that offer side-by-side comparisons of the top companies and their offerings of Web sites, e-mail, and even e-commerce sites.

Once you've chosen your Internet connection type and provider, you'll need to decide whether to use e-mail service from your provider (where your name will include its domain name—like an AOL or Yahoo e-mail address). If you want to register your own domain name (such as *www.kellyjamesenger.com*), you may have to use a third party to host your Web site and e-mail account. In that case, I suggest that you have the same provider host both services. It means you only have one number to call with questions (and you probably will have questions!) and one bill to deal with.

If you opt for a Web site, registering your unique domain name on the Internet is easy. It's likely that your ISP can do this on your behalf; if not, there are sites that offer this service. Sites like *www.netsol.com* let you check to see whether your site name is available, and for about $35 per year, you can have a personalized, professional domain name for your writing business. If you don't opt for your own domain name, stick with a basic e-mail address. Avoid cutesy e-mail handles like "luv2RITE" and the like. You're in business, remember? My e-mail address for years was kellyjames@pop.net; it was easy to spell and remember. Now that I have my own Web site, I use kelly@becomebodywise.com.

The Phone

I recommend a second phone line for your writing business. Yes, you can use your home telephone, but unless you live alone, you'll be sharing that number with the other members of your family. You can write off the entire cost of the second phone line as a tax deduction, and I think the convenience is worth the expense. (The cost of a primary phone line cannot be taken as a tax deduction, although you can deduct business-related long-distance calls.)

Your telephone message on your voicemail should be friendly but brief. If you share a phone line with family members, leave a professional-sounding message on your answering machine and teach your kids how to answer the phone. And you should check your voicemail—and e-mail—several times a day. Having your business phone forward calls to a cellular phone when you're out of the office or traveling helps ensure that you won't miss any important calls. If you use your cell phone exclusively for work like I do, you can take that expense as a business deduction as well.

Like land lines, cell phones now offer a host of voicemail, call forwarding, and other options. Due to recent legislation, it's easier than ever to maintain your same phone number even if you change phone or cell companies. You can even use the same number for both your business line and your cell phone so that you're "always" in the office—at least as far as your clients know.

Letterhead and Business Cards

While letterhead and business cards help create a professional image, you needn't spend a lot on them. Choose something simple, and err on the conservative side with design. I used a simple template in Word for my letterhead for several years before switching to a plain gray bond paper with my name at the top and contact information at the bottom. I suggest omitting titles like "freelance writer," "independent journalist," and the like—I think it looks amateurish, and you never know who you'll be writing for (e.g., a business client may be put off by a "journalist" title). If you feel your name looks too bare without a title, consider including a brief explanation of what you do, like "writing and editing services."

Letterhead that can be used for any occasion—whether you're pitching a magazine article, a book proposal, or a corporate marketing brochure—will give you the most bang for your buck. If you decide to incorporate or use a business name instead of your own, you'll want letterhead featuring your business name. Most freelancers do business under their own names, which obviates the need for a tax identification (ID) number; you simply use your social security number as your tax ID number.

Do You Need a Website?

I've already covered how to find an ISP to host your Web site. The question is, do you need one? You may be surprised to learn that I don't think a Web site is necessary for a new writer who simply wants to use it to showcase work. Despite what you might hope, editors aren't trawling the net, looking for potential contributors. The time you might spend developing your Web site could be better spent pitching potential clients.

However, as time goes on, you may want to consider a Web site to publicize you and your work. A well-designed Web site can help you:

- Develop a platform in a particular subject area
- Publicize speaking engagements and other events
- Market yourself to potential clients
- Sell books and other products
- Maintain clips and other work samples online for editors and potential clients to view

Do you *need* a Web site when you're starting out? Nope. But many writers find that as time goes on, a Web site is an effective promotion vehicle, especially if they have books to sell. Victoria Moran's Web site, *www.victoriamoran.com*, is simple in design but has helped her expand her database and netted her speaking gigs. Margaret Littman's site, *www.littmanwrites.com*, helped her promote her first book, *The Dog Lover's Companion to Chicago*. Jennifer Lawler uses her Web site, *www.jenniferlawler.com*, to promote her speaking appearances and to sell copies of her books. Both Sam Greengard's site at *www.greengard.com* and Robert McGarvey's at *www.mcgarvey.net* make it easy for prospective clients to check out samples of their work—in fact, they've both been contacted with assignments by editors seeking writers with their specific areas of expertise.

If you want to help drive other people—like potential readers of your books—to your site, though, it helps to include content other than background information about you and your work. Sarah Wernick's Web site, *www.sarahwernick.com*, not only markets her numerous health books, but also includes information for potential writers and collaborators and samples of her work. My new site, *www.becomebodywise.com*, features a selection of writing-related articles and a free monthly newsletter to encourage repeat visitors. Know what your intentions are for your Web site before you begin designing it, and you'll get more results from it.

Peripherals

When I started freelancing, I didn't have a fax machine; I simply drove to the local UPS store when I needed to fax something, which wasn't very efficient or professional. To save time, I purchased WinFax, faxing software that enabled me to fax and receive documents from my PC using my office phone line. It was better than nothing, but at the time I didn't have a scanner, which meant that I could only fax documents directly from my PC. For anything else, I still had to make that trip to the "real" fax machine.

Finally, I broke down and bought an all-in-one. This combination printer/scanner/fax machine means that I don't have to run out to send or receive faxes, to make copies for clips, or to scan articles. It's been a huge time-saver and well worth the investment. However, I still keep the phone and fax number for the closest UPS store on hand. If I have a problem with my machine, editors can fax documents to me there, and the UPS employees will call when they've arrived.

Other Tools

If you've got the money, there's no shortage of tools available that can help you work more efficiently. The key is to choose the tools that will allow you to recoup your investment through greater productivity, like:

- A telephone headset. Get one. When I started freelancing, I used the crook-of-the-shoulder technique, holding the receiver between my head and shoulder and scribbling notes furiously with my right hand. Buying a headset saved my neck and my sanity—and best of all, I now transcribe all my interviews directly onto my PC as I conduct them.
- A digital recorder. While most writers tape-record their telephone and in-person interviews, a digital recorder may be worth the expense if you do a lot of interviewing. Unlike a tape recorder, you don't have to worry about tapes breaking or being erased, and digital recording allows you to archive interviews for easy access.
- A better computer mouse. A better mouse can make your working life easier. A computer mouse like the Microsoft IntelliMouse Explorer, which has buttons on either side

as well as a scroll button on top, lets you navigate documents and Web sites more quickly. You can also program the buttons to copy, paste, and cut, so your hand never leaves the mouse to edit documents.

- A QuickLink pen. You're on the go and need to take some notes? Run this digital highlighter over text and it will store the data and then let you download it onto your PC when you get home. It syncs to your computer with a simple cable.
- Database software. Trying to manage freelance clients can be a headache. What's the name of that new editor at that home-and-garden magazine? When was the last time you followed up with that copywriting client? Build your own database to track this kind of information, and you'll have everything you need at your fingertips. Software like FileMaker Pro lets you keep track of editors and contacts; software like Access allows you to perform the same functions, but is not as user-friendly.
- Find-it software. Let's say you're looking for a transcript of an interview but you can't recall the name of the person you spoke with. With software like Enfish Find, you can search for particular words or numbers on your computer's entire hard drive.
- Portable word processor. While I have a laptop, I've discovered that I often only need a word processor for drafts. If you travel a lot or write from different locations, an AlphaSmart can be a blessing. You simply turn it on and type onto the full-size keyboard—it holds about 100 pages' worth of writing—and then download your work onto your PC through a USB connector cable when you get home. The drawback is that it has a very small screen, so it's probably most useful for note-taking or draft-writing rather than editing.
- Personal Digital Assistant (PDA). PDAs are now available in a wide selection of models and with a wide selection of

features. Currently, there are two leading OSs for these devices: the Palm OS and the Windows Mobile OS. Both have similar features like the ability to synchronize with your PC's e-mail mailbox and contacts list. Depending on which model and OS you select, expect to spend anywhere from less than $100 for a very basic model to $600 or more if you include additional software and add-ons like keyboards, power supplies, and wireless adaptors.

- RIM Blackberry. The Blackberry is the latest twist on the traditional PDA. Blackberries are becoming very popular—they offer most if not all of the features of the traditional PDA, but they also have other features like interactive paging, Web browsing, and phone service. They range in price from $99 to about $499, which includes software.

Your Desk

Now that you have the necessary technology for your office, don't overlook the basic furniture you'll be using every day. I find writers are more willing to shell out big bucks for technology than for office furniture. When I started freelancing, I used an old office chair of Erik's, and my monitor and keyboard sat on an antique library table. The chair wasn't that comfortable, and the design of the table kept me from being able to slide my chair underneath it. That meant I had to stretch my arms out and up to reach the keyboard, which barely fit on the narrow table. It was an uncomfortable arrangement that was bound to cause problems, but it wasn't until my wrists began to hurt that I realized I needed to upgrade.

After spending several hours trying out chairs at the local office superstore, I came home with a new chair and computer workstation. Once I got home, I spent time arranging my equipment so that I could type comfortably. Despite the fact that I spend hours at my keyboard every day, I haven't suffered any repetitive stress injuries like carpal tunnel syndrome, and I think a good part of the reason is my office setup. I also take breaks every hour or so to give my fingers (and brain) a rest. Even a few minutes of getting up and walking around can make a big difference. Best of all, I've discovered that I can catch up on the laundry, clean the kitchen, and vacuum the entire house in ten-minute chunks throughout the day. If you tend to lose track of time when you're at your desk, set a timer to remind you when it's time for a break.

When setting up your work area, keep these tips in mind:

- Choose the right chair. You want a chair that allows you to adjust it to your body by raising or lowering the seat, changing the angle of the seat back, and raising or lowering the armrests. In general, the seat of the chair should be high enough to support your thighs, but low enough so that you can rest your feet on the floor and so that you can slide underneath your work surface if you want to. The armrests of the chairs should be high enough to support your forearms directly under your arms but low enough so that they don't hit the desktop as you work. The chair back itself should provide support to your lower back, especially if you recline in your chair as you work. Experiment to find an angle that's comfortable for you and that supports your middle and lower back as you work.

- Select the right height for your work surface. It should be low enough that your fingers rest comfortably on the keyboard but high enough to give you a couple of inches clearance between the tops of your legs and the underside of your desk or keyboard tray. In addition to my desk, I have a credenza that I use to store research or, more often, piles of papers I haven't read yet. The setup takes up one entire wall of my office but gives me plenty of open work space when I need it.

- Maximize your monitor. In general, your monitor should be at a height that lets you see the entire screen without having to raise or lower your head. The top of the screen should be just below eye level, and it should be sharp and bright enough that you're able to read the screen when it's sixteen inches away from you without straining your eyes.
- Take a closer look—or rather, feel—at your keyboard. How easy is it to strike the keys? You shouldn't have to pound them. Experiment with the angle of the keyboard to see what's most comfortable. You may also want to check out adjustable keyboards—some are split down the middle to reduce the amount of sideways wrist turning. A padded wrist rest may also make typing more comfortable. The keyboard should be low enough so that as you use it, your forearms and wrists form a straight line, with your fingers at a natural downward curve.
- Arrange your desk so that the equipment you use the most frequently is within arm's reach. My telephone sits on the desk to my right, next to my mouse, so that I don't have to reach to answer it; my daily calendar and Rolodex are within reach on my left side. My all-in-one printer/scanner/fax machine is a quick turn away on my right, and the files I use on a daily basis are kept a few feet away on my left side. I can access everything I need without getting up from my chair—but even then, I still take breaks every hour or so. My back complains if I don't.
- Consider other ambient factors, such as lighting, room temperature, humidity, and noise. In general, the light from your monitor should match the brightness of the room—a screen that's too bright or too dim can cause eyestrain. You also want a room that's comfortable temperature-wise. Most people prefer working in an environment that's about 68 degrees, although I like writing

in a slightly chilly room—it seems to help keep me alert. Also consider the noise level of your office. Some writers enjoy having music or other background noise, while others work better in complete silence.

- Finally, consider how your office makes you *feel*. You're going to spend hours at your desk, so why not invest in a space that contributes to your comfort and productivity? While I hate clutter, I keep a few personal and motivational quotes near my desk, along with a couple of favorite framed prints. I also have a stereo and a stack of CDs ranging from classical to the B-52s for when I need a musical boost, and I burn candles occasionally when I'm working. The key for me is to make my office a place where I like to be.

Keeping Records

When you're setting up your office, don't overlook your need for record-keeping and storage. Forget the idea of a paperless office. You'll need a filing system of some sort to keep track of invoices, submissions, tax deductions, research materials, and story files.

Some writers use database software like Access or File-Maker Pro to track queries, submissions, and current work. These programs also let you maintain contact files. I prefer the old-fashioned paper method and track submissions and assignments by hand. To ensure that I don't forget anything or blow a deadline, I use what lawyers call the "double-diary" system: as soon as I get an assignment, I make a note of it in both my current assignments calendar and my desk calendar. (Again, if you use software like Microsoft Office, you can easily plug in these dates and even program reminders for yourself.)

Many six-figure freelancers use software to manage their assignments and billings, but I remain committed to doing these tasks by hand. I can see the advantages of software, though, and have begun using QuickBooks for invoicing. I plan to employ more software to help manage my business in the future. While your record-keeping system may vary depending on your needs, even the most basic system should allow you to easily:

- Track and follow up on queries/submissions and pitches to potential clients
- Keep track of current work assignments, including deadlines
- Maintain a list of current invoices and payment histories to stay on top of client payments

In addition, you need some sort of system for organizing the thousands of pieces of paper you're going to encounter as a successful freelancer. I'm a big fan of manila folders. When I get a new assignment, I label a manila folder with the story subject, the market, and the deadline. Each corporate project gets a similar folder, as do speaking gigs, book proposals, and other projects. I file any relevant documents in these folders so I have everything in one location.

I also have several filing cabinets in my office and a database that includes a list of all my old story files along with the experts I interviewed. That's made it much easier to locate relevant information from articles I may have written years ago. (Enfish software makes this even easier—it can search your computer's entire hard drive to find relevant documents.) I also maintain research folders for all of the subjects I write about, including women's health, fitness, nutrition, psychology, and relationships. When I see a newspaper article, press release, or news story I may use for an article, I tear it out and drop it in the appropriate folder. Then, when I'm working on new article queries, I revisit the folders for story ideas or supporting information.

Finally, you should have a system in place for keeping track of your income and expenses. (More about this in chapter 5.) I keep two manila folders in the top drawer of the filing cabinet next to my desk—one labeled "income" and the other "expenses." Check stubs from payments go in one, and all business-related receipts go in the other at the end of the day, which means I don't have to worry about tracking down a missing receipt. When I travel for work, I keep an envelope for receipts and maintain a running list of what I spent on the road and record it when I return home. I'd much rather keep track of expenses as I incur them, but some writers find it easier to total expenses on a regular basis—say weekly or monthly.

Spreading the Word

Part of launching your freelance business is setting up your office. It's also critical to start letting people know that you're now in the writing biz. If you're pitching magazines or book publishers, you have to query and contact the publications. But don't overlook word of mouth, especially when it comes to local business. Let your friends, family members, coworkers, and neighbors know that you're available for copywriting projects. Offer to write ads, brochures, or Web site copy for your church newsletter, school publication, or favorite non-profit organization to make contacts and develop your portfolio—businesspeople will want to see samples of your work before they hire you.

Joining the local chamber of commerce or some other business networking association is another great way to find clients. Look for companies that are large enough to afford hiring a writer but small enough not to have copywriters on staff. Businesses that already actively promote their products and services in local media are good possibilities. And finally, introduce yourself at local printing shops and bring samples of your work—they may hire you to do freelance work or recommend you to their customers.

The more people who know about you, the better. If you've already got contacts, that's great. If not, go get them. When Victoria Moran quit her job to freelance full time in 1989, she was living in the Midwest. Her former boss had an apartment in Manhattan, and one of the first things she did was travel there to meet with editors in person. "I came here and met with five magazine editors, and I got two story assignments, which started me off," says Moran, who has published both magazine articles and books including *Creating a Charmed Life* and *Fit from Within*. "You need to network like crazy. I know that's not necessarily second nature to a writer, but you can develop that part of yourself. . . . Whether it's online or by phone or in person, which is always the best, the more people you can know, the better."

For Parents Only: Juggling Freelancing and Kids

Another issue to consider when setting up your office is how you'll handle parenting responsibilities, if you have them. So far, the only child in my family is the four-legged, doggy variety, so my "parenting" duties are minimal. A few breaks during the day to play Frisbee or walk, and my dog is all set. Parents of the two-legged kiddies have it tougher, which makes good day care a must for maximum productivity.

Freelancer Jim Morrison and his wife, Ann Stokes, a landscape architect, both have offices on the third floor of their home in Norfolk, Virginia. They have a nanny during the day, and their six-year-old twins have learned that when their parents kiss them good-bye and tell them, "We're going to work," they're not to be disturbed. "If anything, we're the ones who break the spell, occasionally going down to check on them or encourage their preschool homework," says Morrison. "I read these horror stories of people trying to do child care and work. That's not fair, though I realize it may be an economic necessity. It's not fair to your children. And it's not fair to you . . . you cannot think about structuring a story or forming an interview if you're worried about getting the kids dressed or getting them lunch or stopping their spat."

Jennifer Lawler has had similar challenges juggling parenting and freelancing. She's successfully managed to do both—since she began freelancing, she's published more than twenty books, including *Dojo Wisdom* and *Dojo Wisdom for Writers,* while parenting, and now homeschooling, her daughter, Jessica. Lawler's advice:

> Many aspiring writers approach me with the idea that they can freelance while also being the stay-at-home parent for their child or children. They save the stress and frustration of going to a job, and get to spend time with their young children. It can work—but you have to plan.
>
> I freelance and am a single mother—I have a young daughter I'm homeschooling. She has multiple disabilities so sometimes it's a challenge, but it would be much, much harder on both of us if I had to go off to work each morning. Freelancing can be a viable alternative, but you have to remember:
>
> - You will have to have child care. A lot of people naively think they can dangle baby on their lap while writing the "Great American Novel" or at least *Harry Potter,* but you need to be professional when handling calls from clients and editors (i.e., no little voices in the background chanting, "I want lunch!" and pulling the dog's tail), and you need to have clear time to write and think about writing

when a little munchkin isn't tugging at your hand saying, "Play, Mama! Play!"

- That said, if you're disciplined you can do your work when munchkin is in bed or when another family member is caring for him/her. On the other hand, sometimes you just need to collapse during such a period. Don't underestimate how exhausting it is to care for young children. Preschools accept toddlers and above, and those precious hours a week can add up to a freelance career.

- You have to set clear boundaries on what the child can and can't do with regards to your work. From the time my daughter was an infant, I made it clear that she could not touch my computer or supplies. In order to make this more palatable, I kept a steady supply of stickers (her favorite) on hand so that when she was tempted, I could bribe her. When she was old enough I got a secondhand computer for her and put it on a child-size table in my office so she can come and work on her computer when I'm working on mine. She has a drawer of supplies I'm not allowed to touch with the strict understanding that she can't touch mine either. I can't emphasize how important this is, or else you'll spend six hours looking for your files when you're trying to finish that brochure, only to find them squirreled under your sofa.

- Be flexible. For a long time, when my daughter was seriously ill, I only took on long-term projects, like books. In the course of six months while I was writing the book, she might have ended up in the hospital three times, but I was still able to write the book in between times. If I had been trying to turn around a magazine article or commercial writing for clients when this was happening, it would have added way too much stress to my life. Also, a book editor didn't care if I didn't return a phone call today—tomorrow was fine, too. But business clients and others aren't so patient. As the primary caregiver for your child, you have quite a juggling act, so don't feel like you have to do what everyone else is doing. You have to do what works for you. It may mean a slightly roundabout career path, but that's okay.

- And one bonus tip: you have to take your work seriously. People think you can be imposed upon because you're working at home anyway. This assumption gets even worse when you have children, because they assume you're a stay-at-home parent who's just playing around with writing. Pretty soon you'll be doing all sorts of favors for everyone else and not having any time to write. But take yourself seriously, and guard your writing time (it is not out of bounds to hang up on people who should know better), and you'll be okay.

Getting Serious About Work

One of the reasons I think it's so important for writers to have an office is that it underscores the fact that you're a professional and you're serious about your work. That kind of attitude is essential to success. Whether you're a fledgling writer or a seasoned pro, be confident when you approach new clients or markets for your work. Too many writers undersell themselves because they are afraid of appearing boastful or arrogant. Remember that you're offering the editor something unique— yourself and your skills. When you query about an idea or bid on a project, think about how your experience and background will benefit this editor or client, and point them out.

That also means not apologizing for your work. If someone asks you what you do, don't mumble, "Oh, I'm trying to write." "I'm a self-employed journalist" or "I run my own writing business" is a much more businesslike, self-assured answer. You never know where your next client will come from—that person at the neighborhood get-together may wind up hiring you for a project, so be prepared to explain what you do.

Sometimes, it's easier to take care of the external things—making sure your PC has sufficient memory, setting up a second phone line, and using software to track outstanding queries—than to address the internal aspects of freelancing. Success in this business requires a mental shift from working for a paycheck. It means that you have to believe in yourself and your abilities even when no one else seems to. It also means being willing to work harder than you ever worked for a boss—because you're now working for yourself and because you want to. In the next chapter, we'll talk more about developing a plan to help you ensure a successful freelance career.

CHAPTER 4
Boosting Your Bottom Line: Planning—and Negotiating—for More Money

S o, you've outfitted your office with the necessary technology and equipment and have created an efficient filing system. What's next? Creating a plan for how you'll approach your writing career on a day-to-day basis.

Creating Your Plan for Success

Don't worry: a formal business plan isn't necessary. But devising some kind of marketing and writing strategy from the outset can boost the number of assignments you receive and help you get up to speed as a full-time freelancer much more quickly. In chapter 1, you reviewed your prior writing experience. Keeping this in mind, consider the types of writing you've done, the kinds of clients you've worked for, your writing goals, and the time you have available to freelance.

For example, at the end of each year, I review what types of writing work I performed, for whom, and how much money I made as a result. I also break down my income so I can determine who my biggest clients are; these are the editors I want to pay special attention to in the future. I look at the types of work

I did and determine which jobs were the most lucrative. I also add up the amount I made from selling reprints and from speaking engagements so I know how much I'm making from both activities.

Another issue to explore is how you spent your *time* last year. Look at when projects were assigned and when you turned them in. Are you turning around your profiles quickly but spending hours on shorter, lower-paying pieces? Are those heavily researched business articles really worth spending so much energy on? Remember that it's not how much you make for a particular project—it's what your hourly *rate* turns out to be. (More about that in chapter 8.)

Finally, how diversified were you this year? Were you working for only a handful of clients or for dozens? Did you have lots of short, lower-paying assignments or did you focus more on bigger projects or feature stories? Does your income come from a variety of sources or only a few? I've found that it's easier to do a lot of work for a few steady clients rather than doing one-shot projects for a larger number of editors, but some writers prefer to work with a more diversified client base. While it may be more demanding, having a large pool of clients and editors helps maintain a steady workload and cash flow.

After you've considered these kinds of factors, set an annual financial goal. (It's fine to have other goals—say, publishing a book or having your byline appear in the *New Yorker*. But first and foremost, you're doing this to make money.) Write it down here:

Does it seem insurmountable? Take heart. The next step is to break this number down into weekly and daily goals. For example, a six-figure income might seem like a lot. But if you work five days a week and take two weeks of vacation a year, that leaves you 250 working days (50 weeks x 5 days per week = 250 days). Average $400 a day and you'll make $100,000 by the end of the year.

Based on your annual goal, and the number of days you'll work this year, set your own daily and weekly goals:

_____ per day

_____ per week

Of course, most people don't start out at the six-figure mark, but setting goals like these help you get there. For my second year, I set my income goal at $30,000, which translated to $125/day for 240 days a year, which gave me four weeks of vacation a year. My focus on my daily financial goals also helped me determine how much time to put into different projects. For example, a story that paid $500 shouldn't take me more than four days' total to complete or I'd be losing money. If on the other hand I spent a day working for a corporate client and billed it $250, I was a day ahead of my average.

Get the idea? Having a daily target keeps you focused on your bottom line. As time goes on, you can also adjust your goals upward or modify them to reflect other writing objectives. For example, for my fourth year of freelancing full time, I doubled my second-year goal of $30,000 to $60,000 annually, which broke down into $250/day for 240 days a year. But the next year, I knew I wanted to work on a book proposal, which meant I had fewer hours available to freelance. I decided to maintain the same financial goal that year to give me the time I needed for the proposal.

Setting both long- and short-term financial goals is the first step toward freelancing success. The next is to set production goals that will help you meet those financial ones. Production goals give you a framework to work from, help you work more efficiently, and ensure that you're always marketing yourself. I like to keep my production goals simple. For example, if you're freelancing full time, you may set a production goal of always sending out at least one query per day. That's five queries a week—and it's guaranteed to help bring in work if you maintain it.

As a new freelancer, I also employed what I called the "twenty-four-hour rule." That meant that within twenty-four hours of receiving a rejection (what I call a "bong") from an editor, two things would happen. First, I'd resubmit the query to another market. Second, I'd send a new query to the editor who had rejected me, starting with language like, "Thank you very much for your *response* [not rejection!] to my query about women and weight lifting. While I'm sorry you can't use the idea at this time, I have another for you to consider." Then I'd include my new query.

The twenty-four-hour rule enabled me to turn each rejection into two new opportunities. And getting back in touch with editors immediately helped me build relationships even before I'd written for their publications. It also eliminated the question of "what should I do now?" that I would have otherwise wondered about after receiving a bong. I didn't get derailed by the rejection; I simply used it as an opportunity to apply my twenty-four-hour rule.

If you want to expand your stable of regular clients but dread the cold-call process, a production goal can help you keep on track. You might set a target of making a set number of marketing or pitch calls each week. I find that it's more efficient to make these kinds of calls in batches. It takes less time and as you get warmed up, it's less stressful, too. Hey, I admit that I hate the marketing side of the freelancing business. But sales in any business is a numbers game—the more calls you make, the more likely you are to get work.

That's the nice thing about production goals. They can get you out of the mind-set of worrying about whether to do something and compel you to simply complete the task. You don't have to consider whether you'll brush your teeth in the morning, do you? (As a dentist's daughter, I hope not!) Production goals give you the same kind of framework. If you set a production goal to pitch five queries a week or to query at least one new market every week, you don't get angst-ridden over it. You just meet the goal and move on.

Production goals can also be useful if you want to branch into a new type of writing. For example, you can decide to dedicate a certain amount of time to breaking into this area. If you're a magazine journalist who wants to get into books, you may budget some time to research an appropriate book topic, write a book proposal, and find an agent. Setting a time goal—like spending one hour a day or a certain number of hours each week—on a project like this can keep it from winding up on the bottom of your to-do pile.

If you have particular markets you want to crack, you may want to make that one of your goals as well. Or perhaps you'll choose to find some regular gigs such as an ongoing corporate client or a contributing-editor relationship with one or more magazines. Considering the market and demand for particular types of writing may also help you make this change.

What types of production goals will you set? Make a note of them here:

_____

_____

_____

_____

_____

If you're going to be freelancing full time, you may also want to consider the hours you'll keep. You may wind up working more than forty hours a week, but having a set schedule can make you more productive. Sure, in theory you can work whenever you like, but I find I get more done when I keep regular hours. I also try not to work on the weekends unless I absolutely must to meet a deadline. On weekdays, I work nine to five, more or less; sometimes I'm in my office by seven, some days not until ten, but it generally works out to about forty hours a week. Of course, the question isn't how many hours I spend at work. It's how much work I'm actually getting done.

By setting monthly, weekly, and daily financial targets—along with production goals to help you meet them—you'll be on your way to achieving your overall financial goal this year. But remember that your writing career isn't only about the money. Your writing goals may also include non-monetary ones like spending more time writing fiction or essays, working on a screenplay, or writing that great American novel.

If that's the case, build writing time into your schedule for projects that don't produce income (at least not yet) but are important to you for other reasons. If you focus solely on the bottom line and continually take work that bores or frustrates you, you'll be likely to become bored and frustrated with your career as well. Instead, strive for a balance between the money you want to make and the work you want to do—and both you and your bank account will be better off this year.

Copyright: What Every Writer Needs to Know

Now that you have your plan in place, let's talk about copyright. As a writer, you make your living with words. That's why it's important that you understand the basics of copyright law. Amazingly, many writers—and even editors—don't have even a vague grasp of what it is.

According to the U.S. Copyright Office, "copyright" refers to a form of protection provided by U.S. law to the authors of "original works of authorship," including literary, dramatic, musical, artistic, and certain other intellectual rights. The author has the exclusive right to do and to authorize others to do things including reproducing, distributing, and displaying the work. In other words, if you own the copyright, you can do whatever you want with the work in question—or sell, assign, or transfer that right to someone else. For example, a book contract may provide for first-world publication rights as well as the right to authorize excerpts, which allows the publisher to offer the work to serial markets.

While many writers mistakenly believe they have to register their work to create copyright, it's actually created concurrently along with the work. Copyright protection exists from the time the work is "in fixed form." This means that as soon as you write an article, brochure, or screenplay, you own the copyright to it. (The exception is if you're an employee, where the company you work for may own the copyright to anything you create at work under what's called the "work-for-hire" doctrine. In that instance, your employer is considered the copyright holder, not you, because the writing you're creating is considered owned by the company.) Some freelance contracts also have work-for-hire provisions; technically, though, a work-for-hire can only exist between an employer and an employee, not a freelancer and a client.

Copyright Notice

So, if that's all there is to copyright, why bother to affix a copyright symbol (©) on your work? The reason has to do with something called the "innocent infringement" doctrine.

Let's say you write a fabulous article and distribute it to your family members. If there's no copyright notice and someone copies it, assuming in good faith that there's no copyright notice on it, that person (the so-called "innocent infringer") may not be liable for damages and may even be permitted to continue copying the work! The notice required is the copyright symbol ©, followed by the date the work was first published, and the author's name—for example, © 2005, Kelly James-Enger.

Why Register Your Work?

Creating your work isn't enough to effectively protect your copyright. You don't *have* to register your work with the Library of Congress, but it's easier—and usually more lucrative—to enforce an infringement case if you have registered your work. If you don't register the work "in a timely fashion," infringement that occurs prior to registration will not give rise to attorneys' fees or statutory damages.

What's the big deal? Attorneys' fees (which can easily reach tens of thousands of dollars) and statutory damages are two of your best remedies in a copyright infringement suit. You can introduce your registered copyright at trial to prove you're the legal copyright owner. And if you prevail in a lawsuit and you registered the work within three months of publication, you're entitled to attorneys' fees and statutory damages—a specified amount of money set out by law. If you don't register your work within three months, you may still have a cause of action for infringement, but you're limited to injunctive relief and/or actual damages—that is, the amount of money you have lost because of the violator's actions, which is often a difficult thing to prove.

Once your work is published, you have three months in which to register it. (Registering is retroactive, which means that registering within those three months protects you back to the publication date.) In 2004, it cost $30 to register work with the U.S. Copyright Office, but you can include more than one piece of writing (e.g., a batch of magazine articles) on the same application. For more information about copyright registration procedures, visit *www.copyright.gov/;* forms are available at *www.copyright.gov/forms/.*

Don't Give It Away

Another important aspect of protecting your copyrights is being aware of exactly what you're selling to a publisher. The copyright statute refers to a "bundle of rights": the right to reproduce the work, to sell the work, to publicly display the work, and the like. As a writer, you want to sell as few rights as possible—one-time only rights would be ideal. Then if the publisher wants additional rights—say to reprint the piece in a special issue or post it on its Web site—it has to offer you additional money for these rights.

Not surprisingly, publishers take the opposite approach. They want to obtain as many rights as possible (often, all rights) so that they're free to use and reuse the work in print publications, on Web sites, in books, in electronic databases, and, as one of my contracts reads, in "all media whether now existing and hereafter devised, created, and invented."

Read every contract and make sure that you understand what rights you're selling before you sign it. As a writer, you're probably much more concerned with creating work than protecting it. But by giving notice of your copyright, and registering your work on a regular basis, you'll help prevent it from being stolen or misappropriated in the future. Better yet, it will give you an effective weapon to use against violators if you need to.

The Art of Negotiation: Getting the Most for Your Words

Why spend time discussing copyright? Because it can directly impact the amount of money you make both now and in the future. Remember, when you create any piece of writing, you own the copyright to what's referred to as a "bundle of rights." This bundle includes any use you can think of—from the right to publish the work for the first time in a magazine published in North America (also called "first North American serial rights"), to the right to publish the piece in China, to the right to include the work in an online database, to the right to include it in an anthology, to the right to create a board game for cats based on the piece. (Okay, I'm stretching here, but you get the point.)

Simply put, the more rights you retain, the better. Publishers are usually going to try to grab as many rights as they can while compensating you as little as possible. They may offer an all-rights contract or a work-for-hire contract and simply hope you'll sign it without complaint. Learning to negotiate with editors and clients can boost your bottom line, ensure that you're paid what you're worth, and enable you to retain rights to material that you can resell in the future.

Yet, many writers—even experienced writers—aren't comfortable negotiating with editors. That's a mistake, and one I'm all too familiar with. When I started freelancing full time, I accepted whatever editors offered me and signed work-for-hire and all-rights contracts without complaint. (With a work-for-hire agreement, the publisher owns the copyright to the story; with an all-rights agreement, you own the copyright to the story but transfer all rights to the publisher. Legally, there's a distinction, but from a practical standpoint, the effect is the same. You got nuthin'.) I soon realized, though, that every time I sold all rights, I was also giving up any possibility of making more money from that particular story by reprinting it. I started asking for better rates and more writer-friendly contracts instead of automatically agreeing to editors' offers, and my strategy has paid off. I've made more money on individual stories, and today reprints comprise nearly 10 percent of my income.

Still, negotiating can be stressful, especially when you don't know where to begin. With a handful of useful strategies at the ready, you're more likely to get what you want from an editor—without losing an assignment or hurting your professional relationship.

Set Your Standards

First things first. You cannot negotiate effectively until you know what you want, what you're willing to concede on, and what your absolute bottom line or "walk away position" is. These factors will vary from writer to writer, and may change depending on where you are in your freelancing career. When I started freelancing, I took on every assignment regardless of pay. I focused on developing relationships with editors, building my portfolio, and improving my writing abilities. Today, however, I usually don't write for less than $1/word, and I strive for more.

However, don't get sucked into believing that the most important factor is dollars per word. It's not. It's dollars per *hour* that you should be concerned with. (Much more about that in chapter 8.) I may tell editors that I usually don't write for less than $1/word, but sometimes it's worth it to me to accept less for an assignment. For example, as a contributing editor at *The Writer*, I'm paid less than $1/word but have the benefit of being listed on the masthead as a regular contributor and promoting my books on writing and speaking gigs through my column. And if an editor will pay, say, $500 for a 1,000-word piece that will only require a few hours to write, I'll take the assignment. Do the math: if a story takes four hours to report and write, I'm making $125/hour—not a bad hourly rate.

So, what do you want from the assignment? Consider these factors:

- How much money is being offered? Is this comparable to what you're usually paid (or more)?
- What rights does the editor want to purchase? (In general, the more rights they want, the more they should be paying you.)

- How complicated is the assignment? Is it something that will take a couple quick interviews or several weeks' worth of reporting? Is it a subject you're well-versed in already, or will you have to start from scratch to write the piece?
- How soon does the editor need the assignment delivered? The sooner the deadline, the more you should be paid—especially if you're going to work nights and weekends to meet the deadline.
- How much of a PIA factor is involved? That's a polite way of saying "pain in the ass." Is this an editor who's known for requiring extensive revisions? Is the market known as a slow-paying one?
- Is this assignment likely to lead to more work or is it a one-shot deal?
- Does the story further your career in some other way? (For example, even a short piece in the *Atlantic Monthly*, *New Yorker*, or *New York Times* may garner you more attention than a longer feature in many other publications.)
- What's the state of your bank account? In other words, how desperate are you for the work?
- Is this a subject you can write about more than once, justifying the time you're going to put into the story? Is it a subject that commands your attention?

The best possible situation you're likely to encounter when negotiating an assignment is when you have plenty of work already. I know from experience that when your bank balance is dwindling, you're going to be more willing to take assignments that you would otherwise pass up.

Be Professional, Not Petulant

Remember the old saw about catching more flies with honey than vinegar? The same goes with contracts. I usually start this type of conversation by saying, "I'm really excited about this story, and am happy to be working with you. But there are a few sections of this contract I'd like to talk to you about." This is much more effective than saying, "You expect me to sign this piece of garbage? It sucks!" Editors are people, too—and they may have nothing to do with the language that's been offered to you.

Ask for More Money

Okay. You've determined your personal walk-away point and you're ready to ask (nicely) for what you want—or rather, to ask for more than what you want. Shoot high—that gives the editor some wiggle room. What do you actually say? It depends on the situation, but here are a variety of negotiating techniques to employ:

- Cite your standard. Let's say you've been writing for publications that pay $0.50 to $0.75/word, and an editor at a trade magazine offers you $0.40/word. You'd like to take the assignment, but you know you're worth more. Say so. "I'm excited about this story and I'd love to work with you, but I'm usually paid more than this rate."
- Act depressed. I've heard a number of writers suggest this one. When the editor makes an offer, don't say anything or sigh heavily and ask, "Is that really the best you can do?" If you can pull this one off, it can result in more money simply by brushing up on your method-acting techniques.
- Forget about being liked. "I'm not shy about asking for money. I'm not shy about negotiating—about asking for what I need and asking for more if necessary," says Erik Sherman. "It depends on the editor, the circumstances, and everything else. If someone is offering me enough, say $1.50/word for a business article, I'll probably say yes unless the way they want me to do it is going to be so

ridiculously time-consuming that I just don't think I can
do it. . . . You can't be shy about it, and you can't care
about whether the editor thinks you're nice. I think a lot of
writers are worried about whether they're going to come
across as nice people. Nice versus mean is a totally separate thing. This is what you need to do to make a living."

- Think big from the outset. "If a magazine wants you to
do something, they'll try to get you to do it cheap, and
say, 'if you do it cheap now, and if it goes well, we can
pay you more later,' " says Jim Thornton. "But try to get
as much as you can from the get-go because the first
thing you do kind of establishes your base. If they like it,
they may pay you better in the future but it's better to
start from a higher base." While new writers are often
willing to take less money with their first assignments,
Thornton thinks that's a mistake. "It's contrary to most
people's intuition," he says. "You think you'll do it cheap
so they'll like you, but I think the more they pay you, the
more they're predisposed to liking you. Try to stand up
for yourself financially and get as much as you possibly
can from the get-go."

- Prove your worth. While other writers may ask for more
money right off the bat, if I'm offered a decent deal for
the first story I do for an editor, I take it. Even if you have
hundreds of clips to your name, the editor's taking a
chance on you—there are plenty of talented writers who
are lazy about deadlines or turn in sloppy copy. But once
I've done a great job on my first or second assignment,
I'm in a much better position to ask for a higher per-word
rate for the next story. That's when I almost always ask
for a "raise," using language like, "I'm so happy we'll be
working together again! Because you've worked with me
before, you know I'm going to do a good job for you, and
turn in the story before deadline. Considering that you
know I'll deliver for you, can we bump up my per-word

rate?" (Or, "Can you do better money-wise for me this time around?")

- Make your case. Being assigned a straightforward story that will require minimal research is one thing. If, however, you're asked to write a piece with a tight deadline or one that will entail significant legwork and time, use this fact as a bargaining point. For example, several years ago an editor I'd worked with before called to assign a 2,000-word piece on oral contraceptives that included five sidebars—and then offered $1/word. That's not a bad rate, but it wasn't enough to justify all the time I was going to put into the story. I told her, "I really want to write this piece, but obviously this story is going to take me weeks of research and interviews, especially with all the sidebars. I don't think $1/word is really fair for this particular story. Can you do better than that?" She immediately agreed to $1.50/word, which gave me an extra $1,000 just for asking. (In retrospect, I realize she agreed too quickly—she probably would have gone even higher.)

- Keep your options open. Freelancer Sam Greengard makes his case for a higher rate, but refrains from boxing the editor into a corner. "I try not to get adversarial. If I feel I deserve more money, I'll ask for more money, but if I can't get it, I'll always leave the editor a back door," says Greengard. "In other words, I'll say, 'I'd really like to get $3,000 for this project instead of $2,500,' and I'll give reasons why—it's going to require a lot of research, it's going to require a lot of interviews, or there's a lot of travel involved. I'll give evidence of why I deserve more money, and if the editor says, 'I can't do that,' I'll say, 'I understand where you're coming from and perhaps next time we can go higher.'" That kind of bargaining keeps the negotiations friendly and sets up a possible increase next time around.

- Offer an alternative. Many editors don't understand why writers are resistant to signing all-rights contracts. You may hear words like, "But no other writer has ever complained!" Rather than turning down an all-rights contract flat, tell the editor *why* you don't want to sign it. I'll often explain to editors that I make a fair amount of income by reprinting articles, which is one of the reasons I resist all-rights contracts. If the contract asks for more rights than you want to sell, suggest a compromise. Early in my freelance career, I was assigned a story by a fitness magazine, which sent me a work-for-hire contract. I knew the story had definite reprint possibilities, and I realized that if I gave up all rights, I'd see nothing from this story but one check. I called my editor and suggested that I sell first North American serial rights with the provision that I wouldn't write about the same subject for a competing magazine for six months after the piece was published. The editor accepted that language, and I've reprinted that story twice since it first ran—for an extra $250. (In retrospect, I offered too much off the bat. If I were to do this now, I would only offer first North American serial rights and wait to see if *she* requested exclusivity for a certain time period.)
- More rights equal more money. On rare occasions, I will sign an all-rights contract if certain conditions are met. I consider how much time the piece will take, whether it's unlikely to be reprinted, and how much money the editor is offering. For example, a story on a new technological gadget is likely to be out-of-date in a few months' time. I'm more likely to sign an all-rights contract to a piece like that than to a piece about an evergreen topic. If you're giving up more rights, though, use that as a bargaining chip to get more money. Several years ago, I was offered a story on a subject that I was familiar with, and I knew it would only take me a few hours to research and

write. Because of the time-sensitive nature of the piece (an update on contraceptive options), it would almost immediately be outdated and reprinting it wasn't likely. The editor was offering me $1.50/word, certainly a decent rate. Even then, I explained why I usually don't sell all rights to my work and asked the editor if she could boost her usual rate. She offered an additional $.50/word for the story, and I took it. (Even if she wouldn't have upped the rate, I would have taken her original offer, but it never hurts to ask.) Realize, too, that if you're working for corporations, they may insist on all-rights or work-for-hire contracts. I don't have a problem with that as long as the money is good.

- Be willing to walk. Of course, not every negotiation will go the way you want it to. In some instances, an editor may refuse to offer better terms and/or the money you were hoping for. At that point, you must decide whether the money and clip are worth it to you. A couple of years ago, an editor offered me $800 for a 1,500-word story that would require a lot of research and then insisted on an all-rights contract. If this had been a subject I'd written about before, I might have accepted it, because I'm a relatively fast writer and researcher. The all-rights contract queered the deal and meant I had no qualms about turning down the work. If he had offered $3,000 for the same piece, my decision would have been more difficult. I thanked him for thinking of me, but explained that the assignment was too far below what I usually charge to accept it. "You have to be willing to walk away from work," agrees Sherman. "There were times early on when I was slaving away on lower-priced stuff and I started letting some of that stuff go so I could concentrate on getting higher-paid work. You're never going to be able to make a decent living working for 50 cents a word because you can't do enough work to make that possible."

- Be willing to try. Sure, it's easier to simply say "yes" or "no" to an offer than to try to negotiate with an editor, but that's no reason not to try. Take a deep breath, summon your courage, and ask if the editor can do better. You can usually find a compromise that will make both of you happy—and pay off in the long run as well. Writers are often afraid that if they ask for more money, they'll lose the assignment. In more than seven years of freelancing, that has never happened to me. The worst case scenario is that you'll ask for more money, the editor will refuse, and you'll have to decide whether you're willing to take the work or not. Remember, you're still the one who has the power to turn down work you don't want—or that isn't worth the time and hassle.

Negotiating Other Contract Changes

A contract is a binding legal document. I assume you wouldn't sign an employment agreement or a home loan without examining it carefully (or having a lawyer check it out for you). While you may be most concerned with how much money you're being paid, take the time to actually read the contract and highlight any areas that are confusing or incomprehensible. It may be tempting to simply flip to the signature page and affix your name, but it's worth it to negotiate changes that benefit you in the long run.

"I used to be terrible at changing contracts," admits Margaret Littman, who's based in Chicago. "I used to never do it, but the more I do it, the easier it seems." Don't assume an editor is married to the language in his or her contract. Because editors don't write their contracts, they may not understand the effects of certain provisions. In many cases, they haven't read their own agreements! "Editors don't have an emotional investment in the contract," says Littman. "I don't get confrontational about it. It's more that I have a conversation with an editor. . . . I pick up the phone and say, 'I really want to work on this assignment with you, and I understand you're not the one who came up with this contract, but I don't typically sign these clauses and here's why.'"

That kind of approach often works—and it keeps the discussion from becoming adversarial. If you have questions about what the language actually means, gather more information or ask a lawyer or a more experienced freelancer for help. The American Society of Journalists and Authors offers Contracts Watch, a free service that updates writers about publishing contracts and changes at *www.asja.org/cw/cw.php*. The National Writers Union also has some helpful advice about negotiating contracts at *www.nwu.org*.

Like Littman, I found that once I'd negotiated a few contract changes, I felt more comfortable approaching the issue with new editors. Not every approach works in every situation, but keep these strategies in mind if you're new to this:

- Choose your battles. Insisting on too many changes may give you a reputation for being "difficult." "I won't go to someone for a magazine article contract with twelve changes I want to make," says Littman. "That just seems ridiculous." In situations where she needs a number of alterations, such as with a book contract, she'll ask to work with the contracts department instead of the editor. "I'll try to avoid the editor and say, 'You know I have a lot of specific changes on this. Is there someone in the contracts department I can talk to so you don't have to waste your time?'" she adds. "That way, if there is any tension, it doesn't get the editor involved."
- Use your agent. As a magazine journalist or a freelancer working for businesses or corporations, you don't need an agent. But if you're writing nonfiction books, an agent can not only sell your manuscript, but also act as a go-between if things get sticky with contractual issues. Tell

your *agent* what you want, and then let him or her play
"bad cop" while you maintain a cordial relationship with
your editor. If you don't have an agent yet, don't worry;
many writers don't need them, and most freelancers
don't have agents early in their careers. If you decide that
you want to spend a significant part of your career writing books, however, a good agent is invaluable. (More
about whether you need an agent—and how to get one—
in chapter 10.)

- Ask for the "other" contract. Many publishers use more
  than one contract—often there's an all-rights agreement
  and another, less-rights-grabbing one. You don't get the
  latter if you don't ask for it. "If it's a magazine article, I'll
  usually say, 'do you have a first NA rights contract? I
  don't normally sell all rights,'" says Littman. "They usually have other contracts, particularly big publishers."

- Take the first step. Don't forget, you can always alter the
  contract to fit your specifications, send it in, and hope for
  the best. Believe it or not, this nonconfrontational
  approach often works. "I mark it up and send it in and
  hold my breath. On contract changes, I'm passive-
  aggressive. I'll send things back and see what happens,"
  says New Hope, Pennsylvania–based freelancer Leah
  Ingram, who's also worked as an editor. "Sometimes, it's
  easier to have the contract come back marked up if they
  are reasonable changes. You can't change every single
  clause, but honestly it's been a rare occasion where I've
  had a publisher that wouldn't accept my changes."

- Think outside the box. Freelancer Terry Whalin of Colorado Springs, Colorado, has also worked as an acquisi-
  tions editor for two publishing houses. He says that even
  when a publisher won't offer more in terms of an
  advance, it is often willing to make other changes to a
  book contract, such as including escalating clauses. (An
  escalating clause increases the percentage of royalties

you get as an author at certain sales points—for example, you might get 10 percent of the catalog retail price on the first 5,000 copies sold, 12.5 percent on the next 5,000, and 15 percent on any copies sold over 10,000.) "Another thing for authors to keep in mind is that if you come up with an innovative idea, you can often fit that into your contract," says Whalin. "For example, one of my authors is a real savvy marketer, and she suggested that she pay for up to half of the cost for an outside publicist and gave a dollar amount as to what she was willing to spend on that. She also negotiated that we'd provide several thousand postcards, and agreed that she would mail them out in the long run. A lot of authors don't think to do that kind of thing."

- Think long term. If this is a high-profile magazine, for example, you may be more willing to accept less-than-stellar contract terms for a compelling clip. Brian O'Connell, a business and finance writer, takes this long view with several of the publications he writes for because of the publicity involved. "I don't care about the *New York Times* contract [which is notoriously bad for writers]. . . . I'll write for the *Times* or the *Wall Street Journal* for less money because I know I'm going to parlay it into more assignments," says O'Connell. "It's a respect and cachet thing." In fact, a piece O'Connell wrote for the *New York Daily News* on a financial expert who discussed how to use a 401(k) plan to take early retirement caught the attention of a book editor at Random House early in O'Connell's career, which led to his first book contract.
- Consider potential resale markets. For magazine articles, you want to retain reprint rights. With book contracts, you may to want to retain foreign rights. "If you write a book that's general enough that someone will want to read it in Bulgaria and Taiwan and Italy, you can make a lot of money," says Victoria Moran. "I think *Creating a*

Charmed Life [one of her books] has sold into twenty-eight countries. In Iceland, it topped their best-seller list! You have to be far-sighted. . . . Once you have a little bit of clout with the publisher, see that you keep your foreign rights." Usually, a book contract will provide that for foreign-rights sales, the publisher gets half and the author gets half. That sounds okay until you realize most publishers won't bother with foreign-rights sales unless you're a best-selling author. That's a compelling reason for you to fight for your foreign rights—and either look for an agent who will sell those rights for you or work with a foreign-rights agent who specializes in overseas markets.

• Consider all the factors. It's not just the amount of money and the terms of the contract that influence whether you'll take an assignment. You may want to set a bottom-line figure for work you'll accept, especially when you're busy with work. "I've made a list of my criteria when I'll do an assignment," says Jim Thornton, who has a number of steady gigs with high-profile magazines. "Either it has to pay really well or it's something I really want to do or it's from an editor who is not going to drive me crazy with revisions and who I like to work with."

Because contracts are written for the benefit of *publishers,* in many cases they're going to try to grab as many rights as possible . . . while you as the writer want to keep as much as you can, or be paid handsomely for the rights you do assign. That means that while reading a contract, you should pay special attention to common clauses that can be downfalls for writers. Watch for provisions involving:

• Exclusivity. For example, magazines may want exclusive rights to a story for a certain period of time, maybe three or six months from publication. But sometimes they want to prevent you from writing about a similar subject during that time *for any other publication*. Ouch! See if you can get that provision stricken, especially if you cover a narrow range of subjects.

- Electronic rights. If you're selling rights to a print publication and it also wants electronic rights (most commonly so it can include the article on a Web site or in an online database), ask for more money to compensate you for those rights. More publishers are offering extra money for electronic rights now, but often you have to ask to be paid for those rights as well. Point out that print and electronic rights are two separate things, so it makes sense that you're paid for both types of rights.

- Research materials/transcripts/notes. Some contracts try to demand ownership of your transcripts and other research materials developed in connection with a story. Strike this language—they're purchasing the rights to the *article*, not the research, which you may use for another story. I've even seen contracts that try to prohibit you from writing about the same subject ever again. Whether a restrictive provision like this would stand up in court is debatable, but that's language you definitely want to strike.

- Indemnification. Be very careful. Many contracts contain indemnification language that requires you to bear the legal and financial responsibility if a claim or lawsuit arises from your actions, like if you libel someone. But some provisions require the writer to indemnify the publisher for "any claim" resulting from a story. If I've breached the contract, that's one thing—but I can't insure a publisher against bogus claims. "I won't sign an indemnification clause, particularly one that makes me not only responsible for my legal fees but their own legal fees," says Littman. "I won't sign that. They're a bigger company. It's one thing to say that I'm paying my legal fees, but I'm not paying theirs, and when I explain, 'I don't think we're going to get sued, I'm very careful, but I just don't think I should have to pay the publisher's legal expenses,' the editors always agree. But a lot of times no one's ever bothered to explain to them what that clause means! They haven't read the contract, so it's been really helpful to me to explain *why* I won't sign something."

- Kill fees. A kill fee is a certain amount of money—usually between 20 and 33 percent—that the publisher pays the writer when it decides not to purchase the work. When a story is killed, rights revert to you and you're free to turn around and offer it to another market. In theory, kill fees offer writers some protection if a piece fails to meet an editor's expectations. However, kill fees can be abused— if an editor changes her mind about a story, she can simply invoke the kill-fee provision. That's why many writers don't like them. Think about it—if you meet your contractual obligations, you should be paid the full price of the story, not a percentage of it because the powers that be at the magazine decided to go in a different direction.

In many cases, markets and clients already have set rates they pay writers, but you should also consider what you'll charge for different kinds of writing work. Magazines usually pay by the word; newspapers, by the column inch. If you write for corporations and businesses, however, you're likely to be paid by the hour or on a per-project basis. (More about these lucrative markets in chapter 11.) While billing *per hour* is convenient, in most cases you can make more billing *per project*, especially as you gain experience. Generally speaking, you can charge more if you live in a more populous area, and you don't want to fall into the trap of setting your rates too low. You might think it would garner more work for you, but it's more likely to look unprofessional.

When Bev Bachel started freelancing, colleagues cautioned her against charging too little. She already had several years of writing experience under her belt working for a corporation as an employee, but like many writers, she didn't feel confident setting her rates. "I was originally going to charge $15 or $20 per hour, and a friend said it had to be at least $50," says Bachel. She originally balked at the idea, but forced herself to get comfortable with her rate before she started quoting it to clients. "I remember spending an afternoon in front of the mirror saying versions of, 'my hourly rate is $50 an hour' and 'I charge $50 an hour,'" says Bachel. "I was only twenty-four or twenty-five and it seemed like an outrageous amount of money."

Hourly rates vary depending on your experience, your location, and your customers. When I started freelancing in 1997, I lived in a town of 10,000 people sixty-five miles from Chicago and charged $35/hour for copywriting. By 1999, I increased my rate to $45, and when I moved closer to the city, I upped my rate to $55/hour. Now I charge between $75/hour and $100/hour for business-writing work, which is about average for this area. Regardless of what you'll charge, think about it *before* a potential client asks about your rates. You want to be able to spit out a figure at a moment's notice, rather than fumbling for a number or trying to guess what might be appropriate.

Hey, I know your eyes may be glazing over at this point. Registering work, reading contracts, and attempting to negotiate better ones may not be the most enjoyable aspects of running your freelance career. But that's no reason to ignore them, especially when they can have a dramatic impact on your bottom line. Online resources like the Library of Congress (*www.loc.gov*) and the Internal Revenue Service (*www.irs. gov*), and organizations like the American Society of Journalists and Authors (*www.asja.org*) and the National Writers Union (*www.nwu.org*) can be helpful, but if you still have questions about contracts, consider hiring a lawyer who specializes in publishing. It's a business deduction that may pay for itself many times over.

CHAPTER 5
Think Business, Not
Hobby: The Armchair
Accountant

A s I pointed out in chapter 2, launching a successful free-lance business doesn't require a lot of capital or invest-ment. You don't need a lot of experience. You don't even need a formal business plan. But there are some basic tax issues every freelancer should be familiar with because they can have a sizable impact on your bottom line—and mean the difference between eking out a living and flourishing as a writer.

The problem is that most books on writing focus more on craft and marketing than on some of these less-than-thrilling topics. This chapter isn't meant as a substitute for the advice of an experienced accountant or tax attorney, but it will give you an overview of what every writer should know about taxes.

Talking about Taxes

When I started freelancing full time, taxes were the last thing on my mind. I was more concerned with getting assignments and building my portfolio than with what I would eventually pay to both the U.S. Treasury and the State of Illinois. I did understand, though, that I could take legitimate business expenses as tax deductions, and I kept track of them. Etch these words into your head: *Take every deduction you're legally entitled to!*

As a freelancer, every penny you make from your writing business (including reimbursed expenses) is reportable income. Some writers mistakenly think that because businesses are not required to file a form 1099-MISC unless they hit the $600 minimum, any amounts less than $600 need not be reported on their federal and state income tax returns. That's not the case. According to the Internal Revenue Service (IRS), businesses and individuals who pay more than $600 in services to another person or business must file a form 1099-MISC with the IRS and the person or business who received the payment. (The 1099 form is used to report payments to nonemployees—employees receive a W-2 form at the end of the year.) Even if you don't receive a 1099, you're required to report the amount as income on your taxes, regardless of whether your writing is considered a business or a hobby.

That's a critical distinction. If you operate as a "business" rather than as a "hobby," you're entitled to deduct legitimate business expenses, which reduces the amount you pay in taxes at the end of the year. The key, as far as the IRS is concerned, is having a profit motive. If you're writing with the intention of getting paid for your work, you've got profit in mind. You don't have to be freelancing full time or writing solely for the bucks to have a profit motive—the fact that you get some kind of psychic reward in addition to a monetary one from your work doesn't count against you. Going for the green (instead of merely writing for fun or to get published) is a major factor the government considers when deciding whether you're a legitimate business.

"The government looks much more favorably on enterprises that are conducted with the intention of making a profit—like a business—than enterprises that are conducted for one's personal pleasure, which is to say a hobby," explains enrolled agent Joe Anthony, a tax professional specializing in planning and returns for self-employed people and small businesses in Portland, Oregon. "If you're a business, which is to say an enterprise with the intention of trying to make a profit, you can deduct all the expenses related to that business whether or not the result is that you show a loss. If you're a hobby, the government says you can only deduct expenses up to the income you receive." Here's the rub: if you're operating as a hobby, you're probably not making any income from it, so as a practical matter you can't take any deductions.

Keep in mind that profit *motive* is more important than actually making a profit—ending up in the red doesn't mean your deductions will be disallowed. You may have heard of the "three-in-five rule," which is often misinterpreted to mean that a venture *must* make a profit three out of five years to be considered a business. That's not quite what it means. "The three-in-five rule actually says that if you make a profit in at least three out of five years, the *presumption* is that you are conducting a business, which means in an audit the burden of proof is on the government [to show that you aren't]," says Anthony. "If you do not make a profit, in an audit the burden of proof that you are in a business and conducting yourself as a business is on you." In other words, the presumption will be that you're only a hobbyist and you'll have to overcome that at an audit.

According to attorney and tax expert Julian Block of Larchmont, New York, the IRS takes a number of factors into account in determining your intention to make a profit, including:

- The manner in which you conduct your writing activities. For example, a person who submits articles that "pay" in copies is more likely to be considered a hobbyist than someone who submits to markets that pay with money.

- The amount of time—and effort—you spend on your writing career. "The burden of proof to establish that is on you, not the IRS," says Block. "To back up your deductions, in the event of an audit, save such records as queries to publishers and programs from writers' conferences. Note, too, that employment full time in some other field (as is the case with most freelancers) does *not* trigger an IRS refusal to classify you as a professional writer."
- Your history of income—or losses—from writing. If you've been making some income from your writing for several years, you're more likely to be considered a business than if you're always spending more on a writing career than you make from it.
- Your reliance on expert advice. For example, have you sought the assistance of an accountant? Have you taken courses to help you develop expertise as a writer?
- The expectation that the assets used in your business may appreciate in value.
- Your success in other business endeavors.

When determining whether you have a profit motive, the IRS may also consider your financial status and how much "personal pleasure" you receive from pursuing your writing. (Block provides an interesting analysis of IRS cases that have considered the business-versus-hobby question in his e-book, *Tax Tips for Freelance Writers, Photographers, and Artists, 2004,* which he updates each year. See the appendix for ordering information.)

Deductibles

So, what's deductible? All ordinary, necessary, and reasonable expenses related to trying to make a profit in your business. According to IRS regulations, you can deduct expenses that are both ordinary and necessary. An "ordinary" expense is one that is "common and accepted in your trade or business" and a "necessary" expense is one that is "helpful and appropriate for your trade or business." For freelancers, that usually includes:

- Office supplies like letterhead, paper, pens, printing cartridges, and the like
- Postage and mailing expenses
- Membership fees for writing and professional organizations
- Computer and peripherals (e.g., scanner and fax machine) used for your business
- Office equipment like filing cabinets, a desk, a chair, lamps, and the like
- Telephone expenses (you cannot deduct the expense of a primary phone line, but you can deduct long-distance charges related to your business as well as the cost of a second phone line solely used for business)
- Travel and entertainment (meals are subject to a 50 percent deduction)
- Cost of attending writing-related conferences
- Automotive expenses (If your office is in your home, every business-related trip you take can be deducted. You can take a standard mileage deduction—in 2004, it was $0.375/mile—or use a more complicated formula to take a percentage of your total car expenses at the end of the year. See more about this, below.)

If you're self-employed, you can also deduct the cost of medical insurance premiums for yourself, your spouse, and your family. You may also be entitled to a home office deduction if you use a section of your house or apartment solely and exclusively as your place of business. While ideally your home office will be a separate room, it can be part of a room if you have a designated area where you perform work and *only* your work. "To qualify for the deduction, you must use a portion of your home exclusively and regularly for your business. Generally, this is a separate room," says Block. "However, the IRS concedes it can be part of a room, as long as the division is clear and you establish that no personal activities take place within the business area."

Second, your home office has to be your principal place of business. "That means the place where you (1) regularly meet clients or customers or (2) use for your business's key administrative or management activities, provided there is no other fixed location where you conduct substantial administrative or management functions for that business," explains Block. Having a home office still allows you to work in other locations—say at Starbucks or the local library—as long as you perform most of your work at home. Then, you can take a percentage of your rent or mortgage interest and utilities as an expense at the end of the year.

Even if you don't take a home office deduction, remember that you can still deduct the cost of traveling from your home office to other locations for business reasons. Trips to the library for research, to meet with clients, to attend conferences, to purchase office supplies, and to lunch with editors all qualify as business driving. If your office is outside your home, however, you can't take a deduction for commuting to and from work because the IRS considers commuting a nondeductible expense.

With automotive expenses, you can choose between the actual-expense method or the standard mileage deduction to write off allowable operating costs. If you select the actual-expense method, you can deduct items including gas, oil, repairs, license and registration fees, car insurance, lease payments, car payments, parking, tolls, and depreciation. There are a couple of drawbacks to this method, however. "Opting for the actual-expense method in the first year the car is used for business requires you to stick with that method as long as you have that car," says Block. "Moreover, there are restrictions on depreciation deductions for cars used less than 50 percent of the time for business driving. Another limitation applies to cars used for both business and personal driving. You have to divide total costs between the two purposes; the cap on your deductions is the percentage of costs attributable to business use."

That's why many freelancers choose to use the standard mileage deduction, which is designed to cover the actual cost of operation plus depreciation, insurance, and other related expenses. The mileage deduction is adjusted upward every year or two to adjust for inflation. If you use this method, I suggest keeping a mileage log in your car to record the business-related trips you took, dates, purpose, and mileage—that way you're less likely to forget to record them. And note that you can still deduct additional travel expenses like tolls and parking expenses even if you choose the standard mileage deduction.

Keeping track of all writing-related expenses and maintaining receipts for them will reduce your tax liability and support your argument that you are in fact a business, not a hobby, should you get audited. And if any questions arise about deductions, you'll have proof of what you spent, when, and why.

You may want to talk to a tax professional about how to set up a record-keeping system for income and expenses. It needn't be anything fancy—I keep my expenses in a notebook and then store the receipts in a folder in my office. I don't necessarily need a receipt for $5 worth of copies, but if I ever get audited, I should have no problem backing up my deductions. "In an audit, the things that are most important are the documentation," says Anthony. "For example, the government says that meals and entertainment of less than $75, you don't need a receipt. However, they then go on to say that you need to be able to provide all the information to substantiate the deduc-

SCHEDULE C (Form 1040)	Profit or Loss From Business	OMB No. 1545-0074

Profit or Loss From Business
(Sole Proprietorship)

► **Partnerships, joint ventures, etc., must file Form 1065 or 1065-B.**

Department of the Treasury
Internal Revenue Service

► **Attach to Form 1040 or 1041.**   ► **See Instructions for Schedule C (Form 1040).**

2004

Attachment
Sequence No. **09**

Name of proprietor | Social security number (SSN)

A Principal business or profession, including product or service (see page C-2 of the instructions) | **B** Enter code from pages C-7, 8, & 9 ►

C Business name. If no separate business name, leave blank. | **D** Employer ID number (EIN), if any

E Business address (including suite or room no.) ►
City, town or post office, state, and ZIP code

F Accounting method: **(1)** ☐ Cash   **(2)** ☐ Accrual   **(3)** ☐ Other (specify) ►

G Did you "materially participate" in the operation of this business during 2004? If "No," see page C-3 for limit on losses   ☐ Yes ☐ No

H If you started or acquired this business during 2004, check here   . . . . ► ☐

Part I   Income

1	Gross receipts or sales. **Caution.** If this income was reported to you on Form W-2 and the "Statutory employee" box on that form was checked, see page C-3 and check here . . . . . . ► ☐	1	
2	Returns and allowances	2	
3	Subtract line 2 from line 1	3	
4	Cost of goods sold (from line 42 on page 2)	4	
5	**Gross profit.** Subtract line 4 from line 3.	5	
6	Other income, including Federal and state gasoline or fuel tax credit or refund (see page C-3) . . .	6	
7	**Gross income.** Add lines 5 and 6 . . . . ►	7	

Part II   Expenses. Enter expenses for business use of your home **only** on line 30.

8	Advertising	8		19	Pension and profit-sharing plans	19	
9	Car and truck expenses (see page C-3).	9		20	Rent or lease (see page C-5):		
10	Commissions and fees . .	10		a	Vehicles, machinery, and equipment .	20a	
11	Contract labor (see page C-4)	11		b	Other business property . . .	20b	
12	Depletion	12		21	Repairs and maintenance . .	21	
13	Depreciation and section 179 expense deduction (not included in Part III) (see page C-4)	13		22	Supplies (not included in Part III) .	22	
				23	Taxes and licenses	23	
				24	Travel, meals, and entertainment:		
14	Employee benefit programs (other than on line 19). .	14		a	Travel	24a	
15	Insurance (other than health) .	15		b	Meals and entertainment		
16	Interest:			c	Enter nondeductible amount included on line 24b (see page C-5) .		
a	Mortgage (paid to banks, etc.) .	16a					
b	Other	16b		d	Subtract line 24c from line 24b	24d	
17	Legal and professional services	17		25	Utilities	25	
				26	Wages (less employment credits) .	26	
18	Office expense	18		27	Other expenses (from line 48 on page 2)	27	
28	**Total expenses** before expenses for business use of home. Add lines 8 through 27 in columns . . ►					28	

29	Tentative profit (loss). Subtract line 28 from line 7	29	
30	Expenses for business use of your home. Attach **Form 8829**	30	
31	**Net profit or (loss).** Subtract line 30 from line 29.		

- If a profit, enter on **Form 1040, line 12,** and also on **Schedule SE, line 2** (statutory employees, see page C-6). Estates and trusts, enter on Form 1041, line 3.
- If a loss, you **must** go to line 32.

| } | 31 | |

32 If you have a loss, check the box that describes your investment in this activity (see page C-6).

- If you checked 32a, enter the loss on **Form 1040, line 12,** and also on **Schedule SE, line 2** (statutory employees, see page C-6). Estates and trusts, enter on Form 1041, line 3.
- If you checked 32b, you **must** attach **Form 6198.**

| } | 32a ☐ All investment is at risk. |
| | 32b ☐ Some investment is not at risk. |

For Paperwork Reduction Act Notice, see Form 1040 instructions.   Cat. No. 11334P   Schedule C (Form 1040) 2004

Schedule C (Form 1040) 2004   Page **2**

Part III   **Cost of Goods Sold** (see page C-6)

33	Method(s) used to value closing inventory: **a** ☐ Cost **b** ☐ Lower of cost or market **c** ☐ Other (attach explanation)
34	Was there any change in determining quantities, costs, or valuations between opening and closing inventory? If "Yes," attach explanation . . . . ☐ Yes ☐ No

35	Inventory at beginning of year. If different from last year's closing inventory, attach explanation . .	35	
36	Purchases less cost of items withdrawn for personal use	36	
37	Cost of labor. Do not include any amounts paid to yourself	37	
38	Materials and supplies	38	
39	Other costs	39	
40	Add lines 35 through 39	40	
41	Inventory at end of year	41	
42	**Cost of goods sold.** Subtract line 41 from line 40. Enter the result here and on page 1, line 4 . .	42	

Part IV   **Information on Your Vehicle.** Complete this part **only** if you are claiming car or truck expenses on line 9 and are not required to file Form 4562 for this business. See the instructions for line 13 on page C-4 to find out if you must file Form 4562.

43   When did you place your vehicle in service for business purposes? (month, day, year) ▶ . . . . / . . . . / . . . .

44   Of the total number of miles you drove your vehicle during 2004, enter the number of miles you used your vehicle for:

a   Business . . . .   **b** Commuting . . . .   **c** Other . . . .

45   Do you (or your spouse) have another vehicle available for personal use?. . . . . ☐ Yes   ☐ No

46   Was your vehicle available for personal use during off-duty hours? . . . . ☐ Yes   ☐ No

47a   Do you have evidence to support your deduction? . . . . ☐ Yes   ☐ No

b   If "Yes," is the evidence written? . . . . ☐ Yes   ☐ No

Part V   **Other Expenses.** List below business expenses not included on lines 8–26 or line 30.

. . . .	
. . . .	
. . . .	
. . . .	
. . . .	
. . . .	
. . . .	
. . . .	

48	**Total other expenses.** Enter here and on page 1, line 27	48

Schedule C (Form 1040) 2004

tion such as where you were, who you were with, when you did it, what you discussed, what was the business purpose, and how much you spent. . . . I advise people to keep the receipts. If you don't have the receipt, document it in your calendar, your day planner or PDA."

You'll file a Schedule C at the end of the year for your writing business, a sample of which appears on pages 102–103. While you may take a variety of deductions, as a freelancer, you're likely to make the most use of the deductions on the following lines under Part II, "Expenses":

Line 8—Advertising. Did you pay to advertise your writing? Enter it here.

Line 9—Car and truck expenses. Choose either the actual-expense method or the standard mileage deduction and don't forget to fill out Part IV, "Information on Your Vehicle," on the second page of Schedule C.

Line 13—Depreciation and section 179 expense deduction. Here's where you'll deduct the cost of equipment you purchase to run your business. You can take the entire cost of the equipment or depreciate the property over a certain number of years.

Line 17—Legal and professional services. Fees you pay your accountant or lawyer in connection with your business are entered here.

Line 18—Office expense. This may be a sizable expense, including the cost of letterhead, business cards, office supplies, postage, photocopies, sample issues, connectivity charges, software, and telephone expenses.

Line 24—Travel, meals, and entertainment. If you travel to meet with a client, attend a business-related conference, or do business-related entertaining, you'll take the deductions here. Remember, though, that while you can take the full cost of travel expenses such as airline tickets and hotel charges, you can only deduct half of the cost of your meals and entertainment.

Line 27—Other expenses. Miscellaneous expenses are totaled here and detailed on the next page under Part V, "Other Expenses." Here, I deduct expenses like the cost of writers' conferences, temporary help, and professional dues.

A note about line 13: If you purchase equipment to be used for your business, you have two options. You can depreciate it over time, or you can take it as a section 179 deduction and deduct the entire amount for that year. "Freelancers who go the 'standard route' at Form 1040 time recover what they spend on equipment through depreciation deductions over varying periods. The general rules for depreciation of various kinds of personal and real property specify periods that range from as low as three years to as high as thirty-nine years, with the majority closer to three than to thirty-nine," says Block. "Most equipment gets depreciated over five years (computers, copiers, and the like) or seven years (furniture and fax machines, for example). Usually, the cap on the amount allowable as a deduction for the first year is only 20 percent of the cost of five-year property and about 14 percent of the cost of seven-year property." This means that it will take several years before you can deduct the total cost of your equipment.

Under section 179, sometimes called "first-year expensing," however, you can write off the entire cost of the equipment in the first year it's "placed in service." The IRS interprets "placed in service" to mean available for a specific use, so if you bring home a new office chair on December 31, you can write off the entire cost as a section 179 deduction on that year's taxes. If you buy software on December 31, but don't install it until January 2, though, you'll have to wait and take it as a deduction for the following year. There is a cap on section 179 deductions; for 2004, the maximum was $102,000, which is probably far more than you'll spend on equipment in any given year. Also, you can't deduct an amount under section 179 that's more than the amount of your net taxable income before you apply the 179 write-off.

Subtracting your total business expense deductions from your gross income leaves your tentative profit (or loss). After deducting the amount of your home office deduction (which is calculated using Form 8829), you're left with your net profit. It's this amount that you'll pay self-employment tax on, which is 15.3 percent of your profit up to $87,900, and 2.9 percent of your profit above that. You'll also pay any applicable federal, state, and local taxes based on your net profit, so the more legitimate expenses you can deduct, the less you'll shell out to Uncle Sam.

This chapter meant to give an overview of what you'll need to know about taxes as a freelancer. For more information, check out the IRS's *Tax Guide for Small Business* (Publication 334). It and other helpful publications are available at no charge at *www.irs.gov*. For other questions and advice specific to your unique situation, talk to an accountant who specializes in small business and self-employment issues.

Section 2
Efficiency

CHAPTER 6
No Need to Re-create the Wheel: Designing Effective Writing Templates

As a new freelancer, you may be surprised to discover that only part of your days are spent doing work for which you are paid. In addition to working on assignments, you must devote time to marketing, billing, and record-keeping tasks that can easily eat up hours better spent producing income. That's why developing and maintaining a selection of writing templates or forms on your hard drive can be invaluable.

Take query letters. If you write for magazines, you can count on spending a lot of time working on queries, at least when you're pitching editors who are new to you. A query letter serves as a letter of introduction, a sales pitch, and a writing sample—and hopefully convinces the editor to give you an assignment. It's often the first impression you make on the editor and showcases your ability to analyze the magazine's audience and to come up with compelling article ideas.

That doesn't mean it must be perfect. When I started freelancing, I agonized over nearly every query, struggling to come up with the *perfect* pitch each time. I was spending untold hours creating queries. Worse yet, many didn't sell—I wasn't doing a very good job of analyzing markets before I queried them. That added up to an enormous waste of time, especially when you consider that marketing only pays off when it actually leads to work.

Now, I can write a query—a good, salable, successful query—in twenty minutes or less. Part of the reason is that churning out hundreds of them has certainly made me a faster query writer. But I also use the same basic template each time—a four-paragraph format that rarely changes:

- The first paragraph is the lead, designed to catch the editor's attention
- The second is what I call the "why-write-it" paragraph, where I briefly explain the appeal of the story to the publication's readers
- The third is the "nuts-and-bolts" paragraph where I include information about who I plan to interview, suggested word count, appropriate section of the magazine, possible sidebars, and working title
- The fourth is what I call the "I-am-so-great" paragraph, where I demonstrate why I'm uniquely qualified to write the piece

Because I have the structure down, I can pound out queries in a matter of minutes, which saves me countless hours.

When you start freelancing, you may not have templates to work from. Creating your own saves you time and lets you work more efficiently, but you don't have to do it from scratch. In the pages that follow, you'll find examples of templates for a variety of documents you may use in your freelance business, including:

- Magazine queries
- Follow-up letters
- Cover letters
- General pitch letters
- Book proposal queries

- Corporate/business writing pitches
- Proposals
- Invoices

Magazine Queries

Remember, with a magazine query you want to capture the editor's attention, demonstrate the appeal of the story, give an overview of what your completed piece will look like, and prove you're the perfect writer for the story. It's also an opportunity to let the editor know you've read her publication by saying something like, "Interested in this idea for your 'Today's News' section?" Or mention a recent article in your query by saying something like, "I noticed you published a piece on easy ways to save money last month and thought my piece on successful garage sale strategies might interest you." Let the editor know you've done your homework by reviewing her magazine.

When you can, suggest possible sidebars, quizzes, or resource boxes to complement the main piece. Include the section of the magazine the story's appropriate for, proposed word count, and give her an idea of who you plan to interview for the story. Think like your editor and offer her a package that will make her job easier. If she likes the idea, and the angle, all she has to do is call you and assign the story.

Finally, highlight your relevant writing experience and background, and if you can, demonstrate that you're uniquely qualified to write this article. Don't be shy about touting your qualifications. I've received work from editors who didn't like my original query idea but were impressed with my background and assigned other work to me instead.

See the following pages for some sample queries. While the dates and addresses have been removed, normally these queries would be sent on letterhead, in business-letter form.

The first is an example of pitching a magazine that is a new market for me. Note that I've suggested the appropriate section of the magazine for the story to let her know I've studied her publication. Because I'm a new writer to her, I've listed some of my writing credits and included clips.

> Dear Ms. Ferraro:
>
> Breakfast: double latte, no whip. Lunch: Half of a chicken salad sandwich (from a generous coworker!), an apple, and a bag of M & Ms. Mid-afternoon/pre-workout snack: Slightly stale cinnamon roll from the pastry cart (hey, you're starving!). Dinner: Cashew chicken take-out. Dessert: Four spoonfuls of Ben & Jerry's Chubby Hubby.
>
> Sound familiar? If you're like most of us, you consume too much caffeine, too much fat, way too much sugar, and not enough fruits, veggies, and complex carbohydrates. But although we know we *should* eat better, we may mistakenly believe that healthful eating means completely overhauling our diets—and who wants to eat tofu and bean sprouts every day? Fear not! Eating better *doesn't* mean forgoing all the food you know and love—it just means making a few smarter choices.
>
> "Fix Dietary Disasters: How to Eat Healthier—Easily" will describe the most common dietary mistakes young women make and suggest small eating-habit changes to correct those mistakes. The story will include expert advice and suggested healthier substitutions for a "typical" day of meals and snacks, and will discuss how eating better will help readers look, feel, and perform at their peaks. I have several experts already in mind for this story, including registered dietitian Susan Kleiner, author of *Power Eating* (Human Kinetics, 1998) and *High-Performance Nutrition* (John Wiley & Sons, 1996), and will also use "real women" examples if you like. Possible sidebars might include how to make the change to

a vegetarian diet and a list of pre-workout snacks. While I estimate a length of 1,500 words, that's flexible depending on your needs.

Interested in this topic for your "Food for Thought" department or as a feature? I'm a full-time freelancer who's written about health, fitness, and nutrition for magazines including *Fitness, Fit, Shape, Self, Oxygen, Redbook, Family Circle, Marie Claire,* and *Woman's Day;* clips are enclosed. Let me know if you have any questions about this story idea; I look forward to hearing from you soon.

Very truly yours,

Kelly James-Enger

If you've written for an editor before, you can usually get away with shorter, less-developed queries. I've received assignments from queries as short as three sentences. For complex subjects, though, a fully fleshed-out proposal is still a good idea. With the next query, I'd worked with Stephanie Young, then health editor at *Redbook*, before, so I didn't have to remind her of my writing qualifications. Note that this query includes a time peg (the mention of the recent advertising campaign) and also cites recent research and statistics.

Dear Stephanie:

According to the American College of Obstetricians and Gynecologists, 85 percent of menstruating women experience one or more premenstrual symptoms every month, including irritability, headaches, and depression. Most women experience cramps and breast swelling or tenderness as well.

But to see the recent television commercials for the antidepressant drug Sarafem (fluoxetine), recently approved to treat premenstrual mood disorder ("PMDD"), you'd think that every woman turns into an irrational lunatic the week before her period. One ad shows a woman frantically searching for her keys, growing more out-of-control as she does so. One innocent question from her husband and she turns on him in fury. In another, a woman at the grocery store has trouble pulling a shopping cart out and looks as though she'll have a meltdown as a result.

These commercials would be funny if they weren't so misleading. While most women do experience PMS, only a small percentage—3 to 8 percent—appear to have PMDD. Yet these commercials imply that if you're tired of PMS, help is only a pill away.

For women with serious PMDD, Sarafem may be an appropriate treatment. But women shouldn't simply reach for an antidepressant without considering the severity of their symptoms and other treatment options including dietary modifications, lifestyle changes, and calcium supplements. In fact, the cause of these symptoms may not be PMDD or PMS at all; according to a study published a year ago, 40 percent of women who thought they had PMS met the criteria for a mood or anxiety disorder instead. So how do you know if your "PMS" is PMS, PMDD, or something else entirely?

"The PMS-Preventing Pill: Too Good to be True?" will look at this recent development in treating PMS and PMDD and explain the difference between the two conditions and describe other possible causes of these types of symptoms. The piece will explain why Sarafem isn't appropriate for every woman with PMS and will report on the recent research being conducted in this area. Readers will learn how to determine whether their physical and emotional changes are menstrual-related or due to another cause and learn of other ways to reduce the severity of their symptoms. I'll rely on experts such as Steven Sondheimer, MD, professor of obstetrics and gynecology and codirector of the Premenstrual

Syndrome Program at the University of Pennsylvania for this story; a possible sidebar could include a rundown of the five major symptom clusters of PMS. While I estimate 2,000 words for this story, that's flexible depending on your needs.

Stephanie, let me know if you're interested in this topic for your "Health" section or have any questions about this query.

Thanks for your time; I look forward to hearing from you soon.

Best,

Kelly

With the next query, I've reminded the editor of who I am (always mention an "in" or connection in your first paragraph) and highlighted my relevant writing experience. Note that I mention my writing-related publications first in the list of magazines where my work has appeared because *Pages* is a publication about writers and their books. If I were pitching a fitness publication, on the other hand, I would have mentioned magazines like *Self* and *Fitness* first.

Dear John:

It was a real pleasure meeting you in Chicago, and I hope you enjoyed your visit with your parents. I'm writing to follow up on one of the ideas I pitched during our one-on-one:

You've written your first book—a novel, perhaps, or a work of nonfiction. In search of a potential publisher, you pore through books like *Writer's Market* to find the perfect one. Sure, there are hundreds of publishers listed, but did you realize that many of the apparently different houses and imprints may actually be subsidiaries of the same corporation? In fact, according to *Guerrilla Marketing for Writers*, six conglomerates currently dominate

English-language publishing: AOL Time Warner; Bertelsmann; Rupert Murdoch's News Corporation; Pearson, Penguin; Viacom; and Dieter Von Holtzbrinck.

Does the move toward conglomeration in the publishing industry mean good news or bad news for first-time authors? Are there fewer chances for success with the larger houses or are smaller houses picking up the slack? And how does this affect how authors pitch and present their work? "Under the Umbrella: What Mega-Publishers Mean for First-time Authors" will look at this trend and report on how it affects authors and what changes writers may expect in the future. I'll interview publishing-industry experts, including editors and agents, for the story; while I estimate 1,500 words for the piece, that's flexible depending on your needs.

John, are you interested in this topic as a feature for *Pages*? As you know, I'm a full-time freelancer who has written for more than forty national magazines including *The Writer, Writer's Digest, Redbook, Marie Claire, Woman's Day, Self, Shape, Parents, Fitness, E-merging Business,* and *Chamber Executive.* As I mentioned, I was originally a lawyer (ugh!) but now write mostly health, fitness, diet/nutrition, bridal/relationships, and writing-related articles; clips are enclosed.

Let me know if you have any questions about this idea or have other pieces I might be right for; otherwise, I'll follow up on this query in a couple of weeks.

Have a great August!
Best,

Kelly James-Enger

Your query gives an editor who's new to your work a feel for your writing style and voice. It's also a chance to showcase your reporting ability. In the next query, note the amount of detail and the heart-tugging elements longtime freelancer Lisa

Collier Cool includes in her query to Kate Lawler at *Parents* magazine. Her query to *Family Circle* reveals that she's already done extensive reporting on the subject and highlights the threat to parents and readers of the magazine. (Cool also included an extensive biography at the end of the query listing her numerous credits, publications, and awards, which has been omitted.)

> Dear Kate,
>
> Here's a description of a story I think could be great for the December issue, since it involves a touchingly generous holiday gift.
>
> Five-year-old Madisen Jackan was born with white-blonde hair, but by the time she was two, it all fell out, due to an inherited condition called alopecia totallis. She also lost her eyebrows, eyelashes, and all her body hair. In preschool, Madisen was painfully shy, suffered from severe separation anxiety, and was extremely self-conscious, due to the stares and rude comments she received. To ease their daughter's transition into kindergarten, her parents, Chris (a stay-at-home mom) and Jeff (an aircraft mechanic) who also have two older kids who aren't affected by alopecia, sent a letter to all the parents and teachers, explaining Madisen's disorder.
>
> Chris also went to school the first day and talked to the kids. "I wanted everyone to know that she wasn't dying of cancer and hadn't had chemotherapy," says Chris. "I told the children that alopecia wasn't contagious, so they wouldn't lose their hair if they played with Madisen." She showed the children Madisen's large collection of scarves and hats, since the little girl doesn't like to go out in public with her head uncovered. Most of all, says the mom, "I prayed Madisen would find a best friend, because she hadn't made any friends in preschool, and was always clinging to me."
>
> Her wish came true. Soon after school started,

Madisen became fast friends with five-year-old Taylor Schmidt. Taylor, who had waist-length blonde hair, didn't care that her new best friend was bald. Instead, she wanted to help. When she heard about a relative who had donated hair to a group that makes wigs for people who've lost their hair due to cancer treatment, alopecia, or other medical problems, the kindergartner decided that she wanted to give her hair to Madisen. When Taylor told her parents, Jodi (a stay-at-home mom) and Chris (a firefighter), they were amazed by their daughter's generosity, since Taylor was extremely proud of her thick, golden hair, and loved to have her mother style it.

On December 17 of last year, a crowd of relatives, kindergartners, teachers, and firefighters who worked with Chris Schmidt gathered to witness the haircut, the first of Taylor's entire life. Following the instructions from Hip Hats, a company that makes hats with real hair attached for bald-headed girls and women, a stylist tied Taylor's hair into four ponytails, then snipped each of them off at neck length. Jodi was holding her breath, not sure how her daughter would react, but Taylor smiled all through the haircut, then ran over and hugged her best friend when the cut was complete.

On January 30 of this year, the special hat was ready. It's a blue denim cap with long blonde locks flowing down the sides, just as it would if a girl with hair was wearing the hat. Says Chris, "It's now Madisen's favorite hat: She loves it because it came from Taylor. She puts clips and ponytail holders in the hair, so she can give herself different styles." And Taylor is equally delighted with her own new look——she says her head feels lighter, and that she's never going to grow long hair again, because she likes her short bob so much. The two girls remain the best of friends, and are always hugging each other, holding hands, and sharing secrets.

I'll look forward to your reaction to this charming

story. I have asked the moms to send pictures, and will forward them to you when they arrive.

Best wishes,

Lisa

Dear Marilyn,

As discussed, here's an idea I thought could be an important one for *Family Circle*:

"Moms on Meningitis" is a group of five women whose college-age children were killed or suffered devastating amputations as a result of meningococcal meningitis—a dangerous bacterial infection that can cause shock, deafness, brain damage, loss of limbs, and in up to 25 percent of cases, death. It is often misdiagnosed as something less serious because the initial symptoms—fever, headache, stiff neck, nausea, fatigue, and in some cases, a rash—can be confused with the flu. If untreated within hours of initial symptoms, however, the disease can rapidly progress to shock, death, or very serious complications.

Although the disease is relatively rare, affecting about 3,000 Americans a year, it poses a particular threat to certain college students: Freshmen who live in dormitories have triple the risk of other undergraduates—and seven times the risk of non-students the same age. What's more, the rate of the disease in kids ages fifteen to twenty-four has doubled since 1991, the Centers for Disease Control reports. With thousands of kids going off to college in the fall, this information couldn't be more timely.

Although there's a $65 vaccine against bacterial meningitis that can save lives, many students and their families never hear about it. That's because only fourteen states require colleges to provide educational materials about meningitis; and only eight mandate that students be vaccinated. Judy Miller of Coal City, Illinois, and Lynn Bozof of Marietta, Georgia, wish someone had told them about the shot before their kids went to college. In March, 1999, Judy's daughter, Beth, got sick with classic symptoms of meningitis. Thinking that she had the flu, Beth delayed getting medical care, and died three days later. Lynn's son, Evan, was stricken in 1998, and died after twenty-six days of harrowing complications.

After losing their children, both moms went on a mission to save other kids. Judy began by blanketing Beth's campus with flyers about meningitis, its symptoms, and the potentially lifesaving vaccine that protects against it; then she set up a foundation in her daughter's name to fund vaccination programs. Lynn worked with the dean of her son's school to get legislation passed in Georgia to encourage public colleges and universities in that state to educate students and their families about the disease; set up a vaccine clinic at a local high school; and testified about her son's death before the CDC. The CDC now recommends parents and their kids be informed about the risk of meningitis and the benefits of vaccination.

Page Kach and her son John knew about the vaccine, which was on a list of recommended immunizations the boy's college advised for incoming freshmen. Yet neither their family doctor or other local MDs stocked the shot, so John went off to college in 2000 without it. Although his mom encouraged him to get the vaccine when he was on campus, the 6' 6", 200-pound college basketball star never got around to it, in part because he and his family had no idea how serious the disease was. Similar factors kept Deb Kepferle's son, Patrick, from getting the shot.

Both boys contracted this disease in 2000: Patrick

died, and John survived, but had to undergo amputation of his right leg below the knee. After nine months of treatment, he learned to walk with the help of a prosthetic leg and has returned to college, where he hopes to get a teaching degree. He and his mom also devote themselves to educating other students about the horror of meningitis. So do Candie Benn and her daughter Melanie, now 24, who survived meningitis she caught as a college freshman, but had to undergo amputations. She now hopes that by sharing her story she can help protect others, starting with her younger sister, Jessica, who recently started college—AFTER getting the vaccine.

The MOM group has several goals: They want to raise awareness of meningitis and the elevated risk for college freshmen. They'd also like parents and students to be more aware of the symptoms of this extremely dangerous disease, so kids who do get sick know to get prompt, potentially lifesaving medical treatment. And most of all, they'd like every college to require the shot.

I'll look forward to your reaction with interest. Although you're familiar with my work, I have included my bio below, with details of the eleven awards I've won for my medical journalism and the many magazines I've written for.

Best wishes,

Lisa

When writing a query, consider why the topic is a timely one. Timothy Harper pitched the following query to senior editor C. Michael Curtis at the *Atlantic Monthly* several months after the Columbine shootings. (Note that the idea sprung out of a conversation with a friend. Harper realized the story potential for this subject immediately.) Not only did the pitch earn him the assignment, but the story, "Shoot to Kill," also

won the 2001 Outstanding Article Award from the American
Society of Journalists and Authors.

Dear Mike:

I was in Peoria, Illinois, last weekend on some family
business and went for a beer with one of my oldest
friends, a longtime police officer. He told me that he and
his fellow cops are going through new emergency-
response training aimed at Columbine-like events. My
buddy and the other cops are rattled because the new
training is so different—opposite, he said—from what
they were taught before. In the past, if one or more gunmen ran amok in a school or other building, the first officers at the scene were to secure the perimeters and
wait for help. When more police arrived (often a SWAT
team), they would start going in, carefully securing parts
of the building as they went. If there were injured people,
getting them out and to a hospital was a priority. The
goal was to pin down the gunmen, cut off escape routes,
and then negotiate. The police were not supposed to
shoot except when there was an immediate threat—
shots being fired at them or bystanders.

The new training, according to my friend, requires
the first officers at the scene to move in immediately,
without securing the area. They are not supposed to
stop to help the wounded. If they see a gunman, the
police are to shoot, and keep shooting. If a gunman is
holding a gun to a kid's head, the police should shoot,
and keep shooting. They don't want a gunman to hole up
in a defensible position. The cops are supposed to attack
and pursue, and keep the gunman moving if they can.

An abandoned office building in Peoria is being used
for drills. Instead of those old cardboard pop-out figures,
real people play the bad guys, with those new pepper-
powder bullets. My friend had nasty welts where he'd
been hit. He believes police departments around the

country are being retrained this way. If you like, I can find out more about where, how, and why this is happening. My friend says lawsuits and press criticism after Columbine are a big factor. I have to wonder, though, if this approach is really safer. I wonder what various experts have to say. Would this have saved lives at Columbine? Why wasn't this approach used before? What do cops themselves think of it? My friend wasn't sure, but he seemed uneasy. I've enclosed a clip from a *New York Times* story I saw when I got home from Peoria.

Please let me know if you're interested, and what else you'd need to know before deciding if this is a possible story.

Cheers,

Tim Harper
www.timharper.com

High-profile markets like the *Atlantic Monthly, New York Times, New Yorker,* and *Wall Street Journal* are inundated with queries. Jim Morrison's query to Ray Sokolov, the Arts page editor at the *Wall Street Journal,* netted him his first assignment for that section of the newspaper. Note the amount of detail that's included in this query; Morrison also points out that he's well acquainted with the subject, as he's covered one of the potters before—for *Smithsonian,* a magazine known for quality writing.

Dear Ray:

A few years ago, in the midst of firing his wood kiln, North Carolina potter Mark Hewitt reflected on the allure of using the ancient technique to create pots. "This is the hard way of doing it. It's very labor-intensive. It requires skills that you learn only by doing," he said. "I feel like the last of the dodoes."

Hewitt, 43, indeed is a rare breed. While pottery making has grown more popular (and profitable) nationwide, few potters fire wood kilns today because the process is so difficult to master. Fire the kiln too hot and the clay gets brittle. Raise the temperature too high, too fast, and pots may explode. But to Hewitt and others, the downside is worth the unique colors and finish. Hewitt and Jeff Shapiro, two of the best-known and collected creators of wood-fired pottery, will open an exhibit at Dai Ichi Art on 57th Street beginning June 12. I'd like to do a story about the two friends for the Home section pegged to the opening.

Their styles differ drastically. Hewitt, a Brit and descendant of a Spode director, lives off the land in North Carolina, where he has produced museum-quality pieces for nearly two decades. He likes to call his work "Southern Mingei," a mingling (and mangling) of utilitarian styles from rural North Carolina, Asia, and Britain. Customers call it expensive. A simple Hewitt mug costs $35, while his stunning large jugs and planters fetch as much as $2,500. He fires his kiln three times a year (it takes four days), making about 1,500 pots each time. He sells them at a kiln opening on his farm a few weeks later. Often, they are all gone the first day. Shapiro, 51, a New York native, spent eight years studying in Japan before returning to the United States to build a kiln in Accord, New York, nearly two decades ago. His scarred, craggy work draws strongly on the Japanese aesthetic and bears little resemblance to Hewitt's soft lines. He rips, tears, and cuts clay to create both utilitarian pots and sculptural works resembling abstracted landscapes.

Their stories have similar touchstones. Each apprenticed with a master, then left to build a kiln and live a rural lifestyle. Hewitt jokes that he is the "black sheep" of his family for abandoning Britain and his family's tradition in fine china for a vein of clay in the North Carolina Piedmont.

Shapiro found a patron and mentor in Japan in the 1970s. Eventually, he created a home and a studio in a small coastal town named Hamaska. One day, however, he was abruptly asked to leave by his mentor, who offered no explanation. That experience sent him back to the States, where he built an anagama kiln and quickly began creating the irregular, asymmetrical pieces that have found an audience here and in Japan.

Both men have work in several museums, including the Brooklyn Museum, the Mint Museum, the Chrysler Museum, and the Ackland Museum. I know this subject well, having done a *Smithsonian* magazine story two years ago about North Carolina potters featuring Hewitt as its central character. Images of their work can be found at *www.markhewittpottery.com* and *www.the-anagama.com/En/shapiro/jeff.html*. Let me give you a little background about me. I've written for *The New York Times, Smithsonian, George, offspring, Family PC, This Old House, Good Housekeeping, Reader's Digest, Utne Reader, Southwest Spirit,* and *American Way,* among others.

If this idea appeals to you, I'll be happy to mail or fax clips.

Sincerely,

Jim Morrison

If you'd like to pitch more than one idea at once, you can send them as separate queries or use a double-duty query that suggests two ideas in one letter. If you choose the latter method, make sure that each idea is fleshed out. While free-lancer Sam Greengard includes two ideas in the following queries, each contains a significant amount of detail in only a paragraph. He's also targeted his markets. The first, a pitch to an editor at *Los Angeles* magazine, notes the local angle of each idea; the second, a query sent to *Wired*, highlights the techno-logical aspect of each topic.

Dear Ms. McNamara:

- STRIP TEASE: It may not offer the high-concept snob appeal of collecting art or the adrenaline-pulsing excitement of investing in the stock market, but for a significant subculture of Angelenos, there's nothing quite like owning a tiny strip of undeveloped land. Next to the freeway. Beside an apartment building. Behind a movie theater. Wherever. These odd lots, which aren't big enough to build on and are mostly useless, are bought, sold, and traded with amazing regularity, according to Toni DelliQuadri, director of tax collection operations for L.A. County. In fact, at a public auction on February 3, nearly 200 parcels changed hands. In some cases, sales were due to foreclosure (many of those who buy the lots don't pay the taxes); in other cases, these mini-land barons simply wanted a new piece of turf. Remarkably, some of these individuals travel from county to county throughout the state snapping up parcels at auctions and from other landowners as if they were collecting baseball cards.
- DISASTER MAN: Just watched one of your airplanes skid off the end of the runway? Witnessed yet another armed robbery, but this time with a shooting? Seen your oil refinery blow sky high? Who you gonna call? Kevin Flynn. The Los Angeles psychologist is one of the nation's leading experts on debriefing and comforting victims of trauma and disasters. He counseled survivors and employees at the LAX USAir crash a couple years back, the horrendous ARCO oil refinery explosion in Houston, and has worked with the likes of First

Interstate and the Los Angeles Police Department. Usually, he is called to the scene only moments after an event, and can spend anywhere from a few hours to weeks working with victims—who typically display a wide range of behavior. "Some people can handle traumatic situations better than others, but everyone is affected," he says. "My job is to help people cope and prevent them from having their life fall apart. It's not easy."

I'm a contributing editor at *Los Angeles* magazine, and have written for *Travel and Leisure, Playboy, Home, Family Circle, American Health*, and many others.

Sincerely,

Sam Greengard

Dear Jim:

I have two ideas that might work for *Wired*. Over the last 12 years, I have penned articles for *Discover, Playboy, Travel and Leisure, Home, Family Circle, American Way* (American Airlines), *USAir, Los Angeles* magazine, and the Los Angeles *Times*. I can provide clips and references upon request.

PLUGGING INTO THE BRAIN: In the film *Johnny Mnemonic*, Keanu Reeves starred as a futuristic messenger whose brain had been equipped with an electronic port through which information could be fed directly into his memory. That might seem to spiral into the far reaches of sci-fi, but a group of scientists at the University of Southern California, led by biomedical engineer Theodore Berger, have recently made the idea of implanting microchips in gray matter seem entirely possible. Such a device, now in the embryonic stages of development, would restore and enhance myriad capabilities—particularly among those suffering from strokes, head traumas, seizures, Alzheimer's, and an array of other afflictions.

Studying the brain's hippocampus region and using computers to model the function of its five sub-areas, Berger has developed complex mathematical models that mimic the way the brain works. In fact, he has already concocted a computer program that precisely duplicates natural dentate gyrus tissue found in the hippocampus. Problem is, the software would have to execute millions of instructions in order to work, and that would transform a brain prosthesis into a glacially slow device. "Today's computers simply don't have the necessary processing power," he points out.

Instead, he is directing his efforts to building a neural network of microchips, with a silicon wafer able to handle the work of 100 or more neurons. Using fiber-optic lighting signals to connect tens of thousands of one-millimeter-square chips stacked in layers across a small board, he is able to replicate the brainpower of millions of neurons. "At that point, you can easily get to the volume you need to replace the brain system you are trying to simulate," he explains. "A surgeon will remove the damaged portion of the brain and replace it with an implantable device that's about the same size. The fact is, a microchip doesn't have to perfectly mimic every function of the brain that's been lost. The brain is an adaptive organ and it will rewire itself to work with the added instructions from the microchip." So far, preliminary experiments on rabbits have proven that the concept is viable, and Berger believes that he's just over a decade away from engineering an artificial brain.

THE NATIVE WORD: When we ponder all the endangered things on Planet Earth, the spoken word usually isn't included on anyone's list. But Kenneth Hale, an MIT linguistics professor, is making noise when it comes to unusual sounds. In fact, he battles to preserve a resource just as endangered as the rain forests or exotic animals that inhabit them: *languages.* Turns out that the number of existing languages is decreasing rapidly due to economic pressures, television, and the policies of governments. The disappearance of language is threatening our understanding of different societies and their customs, and it is making it almost impossible for these cultures to retain their own sense of history. Using computers and sophisticated technology, Hale compiles dictionaries and grammars with the greater goal of preserving languages—and the cultures tied to them. His latest project is a dictionary of Ulwa, which is spoken by only about 400 people on the east coast of Nicaragua. He has also studied Damin, an auxiliary language invented by the Lardil people of Mornington Island off Queensland, Australia. The tribe produces sounds found nowhere else in the world. He is now working to develop a program to train speakers of local languages in applied linguistics, so they can take language preservation skills back to their own communities.

Sincerely,

Sam Greengard

Another question that often arises among writers is how much information to include in a query letter. In general, you want to give enough detail so the editor has a strong idea of where you plan to take the piece. However, many writers don't want to "give away the store" in a query letter. Note how Greengard approaches this dilemma in the following query to an editor at *Acura Style*, a custom publication. He includes some possible sources without naming *all* the people he plans to interview.

Hi Susan:
Here's the story idea we discussed:
The Next Frontier: Since the beginning of time, humans have stared upward and pondered the dark and mysterious void known as space. And now, finally, the

idea of venturing into the universe is becoming more than a *Star Trek*–inspired fantasy. A slew of current projects—including the International Space Station, powerful space-based observatories, and deep-space missions testing futuristic propulsion methods—promise to revolutionize the race toward space. Combine all this with serious scientific research into wormholes and space-time distortions—mind-bending physics concepts that, if true, could provide shortcuts through the universe—and it's clear that humans might finally be knocking at heaven's door.

I'd like to propose an article that offers the perspectives of five luminaries on how the exploration of space is evolving and what lies ahead. The story would open with an introduction, and then include 300-word first-person narratives describing a specific aspect of space exploration (each could be accompanied by a photograph of the person). The experts would include:

- A high-level NASA administrator, perhaps Dan Goldin (head of NASA) or Joseph Rothenberg, NASA Associate Administrator for Space Flight. One of them could discuss the overall direction NASA is taking and what lies ahead with the International Space Station and other projects.
- A current or former astronaut, who can talk about how space travel is changing and how the International Space Station and other projects are allowing humans to inhabit space on a more permanent basis.
- Doug Stetson, head of the Solar System Exploration Office at JPL. He could discuss unmanned missions planned for the next ten to twenty years as well as new and experimental technologies, such as ion propulsion and harnessing solar winds.
- One of Space.com's corporate officers (which include Neil Armstrong and Lou Dobbs) or the edi-

tor of the Web site, which is a leading source of news and information about space. This person could provide a general perspective on overall space research and discovery.

- The CEO or president of one of the private companies venturing into space. He/she could discuss the role of the private sector in space, including manufacturing and space tourism.

I'm open to any ideas, thoughts, or suggestions on how to structure the piece. I'm looking forward to working with you on this. It should be a fascinating article.

Best,

Sam Greengard

Follow-Up Letters

What comes after a query letter? If you don't get a response, follow up by calling, e-mailing, or sending a letter to check on the status of the query. When sending a follow-up letter, it's a good idea to include a copy of the earlier query in case it's been misplaced. If you're e-mailing, drop the original query in the message below your follow-up note; don't attach it. Usually, I don't query competing markets with a similar idea at the same time, but this kind of letter serves notice that if I don't get a response, I'm taking the pitch elsewhere.

Dear Mr. Divina:

I'm writing to follow up on a query I sent you six weeks ago about violence prevention programs; a copy is enclosed for your convenience. Would you let me know at your earliest opportunity if you're interested in this story for *Parade*? If I don't hear from you within two weeks, I'll assume you're not interested in the idea at this time and may market it elsewhere.

Thank you very much for your time and consideration.

Very truly yours,

Kelly James-Enger

Cover Letters

For some submissions, such as essays, humor, and short fiction, a query isn't used—you submit the work itself. In these instances, include a cover letter to introduce the piece. (A sample cover letter for reprinted material is included in chapter 7.)

Dear Ms. West:

I'm writing to submit an essay, "A Taste for Sex," for your "First Person" section. It explores the chasm between lovemaking and baby-making, and I think women will enjoy the piece.

I'm a full-time freelancer and author who's written for more than forty national magazines including *Woman's Day, Redbook, Parents, Marie Claire, Family Circle, Fitness, Self, Shape, Oxygen,* and *Energy for Women.* If you have any questions about the essay, please let me know.

Thank you very much for your time. I look forward to hearing from you soon.

Sincerely,

Kelly James-Enger
Enc: essay, SASE

General Pitch Letters

Rather than sending a specific query, some writers prefer to use a letter of introduction that sets out their qualifications, writing experience, and background. These are particularly

effective when you're pitching to an editor of multiple publications, a custom publisher, or a magazine that doesn't solicit
queries. Note that the length and formality of these letters can
vary, as will the content depending on the type of market
you're contacting. The first letter was sent via snail mail to the
director of editorial services at a custom publisher; the second
was e-mailed to the editor of an online magazine. (Note that I
mention my "in" in the first line of the query. I also included it
in the subject line of the e-mail.) The third sample is Sam
Greengard's marketing letter, which he often uses instead of
sending traditional queries. Using it, he gets an assignment
about 50 percent of the time—an excellent rate for "cold calling." While he uses the same basic structure, he tweaks it
depending on the market he's contacting.

> Dear Mr. McCarthy:
>
> I'm writing to express my interest in writing for the
> custom publications you produce at The Magazine
> Group. As a full-time freelance writer and former attor-
> ney (I still have my license to practice law but only use it
> for family members' traffic tickets!), I'd appreciate it if
> you'd consider me for possible writing assignments both
> now and in the future.
>
> A little bit about my background: During the past four
> and a half years, my work has appeared in more than
> forty national magazines including *Redbook, Parents,
> Family Circle, Woman's Day, Fitness, Shape, Cos-
> mopolitan, Good Housekeeping,* and *Bridal Guide.* I
> specialize in health, fitness, diet/nutrition, and bridal/
> relationships, but I've also written about legal and busi-
> ness topics for magazines including *E-merging Busi-
> ness, Chamber Executive,* and *www.smalloffice.com.* In
> addition to writing for magazines, I also draft press
> releases, ad copy, newsletters, brochures, and other
> pieces for businesses, as well as edit and proofread
> manuscripts for clients.
>
> I've enclosed my resume and a variety of clips to

give you a feel for my writing style; you can also visit *www.kellyjamesenger.com/page8.html* for additional samples of my work. I've interviewed hundreds of business, health, fitness, nutrition, and other experts over the years and am a tireless researcher; also, as a self-admitted "type A", I *never* miss a deadline.

Please keep me in mind for any assignments that match my qualifications, and let me know if you have any questions about my background or experience.

Thank you very much for your time.
Sincerely,

Kelly James-Enger

Dear Ms. Oakes:

I'm a friend and colleague of Linda Formichelli's, who mentioned several weeks ago that you're looking for freelancers to write for your soon-to-come health magazine. I'm e-mailing to express my interest in working for you. I'm a full-time freelancer who specializes in health, fitness, and nutrition topics; my work has appeared in magazines including *Fitness, Fit, Shape, Self, Oxygen, Energy for Women, Redbook, Family Circle, Marie Claire, Bridal Guide, For the Bride, Wedding Bells,* and *Woman's Day*; I've also written for Web sites including *www.onhealth.com.*

If you like, I'd be happy to send some clips via e-mail or snail mail, or you can visit *www.kellyjamesenger. com/page8.html* for samples of my work. If you're interested in receiving query ideas, let me know and I'll come up with some for you.

Thank you very much for your time and let me know if you have any questions about my background or experience; I look forward to hearing from you soon.

Sincerely,

Kelly James-Enger

Dear Rhonda:

If you're looking for writers for *USAA Magazine,* I'd be interested in talking to you. I'm a business, personal-finance, and technology writer with twenty years of experience in the publishing field. Currently, I'm a contributing editor for *IndustryWeek, Workforce,* and *Business Finance,* and have contributed to many other business and trade magazines, including *Internet World, InformationWeek, M-Business,* and *Bloomberg.* On the consumer side, I'm a contributing editor at *FamilyPC* and *Home,* and have written stories for in-flight magazines and many others, including *Discover, Wired, Westways,* and *Modern Maturity.*

If you'd like to view my Web site, please click to *www.greengard.com.* There's a complete bio page and clips available for review. I assure you that I provide the highest-quality writing and a dedication to completely serving the needs of my clients.

Hope to hear from you soon.
Best regards,

Sam Greengard

Book Proposal Queries

Book queries are similar to magazine queries. When pitching an agent or editor about a nonfiction book, you want a letter that hooks the editor, demonstrates the potential audience and market for your title, and highlights your relevant qualifications. If an agent or editor is interested, she'll request a book proposal. The typical proposal includes the book premise, outlines the material to be covered, describes the competition and market for the book, suggests publicity and promotion ideas, and highlights your relevant experience. Usually, a proposal includes one or two sample chapters as well.

If you haven't written a proposal before, check out books like Elizabeth Lyon's *Nonfiction Book Proposals Anybody Can Write: How to Get a Contract and Advance Before Writing Your Book*, Michael Larsen's *How to Write a Book Proposal*, Third Edition, and Jeff Herman and Deborah Levine Herman's *Write the Perfect Book Proposal: 10 That Sold and Why*, Second Edition. Book proposals take considerable time, but a well-researched, well-written proposal can make for a much larger advance.

Dear Ms. Harper:

I've heard good things about you from fellow ASJA member Tina Tessina and am writing to query you about a nonfiction book proposal you may be interested in:

Falling in love is the *easy* part—it's the day-to-day challenges that really put a relationship to the test. But while maintaining a strong, loving bond is difficult for even the most committed couples, those in long-distance relationships face an even greater challenge.

According to recent statistics, at least 1 million Americans currently have commuter marriages and maintain two separate households. Millions more—including the more than 1.3 million men and women in the U.S. armed services—face extended time away from each other because of jobs that require frequent travel. And every fall as students leave to attend college and graduate school, hundreds of thousands of dating and engaged couples face the prospect of long-distance love as well.

Any couple faced with a long-distance relationship faces a multitude of concerns. Will distance threaten their relationship? How will they maintain intimacy? What kind of financial burden will it cause? How will it affect the couple's future? Is infidelity more likely? What if children are involved? How do they know if this is the right decision? How will they cope with the inevitable stress of being apart?

My book, *Make the Heart Grow Fonder: How to Survive—and Thrive in—Your Long-Distance Relationship*, will answer all of the questions and concerns that these couples face. *Heart* will include the experiences of hundreds of long-distance relationship "veterans" as well as expert advice from psychologists and relationship experts. The book will also feature quizzes and activities for couples to use to determine whether a long-distance relationship is a healthy option for their relationship, as well as ways to cope with loneliness and separation, tips on dealing with the financial burden these relationships can cause, and advice for parents who want to maintain a close relationship with their children regardless of physical distance. *Heart* will also look at the reasons for the growing trend in long-distance relationships and report on recent research on the factors that influence the success and stability of such relationships.

This down-to-earth, anecdote-filled book will be both a source of strength and encouragement as well as a wealth of practical information for the millions of people facing this increasingly common challenge. As a full-time freelance journalist and a veteran of three long-distance relationships, I can bring a unique perspective to this timely subject.

I hope you'll be interested reviewing my book proposal for *Heart*—please let me know if I may send it to you immediately. Thank you very much for your time; I look forward to hearing from you soon.

Very truly yours,

Kelly James-Enger

Typically, book queries are a page in length, but they can be longer. While I like a fairly detailed query, Jennifer Lawler has had great success with more concise pitch letters, several of which follow.

Note that her first query letter focuses on the potential audience and briefly describes its scope. At the time, Lawler only had a few clips, so she highlights her unique qualification: her black belt in Tae Kwon Do.

Her second query builds on her experience. Her experience and new book qualify her as an expert, and she notes the lack of competing titles and audience for this title. Again, her personal experience helps set her apart from other writers.

While Lawler specializes in writing about martial arts, she covers other subjects as well. The third query describes the specific audience for the book and the lack of books serving this audience. In this case, she didn't mention her writing credentials because they were in other areas, but instead focused on her personal experience.

Do short queries like this work? Certainly—all three of the books pitched in these queries sold.

> Dear Ms. Doe:
>
> There are two million black belts in Tae Kwon Do, worldwide. (I happen to be one of them.) Multiply that number by the number of martial-arts styles available (Karate-Do, Jeet Kune Do, Jujitsu, and so on) and you realize just how large the martial arts community is. And how diverse.
>
> I am interested in compiling a martial-arts encyclopedia as a general reference tool. Anyone from an individual with a little interest to a fourth-degree Wushu stylist could find valuable information on various styles, techniques, philosophies, countries of origin, history, and so on.
>
> Would you be interested in seeing a proposal for such a book? I have enclosed an SASE for your reply. I look forward to hearing from you.
>
> Sincerely,
>
> Jennifer Lawler

Dear Ms. Doe:

   As a martial artist, I often try to improve my skills by following the instructions of others, often using videos and books to do so. What I have discovered is a lack of practical advice for female martial artists. In many ways, female martial artists differ from male martial artists and could use information directed specifically toward them. For instance, women are prone to different injuries than men; because of our build, in general, martial arts can be very hard on our hips. Other injuries are also gender-specific. It would help to have information on avoiding such injuries.

   However, little in the literature addresses the needs and questions of female martial artists—from how to make the uniform fit better to whether it is safe to practice while pregnant. I have seen plenty of advice on sparring, but what if you are shorter than everyone you spar (as is often the case with women)? I have learned, through trial and error, the value of fighting "inside," but I have always wanted to know more about how women should spar, capitalizing on their strengths and overcoming their weaknesses. I am certain that other female martial artists feel the same.

   Would you be interested in seeing a proposal for a book on *Martial Arts for Women: A Practical Approach*? I am a black belt in Tae Kwon Do (black belt, October 1994; first degree, June 1995). My book, *The Comprehensive Martial Arts Encyclopedia* is being published this spring by Master's Press.

   I have enclosed an SASE for your reply. Thank you for your time and attention.

Sincerely,

Jennifer Lawler

Dear Ms. Doe:

   I'm a full-time writer. That means I'm also a full-time small-business owner. If I don't run my freelance-writing career as if it were a business, I'll lose money, customers, and, eventually, my job. Yet, like many creative people, I never bothered to listen during accounting class. When a helpful friend asked me what my business plan was, I answered, "I plan to make a lot of money with my business."

Frankly, the idea of keeping books and tax records terrified me; I need a calculator to figure out 10 percent off at the grocery store. But with the help of some very patient friends and family, I learned how to run my business like a business. I learned what projects were best bets for my bottom line, and which weren't worth the time I spent on them. I learned to value my time so I could bill more realistically, and I learned how to market my "product" effectively.

Although I consulted small-business books, most of them weren't for me. Creative people are in service professions, even though they do make a product. They own single proprietorships, so the question of business organization is moot. They don't have helpful assistants to manage (usually), so they don't need to know how. And they don't sell their businesses in order to retire; they are their businesses.

For these reasons, I am writing a guide called "Small-Business Ownership for Creative People," targeted at writers, artists, photographers, and others in similar professions. Would you be interested in seeing a proposal for this book? I have enclosed a SASE for your reply.

Thank you for your time.
Sincerely,

Jennifer Lawler

Corporate/Business Writing Pitches

When seeking corporate gigs, it's helpful to have a standard template that you can tweak depending on the nature of the client you're contacting. Don't forget to demonstrate your familiarity with the company, organization, or client you wish to work for. Don't send a letter like this to human resources; call the company to ask who's responsible for hiring free-lancers for writing work.

Dear Ms. Bokar:

You've only got three days to finish that important new brochure—but the writers in your corporate communications department are backed up with other work. Wouldn't it be great if you had another writer you could rely on? A writer who would deliver compelling, persuasive copy on deadline when you needed it? I'm sending this letter because I'd like to be that writer. I know that your company has run ads seeking a writer in *The Chicago Tribune* several times during the past year and a half, and would like to offer my freelance services for any writing projects you're currently working on.

A little bit about my background: During the past four and a half years, my work has appeared in more than forty national magazines including *Redbook, Parents, Family Circle, Woman's Day, Fitness, Shape, Cosmopolitan, Good Housekeeping,* and *Bridal Guide.* In addition to writing for magazines, I also draft press releases, ad copy, newsletters, brochures, and other pieces for businesses, as well as edit and proofread manuscripts for clients. I believe that copy and design should complement each other, and I enjoy collaborating with graphic designers to produce attention-getting advertisements and brochures.

As my resume indicates, I received my bachelor's degree in rhetoric. I also practiced law for five years before changing careers to write full time, and my legal training has given me a unique perspective on the importance of accuracy and clarity in written communication. Finally, because I own a variety of The Pampered

Chef cookware and utensils, I'm aware of the quality of your product line.

I've enclosed my resume and some clips, and will be happy to provide you with additional writing samples if desired. I'd love to meet in person so that I can bring my portfolio and we can discuss freelance opportunities with The Pampered Chef; I'll call to follow up on this letter in the next two weeks.

Thank you very much for your time, and please let me know if you have any questions about my background or experience.

Very truly yours,

Kelly James-Enger

Remember, when you're pitching a new client, don't be modest. You want to write the most compelling letter you can. Look at the way Bev Bachel, a corporate writer based in Minneapolis, highlights her background and experience in the "cold-call" letter. In the second letter, she uses her follow-up after a personal meeting to describe what she offers the client and recaps her relevant background and experience.

Lissa and Pam:

Since I understand Anne Nicolai and Doug Kline have already been singing my praises, I wanted to follow up and introduce myself.

As Anne mentioned in an earlier e-mail, I'm the author of *What Do You Really Want? How to Set a Goal and Go for It! A Guide for Teens.* I'm also a public speaker and do a lot of other writing that is motivational and focused on helping people, particularly young people, reach their potential.

More than anything, however, I'm a business writer who specializes in employee communications, including benefits communication.

Based on what I know, I think Anne is right: I would have a great mind-set for working with Target, Marshall Field's, and Mervyn's and I hope I'll have the opportunity to do so.

I am a strategic thinker with a strong background in all areas of communication. I started and ran my own marketing and employee communications firm, Words At Work (I understand you know Charlie Quimby, my former partner). Our clients were primarily Fortune 500 companies, including 3M, Aetna, Honeywell, International Multifoods, Northwest Airlines, and St. Paul Companies. I sold my share of the business a few years ago and now work on my own, typically for three to five clients each year, although I do take on a few select projects along the way.

Highlights of my career include:

- Working as the director of corporate communications for a publicly held publishing and printing company; I reported directly to the CEO and was responsible for employee communications, public relations, and investor relations
- Owner of Words At Work, one of the Twin Cities' top marketing and employee communication firms
- Senior benefits communications manager at Deloitte & Touche
- Managing and writing for Ceridian's award-winning Web site and developing and managing its intranet (a two-year project)
- Investor and public relations for Ceridian (wrote quarterly financial releases and helped prep the CEO, CFO, and other executives for quarterly teleconference calls with analysts)
- Award-winning corporate image, recruiting, and marketing materials for Cargill, Piper Capital, Mutual of Omaha, St. Paul Companies, and other clients

- Speechwriting and ghostwriting of articles and letters for senior-level executives, including CEOs of Cargill, Ceridian, and St. Paul Companies
- Managing and writing for dozens of employee publications for a variety of companies, including Ceridian, GNB, Schreiber, and St. Paul Companies
- Communications consulting, strategy development, and project management on various corporate initiatives, including a twelve-month benefits conversion project for Ceridian and an eighteen-month business redesign project for St. Paul Companies
- Various communication for Schreiber, including articles for a daily online newsletter and video scripts for a 24/7 in-plant company news program
- Variety of benefits communication, including annual enrollment materials, financial education, and monthly health improvement campaign for Apogee, Ceridian, Mutual of Omaha, and US Bank

I would love the opportunity to make an ongoing contribution to your internal communication efforts. And because I'm a strong writer who knows how to work independently and meet deadlines, I can also make your job easier.

I'm looking to add one additional client this year and would love the opportunity to talk with you. Please call me at 612-555-5555 at your convenience.

Thanks very much for your time.

Regards,

Bev Bachel

Kay and Becky:

It was such a treat to meet you on Tuesday. I loved the energy of our meeting and hope that we'll get the chance to talk further about the many ways I can use my writing, marketing, and public-relations skills to help Search Institute develop its trade publishing business.

As you know, I'm the author of *What Do You Really Want? How to Set a Goal and Go For It! A Guide for Teens*, published by Free Spirit in 2001. The book, which has already been reprinted twice, is written for eleven to eighteen year olds. In the process of writing it, I learned how to both entertain and inform young readers, and I've developed a strong network of youth, parents, and teachers from whom I can draw real-life examples for future books.

As I mentioned (and I'm sure you could tell), I'm passionate about helping people become financially savvy and am particularly interested in writing a book that would help educate kids and their parents about saving, spending, investing, and giving, all practices that I've adopted in my own life.

Because teenagers have money (at least one-half of all youths ages sixteen to eighteen are employed) and spend it (teens are expected to spend over $100 billion this year), they represent one of the fastest-growing and most-powerful consumer groups in today's society. However, like many of their parents, teens have no idea how to save or manage their money, a skill particularly important for teens who have goals.

As we discussed, I have a strong background in communications, including marketing and public relations. I've been providing these and other services to my clients since 1980. I've owned my own million-dollar employee and marketing communications firms, worked for an international consulting firm, and held several senior-level positions within corporations. I now work as an independent writer and consultant for a number of Fortune 500 companies, including Cargill, Ceridian, St.

Paul Companies, and US Bank. I specialize in financial communication, helping companies educate their employees about the exact concepts Search is interested in developing for its target market.

I'm also the founder of Idea Girls, a group of entrepreneurs dedicated to developing products that inspire others to pursue their dreams, and the author of several Idea Girls Guides, including the *Idea Girls Guide to Creativity* and the *Idea Girls Guide to Net-weaving: Make Your Contacts Count.*

In addition, I've written articles about goal setting, creativity, and other topics for teens for various publications, including *Girls' Life* magazine, *New Moon Network*, and *Scholastic Choices.*

Assuming I'm given the opportunity, I'm interested in using my expertise to help Search think about how the books I write can be part of a larger, strategic plan that includes companion products, such as parents' and teachers' guides.

I've already given you a copy of my book. I've enclosed the press release for my book, several book reviews, samples, and a resume.

I'd love to meet with you again to discuss writing, and perhaps doing other work, for Search. Please call me at 612-555-5555 or write me at [omitted e-mail] to discuss next steps.

Again, thanks for your time on Tuesday.

Regards,

Bev Bachel

Proposals

Often, a client will ask for a written proposal before you're offered a job. Again, I like to use a standard template for this kind of letter. I also describe the scope of the work involved to back up my bid. (This brochure was an early project—now my hourly rate is between $75 and $100 for this kind of work.) Sometimes, it's beneficial to list the amount of hours you're basing your bid on; in other situations, you may want to simply set out one number for the entire project. Bev Bachel uses both approaches, depending on the project; samples of each follow.

Dear Diane:

It was a pleasure speaking with you this morning about the referenced project; thank you for giving me the opportunity to bid on the Tri-State Stone brochure. I've spoken with Joel van de Kamp about the brochure and submit this letter as my bid on the project.

My bid to do the copy on the project is 17.5 hours; my billable rate is $35/hour, for a total of $612.50. This figure includes the following:

- Meetings with you to discuss copy, layout, etc.;
- Research/review of background materials to discuss copy and prepare bid;
- Phone calls with client re: theme and purpose behind brochure;
- Trip to Frankfort to visit Tri-State;
- Initial draft of copy;
- Reviewing and discussing copy with client;
- Phone calls with you and client re: copy, layout, etc.;
- Editing and revising copy;
- Final copy for production.

As you know, I keep detailed time records and will supply you with an itemized statement at the conclusion of this project; if the project comes in "under budget," my statement will reflect that. If you have any questions about this bid, please give me a call.

Thanks again for letting me bid on this project; I hope we'll have the chance to work on this brochure together.

Very truly yours,

Kelly James-Enger

Melanie:

Thanks so much for asking Idea Girls to put together this proposal for ABC Industries. It's clear that you're an Idea Girl with a lot of energy (my favorite type of client), and I look forward to working with you. And just in case we need more Idea Girl power, I've already pulled together a team of other creative women who I know will work hard to ensure we meet your objectives.

I'm in town until Sunday, February 29. I'll be working the first two weeks while I'm gone, but then will have only limited e-mail access through the end of the month (I return on March 30).

I know you're just getting back into town and expect you'll have a busy week, but let's be sure to connect so I can answer any questions and we can plan the next steps.

All good things,

Bev Bachel
Chief Idea Girl
www.ideagirls.com

Step one:
Idea Girls get smart
To ensure that we thoroughly understand your company, its products, market segments, and more, we will gather information in a variety of ways, including:

- Review ABC Industries' existing market research
- Review ABC Industries' current marketing materials

- Review ABC Industries' previous marketing efforts and results
- Interview you (and other key staff, if appropriate)
- Interview customers and potential customers

Estimated fee: $500–750

Step two:
Making a soufflé out of a smorgasbord
One of ABC Industries' strengths is the breadth and depth of its product line: books, videos, DVDs, PowerPoint presentations, activity pads, etc., as well as the breadth and depth of the subjects they cover: nutrition, fashion design, interior design, kitchen safety, sewing, etc.

As it's difficult to be all things to all people—and because it's key that you concentrate your efforts in a few areas that can have a significant impact on your bottom line—we will clearly define objectives, identify key audiences, and develop specific messages for each of these audiences.

Estimate for XYZ overview brochure

Description: 12 pages

Project Management
Client meetings/phone calls/scheduling
Estimate: 10–12 hours @ $100/hour

$1,000–1,200

Concept Development
Brainstorming session with designer
Writing headlines
Estimate: 4–6 hours @ $100/hour

$ 400–600

Research and Interviews
Review background materials
Interview(s) with appropriate XYZ contact(s)
Estimate: 8–12 hours @ $100/hour

$ 800–1,200

Writing (includes three rounds of revisions)
Estimate: 35–45 hours @ $100/hour

$3,500–4,500

Total Estimate: $ 5,700–7,500

      The above estimate includes three rounds of revisions. Additional revisions, as well as additional meeting time and interviews, will be billed at $100/hour. Expenses, such as long-distance and messenger service, will be billed at cost. If I am able to complete the project in less time than indicated here, I will bill accordingly.
      Let me know if you have questions or need additional information.

Bev

Invoices

Many writers use programs like QuickBooks to send invoices, but you can also create a template for invoices. Every invoice should include the date, invoice number, dollar amount, and rights purchased (or you can refer to the language of a written contract by using language like "for rights per written contract of November 15, 2002"), in addition to your name, social security number, and mailing address. If you're billing by the hour, include the amount of time you spent, your hourly rate, and any other expenses the way Bev Bachel does in the following sample invoice.

      DATE
      Re: INVOICE #387
      Dear Sue,
           Please let this letter serve as my invoice for $90 for one-time reprint rights to "Banish the Workout Blues"

per your e-mail of today. My social security number is
xxx-xx-xxxx.

Thank you very much!
Best,

Kelly James-Enger

INVOICE

CLIENT NAME
CLIENT ADDRESS

DATE

INVOICE: XXX-XXX-XXC
For time incurred during February 2004

Source
36 hours @ $50/hour $ 1,800.00

SCOPE Express
18 hours @ $50/hour $ 900.00

Total comp planning
6 hours @ $75/hour $ 450.00

Process excellence writing and projects
3.5 hours @ $100/hour $ 350.00

Work with vendor A
28 hours @ $50/hour $ 1,400.00

Work with Vendor B
1.5 hours @ $50/hour $ 75.00

Access
8.25 hours @ $75/hour $ 618.75

Project Management (i.e., meetings, non–Source/non–SE-related projects, travel): 14 hours @ $50/hour $ 700.00

| | Subtotal: | $ 6,293.75 |

Expenses

Taxi		$ 85.00
Meals		$ 32.07
Long distance	$ 30.00	
	Subtotal:	$ 147.07
	Amount due:	$ 6,440.82

Please submit to Bev Bachel within 30 days.
Social Security Number: XXX-XX-XXXX.
Thank you for your business.

CHAPTER 7
No More One-Story Sales: Getting More out of Everything You Write

As a freelancer, you have a limited number of hours to dedicate to earning money from your work, whether you're writing part or full time. You can make the most of your time by squeezing as much as you can out of your research. Write about the same topic more than once, and you'll spend less time on future stories, which translates into a higher dollar per hour rate as well as more assignments.

It took me several years to grasp this fact, though. Like most freelancers, when I started writing, I dug for story ideas, looked for appropriate markets, and queried magazines. When I got an assignment, I wrote the article. Then it was on to the next idea, the next market, the next story. I wrote about topics ranging from how small businesses could protect themselves from employment discrimination claims, to how to improve your memory, to animal dissection alternatives, to religious weight-loss programs. Each story took a considerable amount of time to research, but once I was finished with it, I never revisited the topic.

If that sounds a lot like the way you've been working, break yourself of the one-idea-equals-one-story habit right now. Instead, start thinking about the different ways you can reslant material to different markets.

Reslanting involves taking your initial story idea, spinning off other angles, and locating possible markets for it. Say your initial idea is a story on the benefits of antioxidants for older people, and you have a health-oriented publication like *Prevention* in mind. That's a great start, but don't stop there. How many different angles can you take with the piece? How about a piece for a parenting magazine on why it's so important for children to eat fruits and vegetables—along with ways to encourage them to consume more produce? Or a nutrition story for a fitness publication about how antioxidants help your body recover from exercise and keep your immune system strong? What about a health piece for a general interest magazine examining the question of whether it's more beneficial to get your antioxidants from food instead of vitamin supplements?

Even seemingly narrow subjects can be spun off for additional articles. For example, several years ago I wrote about the benefits of using a heart rate monitor during exercise for *Fit*. The story, like many featured in women's fitness magazines, had a weight-loss angle. Later, I wrote about how heart rate monitors can help both new and seasoned exercisers start and maintain workout programs for *Experience Life*, a custom publication for members of Lifetime Fitness health clubs. A few months ago, I wrote about monitors again for a men's fitness magazine. This time, the story focused on how readers could turn formerly boring cardio workouts (most guys who lift weights hate doing cardiovascular exercise) into more challenging and productive sessions.

Get the picture? Three stories—admittedly similar ones—out of one basic idea. Each article conveys the same basic information, but in a different way. For example, I never reuse a quote when reslanting an article, and I usually rely on different expert sources. The exception to the rule is when there's an expert I need—because he or she has conducted important research in this field. Even then I use fresh quotes—I don't want to reuse the exact same material in an original piece.

Gamers? Seniors? College students? Frequent travelers? Professionals? People on a limited budget? Hobbyists? Residents of California? African-Americans? People with disabilities? Pet owners? Homeowners? Gourmands?

_____

_____

_____

_____

_____

Considering potential audiences, what markets might be interested in this information? Again, think broadly. Consider consumer magazines, trade publications, and regional magazines and newspapers. Even if some of the markets don't pay that well, a story that takes minimal time to report and write may be worth it.

_____

_____

_____

_____

_____

What angles would be of most interest to each audience and market?

_____

_____

_____

_____

_____

Try this exercise whenever you're hashing out a new story idea. You may be amazed at how many different approaches you can come up with for one seemingly tiny kernel of a story idea. Even if you can't come up with many angles at the beginning, you may discover new approaches and potential markets as you research the idea. The more you know about a particular subject, the more story ideas you can develop.

Remember, you're probably going to wind up with much more research than will make it into the finished article. You may only cull two or three quotes from an interview transcript, and you may amass studies, statistics, resources, and anecdotes that you don't use in the first story. The more information you have at your fingertips, the less work you need to do on the second, or third, or fourth story.

"I would say 75 percent of the work I do is somehow related to something I've done before," says Margaret Littman. "That doesn't necessarily mean it's a straight reslant, but it means I'm not reinventing the wheel with every story." Littman writes for both consumer and trade magazines and has found that many topics that fly in one type of market will also work in the other. "Writing for both trade and consumer mags has turned out to be a really good way for me to reslant and not be in competing markets at all," she says. "For example, I've written a story about a wine bar in Chicago that is kid-friendly. They do wine tastings and they do milk tastings for kids. I wrote that story for a trade magazine as a business story—how restaurants that are geared to adults can attract families and how they can use different parts of the day to their advantage without developing a whole different menu." But she didn't stop there. By considering different markets for this relatively narrow story, Littman wound up writing about the wine bar several times for consumer magazines, including several wine publications, and a local magazine.

When she's working on a story, Littman always looks for other ways to approach the material. Covering topics for trade publications often leads to ideas for consumer magazines. "I find that consumer magazine editors look to trade magazines to confirm that there's a trend, and I may have that information in my notes," she explains. "I may have written an article that confirms the trend. I'm already the expert or I've already got the expert and I can then pitch the idea to a consumer magazine." She's taken the other approach as well, reslanting ideas she first covered for consumer publications for trade magazines. "You can go the other way and start with a consumer magazine, and then go to the trades and say, 'everyone's really interested in this,'" she says. "A good example is the low-carb diet. . . . Everyone and their mother were on the low-carb diet, so I started doing low-carb stories for consumer magazines. Then I wrote about low-carb topics for trade magazines, like how restaurants can have low-carb foods on their menus."

Practical Problems with Reslanting

However, there are some drawbacks to reslanting. First, you need to be careful about writing about the same topics for competing magazines. Normally, I don't pitch competitors with the same idea—if they both want it, I can write two different stories, but my editors may not be pleased that I'm covering the identical topic for their rival. It's not worth upsetting an editor. If I cover a topic for one magazine and then wind up writing about it for a competing magazine later, I'll use different experts. It helps ensure that the story will in fact be different and keeps it from looking like a carbon copy of the first piece. Remember, it's perfectly acceptable to write about the same topic more than once. But it shouldn't *look* like the same story you wrote before—that's the kind of thing that editors get annoyed about.

I ran into this problem when I was writing two very similar stories at the same time. A couple of years ago, I pitched a piece on the health benefits of taking oral contraceptives continuously—instead of taking them for twenty-one days and then taking a placebo for seven days—to *Redbook*. While I was waiting to hear from the magazine, I pitched a similar story to *Oxygen*, a women's fitness magazine. Within three days, both editors called to assign articles on the subject.

At first blush, this might sound like a problem. It's not. Here's why:

1. *Redbook* and *Oxygen* aren't competitors. *Redbook* is a women's magazine aimed primarily at working moms in their mid-twenties to early forties. The magazine covers everything from women's health, to marriage, to parenting, to fashion, to personal finance, to diet and nutrition, to career issues. *Oxygen* is a fitness magazine that focuses on weight training, nutrition, and weight loss. Not too many readers of one will be reading the other, so I wasn't concerned about crossover. If I had been writing about this subject for *Shape* and *Self*, however— or *Ladies Home Journal* and *Redbook*—I would had a potential problem on my hands. These magazines compete directly with each other for readers and advertisers, and if the editors saw that I was writing about the same topic for their biggest competition, they would probably have been upset.

2. More importantly, nothing in either contract prohibited me from writing about the subject for another publication. Some magazines insist on language that prohibits writers from writing about "the same or similar subject" for other magazines for a certain time period—often three to six months. In this case, neither magazine had that type of contractual limitation.

3. I used different sources for each story. Yes, the published research on the benefits and potential drawbacks of continuous taking of oral contraceptives was the same. The statistics on the number of women who use oral contraceptives were the same. But I used different experts for each piece. In this instance, my editor at *Redbook* wanted

me to interview female obstetricians/gynecologists aged twenty-five to forty-two who had used the pill to skip periods. Good enough. I interviewed five of them for the *Redbook* piece. Then, I interviewed and quoted different physicians and researchers for the *Oxygen* story. (Yes, I *could* have used the same sources for the *Oxygen* story. But that looks like lazy reporting to me. In a situation like this, I err on the conservative side.)

4. I took a different approach to each story. The *Redbook* piece was a full-blown feature that discussed all of the potential pros and cons of using the pill to skip periods. The *Oxygen* story focused more on the fitness benefits of skipping periods, especially for women who were fitness competitors or serious athletes. I was researching both stories simultaneously, but when it came to writing them, I worked on the *Redbook* story—the longer, more complicated piece—first. I finished it and turned it in. Before I started writing the *Oxygen* article, I reread the *Redbook* story to make sure that I didn't repeat myself or fall into the trap of unconsciously using the same language, phrasing, or metaphors. It worked—while the basic information and research was the same, I was able to write two very different stories using different experts and angles.

Another drawback of reslanting is the risk of returning to the well too often. Write about any subject more than once and you may get bored with it. Over the last five or six years, I've written a slew of articles on weight-loss strategies. We're talking about at least $70,000 worth of work and hundreds of tips and suggestions—all of which could be summed up in four short words: "Eat less, exercise more." A new writer might only be able to come up with one story from this simple phrase. But by focusing on three aspects of the topic—audience, angle, and approach—I've come up with a slew of different ways to approach this subject:

- "Outsmart Holiday Fat Traps." Avoiding holiday weight gain is a perennial favorite topic in health and fitness magazines. This story in *Fitness* listed the biggest culprits likely to cause readers to put on seasonal pounds—and showed readers how to overcome them.
- "10 Easy Ways to Eat Healthier." This service piece used an "ease-of-eating-healthy" angle to show *Fit* readers how to make simple changes in their diets to boost their nutritional intake while reducing the total number of calories they consumed.
- "5 More Ways to Drop the Pounds." This was the result of research for another diet story—I turned it into a short roundup of five quick tips for *Family Circle*.
- "Drop That Holiday Weight." Geared to a January issue of *Complete Woman*, this piece used a time peg—"get in shape for the New Year"—and included a simple diet with sample recipes to follow.
- "Nutritional Friend—or Foe?" Guess what? Even "bad" foods can be good for you. I used a counterintuitive approach for this story in *Oxygen*, which reported on the benefits of "no-nos" like red meat, eggs, nuts, and choco-late—and how consuming them could help with weight-loss efforts. (Editors love stories like this—and it's a great way to come up with a fresh pitch on evergreen subjects. Think of ideas that play on the opposite of what you'd expect—like "for a better marriage, spend less time with your husband," "less discipline, better-behaved kids," or "eat more, lose more weight!")
- "50 Ways to Get a Hot Holiday Bod." A roundup—basi-cally a collection of short tips, anecdotes, or quotes—is probably the simplest story there is to write. You inter-view a handful of sources, select the best tips, and you're all set. The most time-consuming part of a roundup is doing the research for the story, but then it practically writes itself. I again used a seasonal angle for this list of proven exercise and diet tips that ran in *Complete Woman*.

- "The Top Dieting Pitfalls." Aimed at women in their thirties and forties, this *Woman's Day* piece pointed out the biggest diet busters and how to overcome them. It included plenty of real-life examples in addition to expert advice. Adding anecdotes is an easy way to breathe new life into an evergreen topic because it forces you to use different stories, examples, and quotes. And readers often like to hear from people like themselves, not just experts.

- "Easy Ways to Watch Your Weight this Season." Are you an Apple (round around the middle), a Pear (bigger on the bottom), or a Banana (weight distributed evenly throughout your body)? This weight-loss piece in *Family Circle* started with a quiz to let readers determine their own body shape and included customized advice for each "type." Again, this is a basic don't-gain-weight-over-the-holidays topic, but the approach made it unique—and fun for the reader. Including a quiz with a story makes it interactive for the reader and can be a great way to reslant an idea.

- "Saved by Snacking." All of the nutritional stories in *Weight Watchers* revolve around eating healthfully to help with weight-loss or maintenance efforts. This story reported on recent research on the benefits of snacking and showed how frequent snacking could help dieters' efforts. (Note that, again, this is a counterintuitive idea— you'd think that frequent snacking would make you *gain* weight.) It also included a sidebar with ways to snack healthfully on the go.

- "14 Pounds—Gone!" was a typical weight-loss story, focusing on small, doable things *Woman's Day* readers could do for a weight loss of fourteen pounds in just over two months. Here, the focus was on specific tips that would help women create a daily 700-calorie deficit that would allow them to lose weight slowly but steadily. It also included figures for the amount of calories that could be "saved" (e.g., by drinking skim milk instead of whole milk in coffee) or burned by doing everyday activities like housework and walking, so that readers could calculate how quickly their deficit would add up.

- "Hidden Fat Traps." This evergreen topic was made timely with the addition of new studies—for example, did you know that if you're distracted, you eat more? *Woman's Day* readers gobbled up the advice, which included real-life anecdotes in addition to expert suggestions. (By the way, this story may sound a lot like "The Top Dieting Pitfalls," which proves that evergreen stories are always popular.)
- "What's your GI IQ?" focused on the glycemic index, which garnered a lot of attention in 2004. This story explained what the glycemic index is, and how readers could use it to help them lose weight and improve their training programs. This piece was aimed at a fitness-conscious audience and ran in *Energy for Women*.
- "Good Carb, Bad Carb" again covered the glycemic index, but this time for guys. The story pointed out that carbohydrates are an essential part of any man's diet, particularly if he's trying to gain muscle mass and reduce body fat, and showed readers how to incorporate higher-quality carbs into their nutrition plans. It was published in *Muscle Media*, a men's fitness magazine.
- "Get an Early Start on Weight Loss." Did you know that 78 percent of people who lose weight and keep it off eat breakfast every day? That was the angle for this *Oxygen* weight-loss article, which focused on the importance of eating a nutrient-dense breakfast. The story also debunked some common breakfast myths—like the myth that eating breakfast makes you hungrier all day.
- "What's Your Eating ID?" once again included a quiz for *Family Circle* readers to take that determined whether

they were "Mood Munchers," "Repeat Eaters," "Mad Dashers," or "Die-hard Dieters." It then gave advice specifically tailored for each group. Remember, quizzes are an easy way to offer a new twist on a tried-and-true topic. You can include them as part of the main story, or as a separate sidebar.

- "Eat Right for Your Body Type." This profile-type piece looked at the typical diets of three different women, their lifestyles, and their nutritional goals. Then a dietitian reviewed their diets and made specific recommendations for each woman. It ran in *Oxygen*. With a story like this, finding people who fit the bill can take a significant amount of time, but then it's usually simple to write up.
- "The Real Man's Guide to Holiday Eating." Guys aren't going to limit themselves to carrot sticks and sparkling water at a holiday bash, but they can benefit from the healthy tips in this story in *Muscle Media*. (Does it sound familiar? "Outsmart Holiday Fat Traps" covered the same topic, but for women.)

There you have it—seventeen stories about the same basic subject, yet each is a different story. Some of the information in each article may have been similar, but every piece was tailored to the audience and took a different approach and/or angle to the material. When you're reslanting ideas, don't just consider the different markets you can pitch stories to—consider different *types* of stories as well. For example, let's say you come across a new study that shows that music helps exercisers work out for longer periods of time with less effort. Sounds like a basic, front-of-the-book piece for a fitness magazine, right? You can do more with it. Imagine:

- You could do a quiz on the best ways to maximize your workout motivation for a general fitness magazine like *Self*

- You could interview the researcher and do a profile on him and his work for a local publication, an alumni magazine, or an association publication
- You could pitch a more in-depth piece for a general-interest magazine on how people respond to music and how it's used to boost performance as well as aid in relaxation
- You could write a piece for a parenting magazine on whether music helps students learn or is a distraction when they study
- You could cover the topic for a trade publication for health club owners, and offer instruction about how to choose the types of music they play at their gyms, and whether they should change that music depending on the time of day
- You could pitch a story for a trade publication about the best music choices for retailers, and explore the issue of whether music choice affects the amount of time shoppers spend in a store
- You could query a health-care magazine about using music to help patients reduce their anxiety before surgery, and distract them from pain during recovery
- You could pitch a teen magazine about how to choose music to match your mood, and include a rundown of some of the hot new teen artists today

Wow. All that from one little study. Hopefully you're getting the idea now, but if you're coming up short on different ways to approach a particular topic, don't worry. You may find that you'll come back to the story a year or two later. That's another reason you should save copies of transcripts, journal articles, statistics, background information, and other research in your story folders. You never know when you may revisit a topic, and once you get the hang of reslanting, it can be fun to see how many times you can get paid for writing about the same thing.

Sam Greengard writes about business and technology for a variety of publications and corporations. Because he often covers the same topics more than once, he mines his old story files for background material when working on new assignments. "Sometimes, I'll take interviews and case studies and rewrite or reslant them for another article," says Greengard. "I do reuse a lot of material." He maintains folders in Outlook for every project he works on, and keeps all e-mails, research, and PDF files for that topic in the relevant folder, which makes for easy retrieval later. "I get as much data as I can in my computer, through newsletters and reports, and when analysts send me stuff, I keep it on my computer," says Greengard. "I also do a lot of web clipping. Then I use Enfish Find [a program that indexes your computer's hard drive] and search for material I need."

Note that while Greengard is reusing his work, he's not simply dropping in sections of stories he previously wrote into new ones. "I rewrite the case study so it fits the magazine's style and the flow of that story," he explains. "And I send the source an e-mail or I call and ask if I can reuse material or e-mail them what I'm planning to use and ask . . . if it's accurate. Ninety-nine percent of the time they're fine with it."

Freelancer Leah Ingram takes another reslanting tack: using the same story idea for more than one market. "I did a story for *Bridal Guide* many years ago about how several couples with different wedding budgets had planned for their weddings. I found someone who spent $10,000, $20,000, $50,000, and $100,000," says Ingram. "Now, whenever I enter a new bridal market, I will pitch that same idea but use their target audience. When I do a regional story, I might find four couples in Philadelphia or in Boston, depending on the market. I'm not writing the same story because I'm doing all new research, but the concept is there."

Ingram doesn't limit this approach to magazine articles, either. By thinking on a broader scale, she's written six books about wedding-related subjects. "Every time someone hears that I've written six books about the topic, they say, 'how do you find something else to write about?'" she says. "But if you've developed an expertise in an area, you've got to look at it as if you've never written about it and say, 'Okay. I've done the book on planning your wedding from soup to nuts; what have I not written on?' It's looking at the same topic and figuring out what else can you write about from there." By taking that approach, Ingram has written books on personalizing your wedding (*Your Wedding Your Way*), how brides can physically and emotionally prepare for their weddings (*The Balanced Bride*), and what to do when things go wrong on the big day (*The Complete Guide for the Anxious Bride*). In fact, Ingram's latest project takes into account what's hot and in the news: her agent's shopping a book on the timely subject of gay weddings.

One Story, More Than One Paycheck: Selling Reprints

As much as I like reslanting story ideas to maximize my time and research, there's an even easier way to make more money from your work. Sell reprint rights to your work, and you can get paid twice, three times, four times, or more for the same story. While you may be paid less for reprint rights (also called "second rights" or "one-time rights"), the checks can add up.

While locating and contacting potential reprint markets does take time, selling a reprint is the closest thing I can get to free money. There's usually little work involved. For example, last month I spent fifteen minutes contacting a regional bridal magazine and sending a list of my available wedding-related stories. The editor bought one for $100, which translates to an hourly rate of $400—plus an opportunity to sell more stories to him in the future. It's not going to make me rich, but it's a nice bonus.

Obviously, you have to retain reprint rights before you can sell them to other markets. That means taking a good look at the contracts you sign, and may also mean negotiating better contracts. (See chapter 4 for advice on how to do this.) Read your contracts carefully—even if you retain reprint rights, you may be prohibited from reselling a piece to competing markets, for example. Magazines tend to be more flexible contract-wise, but if you're working for a corporation or business, you may have to sign a work-for-hire or all-rights contract that precludes you from reselling the piece. (This doesn't mean you're prohibited from writing another article about the same subject—just from reselling that particular piece. But the former wouldn't be a reprint—it would be a reslant, as discussed earlier.)

Where Are the Markets?

I've found the most time-consuming aspect of selling reprints is locating markets for them. While annual market guides like *Writer's Market* and *The Writer's Handbook* list magazines that buy reprints, there are thousands of others not included in these publications. I've had the best success simply looking for magazines on local newsstands, both at home and when I travel. Trade publications, specialty magazines, and regional publications are all good potential reprint markets.

I also use directories like *Bacon's Magazine Directory* and *Bacon's Newspaper Directory*, the *Gale Directory of Publications and Broadcast Media,* 138th Edition, and *The Standard Periodical Directory,* 2004, Twenty-seventh Edition, to locate potential reprints. Both *Bacon's* and *Standard Periodical Directory* list more than 70,000 publications; the *Gale* directory includes more than 54,000 periodicals, subdivided by city and state. Every few months, I'll put together a list of potential markets and then call or e-mail them to see if they're interested in my work.

One thing I've learned over time is that, like one-shot stories, one-sale reprint markets aren't really worth the time.

Rather than trying to sell individual stories more than once, I look for potential long-term reprint markets—magazines that will buy reprinted material from me now and in the future. To do this, you need to take a look at what types of stories you have to offer potential reprint markets. If you're writing about a wide variety of subjects, this is trickier, but if you write about several major topic areas—for example, business and personal finance or parenting and health—you can search more effectively for markets that may be interested in your work.

While I've had more success selling to print publications, Web sites looking for content are also potential reprint markets. Sometimes, a reprint market will fall into your lap—for example, editors at *Reader's Digest* contact writers when they want to reprint a story that appeared in another magazine. On some occasions, a company may want reprint permission to distribute an article to customers or to use an article for publicity purposes.

Some writers use a standard "enclosed-please-find" cover letter when offering reprint rights to a piece. I like to jazz mine up a bit to catch the editor's attention, as with the following letter. Include information about where and when the piece was originally printed.

July 10, 2000

Dear Ms. Krueger:
    Most of us have been bitten by the green-eyed monster at least once. Fortunately you *can* keep jealousy from threatening—or even destroying—an otherwise satisfying romance. Read "Slay the Green-Eyed Monster: Keep Jealousy from Ruining Your Relationship," and you'll know how to conquer and overcome jealous feelings for good.
    Interested in purchasing reprint rights to this story? "Green-Eyed Monster" was originally published in the fall 2000 issue of *For the Bride by Demetrios;* a copy is enclosed.

Thank you for your time and consideration; I look forward to hearing from you soon.

Very truly yours,

Kelly James-Enger

Here's a technique to remember when you're selling reprints. "Green-Eyed Monster" was originally written for a bridal magazine. Not surprisingly, I used anecdotes from engaged couples and talked about the importance of trust in marriage. Before I sent the article to *Complete Woman*, however—a magazine aimed at single women in their twenties, thirties, and forties—I tweaked the story to delete any references to marriage, replacing it with "long-term relationship." That made the story more appropriate for the market I was sending it to.

I've done this a number of times, and refer to these stories as "tweaks." A tweak is still technically a reprint, but modified to better fit the second (or third, or fourth) market. For example, I originally sold a piece on fifty ways to eat, work out, and live better to *Oxygen*, a fitness magazine. Before I sent it to a local family fitness publication, I rewrote the lead to make it more timely and revised several sections of the piece to appeal to a broader audience. When I sent the same piece to a bridal magazine, I revised it once again, changing the lead and adding several wedding references throughout the piece. I don't have to do this—I can send out the story "as is" and wait for the editor's response, but I've found that spending a few minutes to tweak a piece for a particular market often results in a quick sale.

As mentioned earlier, some stories can be reprinted over and over. I suggest, though, that you check the factual accuracy of any story that's more than six months old. For example, when I sold reprint rights to a six-year-old story on avoiding legal problems as you plan your wedding, I made sure that the U.S. law I had cited in the original piece was still in effect. It's a minor detail, but one that you should attend to. Do the same thing when including Web sites, contact information, or any other data that is likely to change.

A simple cover letter will suffice when you're pitching one story at a time. If you find a market that may be interested in more than one story, however, it's more efficient to send a letter with a story list like the following:

> January 23, 2002
>
> Dear Lisa:
>
> Thanks very much for your time today; I'm writing to follow up on our phone conversation. As I mentioned, I'm a full-time freelance journalist whose work has appeared in more than forty national magazines including *BRIDE'S*, *Bridal Guide*, *For the Bride*, *Wedding Bells*, *Fitness*, *Fit*, *Shape*, *Redbook*, *Woman's Day*, *Family Circle*, and *Marie Claire*. I currently have bridal-related stories on the following topics available (approximate word count is shown as well):
>
> > "The (Secret) Laws Concerning In-Laws" (coping strategies and suggestions)   1,100 words
> > "Secrets and Lies" (what to tell—and not tell—when you marry)   1,700 words
> > "Playing Doubles" (going from singles to a married couple)   930 words
> > "How to Talk Dollars and Sense" (communicating about money)   1,040 words
> > "What's Your Eating Personality?" (stay slim or trim down for the wedding)   1,130 words
> > "The Better-Sex Report" (tips, resources, and suggestions; includes sidebar)   2,090 words
> > "Formerly Long-Distance Love" (making the transition to being married)   1,000 words
> > "Promises, Promises" (avoiding legal problems as you plan your wedding)   1,190 words

"What's Your Money Style?" (how it affects your marriage; includes quiz)   1,080 words
"Full-Time Employee/Part-Time Bride" (juggling wedding plans and career)   950 words
"Slay the Green-Eyed Monster" (keep jealousy from hurting your marriage)   1,050 words
"Two Tastes, One Home" (blending your styles in your new home)   1,000 words
"When Opposites Attract" (living with your differences)   1,000 words
"The Engaged Girl's Survival Guide" (coping with wedding stress)   1,000 words
"Home, Sweet Home" (using the Internet to buy a home; includes sidebar)   1,000 words
"Girl, Interrupted" (bridesmaids' dish on being in weddings)   2,000 words
"Whose Wedding Is It, Anyway?" (coping with everyone's expectations)   1,300 words
"Bride's Guide to Birth Control" (rundown of options) 1,000 words
"The Taxman Cometh" (how marriage affects your tax status)   1,000 words
"Across the Miles: When You're an Out-of-Town Maid of Honor"   1,450 words

I've enclosed several stories to give you a feel for my writing style; if you'd like to see others or are interested in purchasing one-time rights to any of them, just let me know.

Thank you very much for your time; I look forward to hearing from you soon.

Sincerely,

Kelly James-Enger

Note that I've provided a brief bio, mentioning my bridal-related clips first, along with a list that gives a brief description of each story and word count. With this type of letter, I'll include a story or two to give the editor a sample of my work. This kind of letter often pays off—an editor who might have only purchased one story will often buy more when she sees my complete story list. Last year, one local bridal publication purchased reprint rights to eight different stories at one time after I sent the above letter, and has bought additional stories since then.

I suggest that you create—and maintain—a list of the articles you currently own rights to. Double-check your contracts to make sure that you retained reprint rights, and then divide your work into categories by subject matter. Include the title, a brief description, word count, and when and where the piece was first published. (Also note any restrictions on reprint rights so you don't run afoul of a contract.) Creating the initial list takes some time, but after that, it's relatively simple to update. I have an ever-expanding list, broken down into categories including nutrition, women's health, psychology, fitness, wellness, bridal, and relationship/sex stories. I update it regularly, and then look for markets that would be likely to buy stories in these subject areas.

I've had the most success with regional health and fitness magazines and local bridal magazines. Evergreen topics like "Dollars and Sense: How to Talk about Money" and "What's Your Workout Personality?" tend to sell better than time-oriented pieces like "New Developments in Birth Control," which have a shorter shelf life—unless you're willing to take the time to update them before sending them out.

Freelancer Jennifer Pirtle, who divides her time between London and New York City, sells a lot of reprints and often finds potential markets online. "I tend to find them hunting around on the Web, or by subscribing to e-mail newsletters for writers," says Pirtle. "Most of the writing newsletters are geared toward beginning writers and most of the markets in there wouldn't be things that I would consider for first markets for the pay, but I've found that they're great for finding out about reprints." Pirtle made about $5,000 last year from reprints with very little effort. "It's not a ton of money, but for doing absolutely nothing, it's great!" she says. "That's really what it's about—working less hard and making more money. So if I can make some money by doing nothing but having a brief e-mail exchange, that's fantastic."

How Much to Charge?

Sometimes, editors will ask you how much you charge for reprint rights, but in many cases, the reprint market will have a standard rate. Often, this is less than what it will pay for original stories, but that shouldn't necessarily be the case. After all, the article is still new to the market. If you're asked to quote a price, ask for more than you think (or hope) you'll get—it gives you room to bargain and you may be surprised at how much your work can resell for. (See chapter 4 for more advice on negotiating with editors and other clients.) Because reprints are essentially "found" money, though, I'm much more flexible in terms of what I'll accept than I am for an original piece. While I've been paid as much as $500 for a story that was reprinted in a national business magazine, I've also taken as little as $40 for a reprint that ran in a regional parenting publication. In the latter case, I knew that that was the publication's standard rate for reprinted stories, and it's still an extra $40 in my pocket.

Pirtle takes a similar approach. "If it's a regional magazine, they're not going to have the budget to pay $2/word," she says. "If they're reprinting if for a corporate purpose, they may have more of a budget, but I look at it case by case. If it's something where I'm going to send them the article, and they'll send me money, I'm not too hard-nosed about it." If a market wants to pay a lower rate than she'd like, she'll sometimes agree to it—if the market buys more than one piece. That strategy benefits both her and the publication.

Another way to sell reprint rights to articles is by using a syndicate, which will offer reprint rights to your work to various media. Some share proceeds with you; others pay a flat fee for the license to your work for a certain time period. Featurewell, *www.featurewell.com*, is an example of such a syndication service. Early on, I worked with two syndicators who specialize in selling work to overseas markets, but over the last couple of years I only sold a few articles through them. Now, I prefer to locate reprint markets on my own. If you're interested, though, *Writer's Market* includes a list of syndicates each year; *Editor & Publisher*, a trade publication for newspaper writers and editors, also publishes an annual syndicate directory.

Opting to Specialize

After you've reviewed the work that you own the rights to, you may discover that you've written a lot about a particular subject or area. As a result, you've become an expert of sorts. Developing writing specialties is a natural outgrowth of reslanting material.

Not every writer wants—or intends—to specialize. But like me, many have found that limiting the areas they write about makes them more efficient writers. First, as you research articles, you become well versed in that subject matter. You've developed a background in that area. It's also easier to keep up on a handful of subjects than to try to stay well informed about every possible subject you might cover.

"Specializing is a way that you can easily keep on top of your subjects. It's much easier to keep . . . abreast of advances in the industry and books that are coming out and sources, if you're narrowing yourself down to a handful of topics," says

Pirtle, who writes about health and lifestyle subjects. "It's not as if I'm prevented from writing about something else if I'm interested in [it] or an editor comes up with the idea, but I've found that I feel much more in control of my career [by specializing]."

While Pirtle decided from the outset of her freelance career that she would focus on a handful (albeit fairly broad) of subjects, Jennifer Lawler started out as a generalist. Early in her career, she wrote books about topics ranging from music to drug testing and the Middle Ages. While the subjects were all of personal interest to her, there were drawbacks—like the fact that she wasn't making as much money as she wanted.

Part of the problem was that by covering such a wide range of subjects, she lacked a clearly defined platform or specialty. "Every time I had to find an audience for the book—not only editors and publishers, but reading audiences as well," says Lawler, who's based in Lawrence, Kansas, "I would investigate and do interviews like a journalist would do, but I didn't have the expert status. When I wrote a book on country music, people loved it but I wasn't a music reviewer and I wasn't a musician, so there was no real hook to get the word out about the book. I had a number of books out and all of them were earning royalties, but I wasn't making much money."

Lawler, a black-belt martial artist, had been writing about martial arts for years, when she suddenly realized she already had a platform—as a martial-arts expert. She just hadn't capitalized on it. "I had the black belt. I had written all these books. I had the training," she says. "My current agent helped me see that I wasn't just showing people how to do martial arts or how to do self-defense—I was showing them how the principles of martial arts could help them in their lives. My message isn't that martial arts can change your life, but that the principles of martial arts can change your life." This realization led to Lawler's book *Dojo Wisdom*, which sold well and has led to a series of *Dojo Wisdom* books. "Even though it's a niche and it is specializing, it appeals to a big enough group of people to give me a fairly big platform," she says.

As you develop a background in one area, you can still branch into others as well. Brian O'Connell now writes about a variety of subjects including finance, business, and golf. But when he started freelancing, he relied on his financial background—he'd worked on Wall Street—to nail his first assignments. "Specialization is like building a foundation. When you're building a house, you have to build a foundation first, before you build the second, third, and fourth floor," he says. "You build off your experience. I found a lot of corporate work, like writing newsletters and things like that which fed my family and kept me going until I could gain my footing."

O'Connell focused on financial topics at first, but when he had free time, he wrote about topics that interested him personally, like golf. That led to articles for golfing magazines and a golf column for *Continental*, the in-flight magazine for the airline. "Every step I took on the way up I would use as a means to open more doors," he says. "Now I wasn't just a financial writer, I was also a golf writer. I've also done that in the career management industry and to a lesser extent in health care. . . . It's like a long staircase. There are a lot of doors along the staircase and as you go along, you have to open them up along the way."

Looking at your current specialty and the changing state of the market may encourage you to break into other areas as well. While Leah Ingram has been known for writing wedding-related books, she branched out into the gift-giving area more recently. For her, it was a natural transition and a way to capitalize on some of the speaking and spokesperson work that was coming her way.

"I'd written a bunch of articles and stories on how to give holiday gifts to benefit a good cause, so I had those articles in my clip file" says Ingram. "When I did the bridal registry book and started getting spokesperson work, I was getting hired more as a gift-giving guru than as a wedding expert. People assumed that if I wrote about weddings, I must know about gifts, and that's where that niche developed." Seizing the opportunity, Ingram then wrote a book on gift giving (*You Shouldn't Have!*) to bolster her platform. Now, she's known as a gift-giving expert in addition to a wedding expert, and gets more spokesperson work as a result.

While some writers specialize from the outset, Sam Greengard wrote about a variety of topics before deciding to focus on business and technology when he saw the need for writers who were well versed in the subject. "More than a decade ago, I recognized that business and technology were becoming far more important—at least in terms of media coverage," says Greengard. "I felt as though a vast untapped market was emerging, particularly because most people writing articles on these subjects are either industry experts who cannot write or journalists who lack the knowledge to write articles that provide valuable information and insights."

Greengard's focus on a handful of subjects has made him a more efficient writer. "One advantage to this approach is that I have gained enough general knowledge that writing stories is usually not a stretch. I can turn them out faster while providing a high-quality product," he says. "I can also plug interviews and information into multiple stories, which cuts down on my time further." He occasionally covers other topics, but estimates that 80 to 90 percent of the work he does falls under the umbrella of business, technology, or finance.

Greengard admits that his previous experience as a generalist helped him develop the writing skills he relies on as a specialist today. "As a contributing editor for *Los Angeles* magazine for over a decade and a frequent contributor to airline publications, I really learned a lot of journalistic tricks and techniques," he says. "I can tap into this capability, if necessary, but also write a more straightforward way—if it's a business publication or trade magazine that wants a no-frills writing style. If I hadn't learned this skill, I'm not sure I would be able to achieve as much success as a specialist. My advice: Learn how to write about anything and everything, then choose an area that meshes with your interests, skills, and financial goals."

I used a similar approach when launching my career and gained experience writing everything from profiles, to quizzes, to service pieces, to full-blown features. These days, though, I've found that writing about a narrower range of subjects and focusing primarily on service journalism pieces makes me more productive and saves me time. Whether or not you choose to specialize, reslant more of your work, or decide to start selling reprints, you'll find more ways of making the most of your time in the following chapter.

CHAPTER 8
Watching the Clock: Time Management Techniques for Every Writer

Reslanting your work and focusing on a few specialties helps you make the most of your time. But don't overlook the simple fact that writers who are paid more for their work are going to make more money, on average, than writers who are paid less. That means you need to start targeting higher-paying markets if you're not doing so already. There's nothing wrong with writing for publications or clients that pay less, especially when you're a relatively inexperienced writer and are building your portfolio. But as you gain experience, you should start going after work that pays better. If you spend all your time working on stories that bring in only minimal income, you won't have time to pitch better-paying markets. Make it a goal to average more for the stories you write over time, regardless of the markets you're working for.

Think Per Hour, Not Per Word

There's an important caveat to this, however. Most magazine and newspaper writers are paid per word for their work. (Business writers and copywriters, on the other hand, usually charge by the hour or by project.) This per-word rate, multiplied by word count, tells you how much you'll make for writing the story. By the way, these rates are lagging way behind inflation—in the 1960s, national consumer magazines paid freelancers $1/word and up. And today . . . today, that's the case as well. But anyway, the amount you'll make for the story is just that—how much you'll be paid. It may not tell you whether it's worth it to take it on. The real question is how much *time* the story will take—the assignment amount divided by the number of hours you put into it gives you your hourly rate for the piece.

For example, at first blush a 1,000-word story for a national magazine that pays $2/word sounds like a great deal. That's a $2,000 assignment—and it *is* a great deal if it takes a total of twenty hours (which is $100/hour). (The hourly rate gets even better if I can crank out the story in a mere ten hours!) If the piece winds up taking forty hours, though, my hourly rate has dropped to $50/hour. And if the piece winds up being put through the editorial wringer and costing sixty hours of time, my rate's dropped to $25/hour. That's arguably not a terrible rate, but it's impossible to make a six-figure living if I average $25/hour—unless I work 100 hours a week.

I've seen a lot of writers get hung up on the dollar/word standard. Under that strict logic, a magazine that pays $2/word must be twice as good as a $1/word market, and four times as good as a market that pays only $0.50/word. But that's not necessarily the case. Get in the habit of thinking about the real cost of the assignment—not how much money you're being paid for an assignment, but how much you'll make per hour. I've often found that markets that pay less than $1/word produce a higher per-hour rate because the stories are more straightforward with fewer requests for revisions. While your mileage may vary depending on the assignment, your per-hour rate is a better indication of your productivity whether you're writing for a magazine, a business client, or a book publisher.

Tracking Your Time

Here's the thing: You can't determine what your hourly rates are unless you have an idea of where your time is going. When I was a lawyer, I had to track how I spent my day because that's how my firm billed clients—by the hour. That habit spilled over into my freelancing business. While I don't keep track of how I spend every minute, I usually have a good idea of how I'm spending my time—and how long different assignments take me to complete.

At any given time, freelancer Erik Sherman is working on five or six articles in addition to a book or two. He uses a Franklin Covey time management system to help him juggle the research and writing tasks that the assignments demand. "It can greatly increase the amount you can get done in a given amount of time," says Sherman. "I plan ahead. Maybe I'll need seven or eight sources for a 2,000-word article, so I'll go after the sources ahead of time . . . it doesn't take that much time [to use the system] and you can research a whole bunch of articles at the same time. You have to be realistic about where your time goes and be willing to put in the planning part so that you can overlap your work effectively."

Freelancer Bev Bachel breaks her day into fifteen-minute increments. Part of the reason is for billing purposes, but she finds it also helps her attain other goals. "When I do my corporate client work, I'm generally paid by the hour," says Bachel. "A lot of times, tracking time is a pain in the butt, but it really helps me estimate accurately and helps me to know how I spend my time and determine whether I'm working efficiently. Say I want to make the same amount of money and work 20 percent less. The only way to tell if you're working less is to track your time."

Sure, you can use a spreadsheet, QuickBooks, or specific time-tracking software, but all you really need is a pencil and paper. Use your calendar to record how you spend your day. I like to use a desk calendar that gives a fourteen-hour span (from 7:00 A.M. to 9:00 P.M.) broken into fifteen-minute intervals. While I rarely schedule anything as early as 7:00 A.M. (although I'm usually at my desk, drinking Diet Mountain Dew), a calendar this size allows me to record my entire workday—and other tasks I need to complete as well. Here's a sample entry:

7:00 A.M.

7:15   Drop Erik off/gym

7:30   ↓

7:45   ↓

8:00   ↓

8:15   ↓

8:30   ↓

8:45

9:00   Start *Bottom Line* column

9:15   ↓

9:30   ↓

9:45   ↓

10:00   ↓

10:15

10:30   Work on *Quill* draft

10:45   ↓

11:00   ↓

11:15   ↓

11:30   ↓

11:45   Lunch/Laura

12:00 P.M.   ↓

12:15   ↓

12:30   ↓

12:45   ↓

1:00   ↓

1:15   UPS store—mail copies of RAS/bank/drugstore

1:30   ↓

1:45

2:00   Interview Dawn Jackson/312-555-1212/transcribe notes/send TU

2:15   ↓

2:30   ↓

2:45

3:00   Additional fiber research/request studies

3:15   ↓

3:30   ↓

3:45

4:00   Line up sources for interval training story

4:15   ↓

4:30

4:45

5:00   Walk Sandy

5:15   ↓

5:30

5:45

6:00

6:15

6:30   North Central class (take handouts)

6:45   ↓

7:00   ↓
7:15   ↓
7:30   ↓
7:45   ↓
8:00   ↓
8:15   ↓
8:30   ↓
8:45   ↓

I find that scheduling my day helps me get everything done. And while it may look pretty anal to have to include time to walk my dog on my calendar, I know if I don't make time on my schedule for nonwork tasks, I'm less likely to do them.

This kind of scheduling can also reveal how much time you're spending doing the various tasks that comprise a freelancing career, including marketing, research, writing, speaking, and teaching if applicable, and business management tasks like reading contracts, tracking business expenses, filing relevant paperwork, and sending out—and following up on—invoices. The amount of time you expend on these types of tasks may vary depending on the type of work you do and how established you are in your career. Early on, my time broke down in the following percentages:

Marketing (including research, writing queries, cold calls)	40–50%
Research/interviews for current assignments	10–30%
Writing for pay (magazine, newspaper, and business work)	10–20%
Business management tasks	5–10%
Speaking/teaching	5%

A few years into my writing career, however, these percentages shifted. I still had to market myself, but I was writing for a number of steady clients, which significantly reduced the amount of time I spent looking for new markets and researching and writing queries. The percentages looked more like this:

Marketing (including research, writing queries, cold calls)	10–20%
Research/interviews for current assignments	20–30%
Writing for pay (primarily magazine and business work)	5–35%
Business management tasks	5–10%
Speaking/teaching	5–10%

Notice that as my marketing time decreased, I was able to devote more time to researching and writing assignments. That's a good thing. The next major shift occurred about a year ago, when I began spending less time writing magazine articles, and more time working on books. Currently, my time breaks down like this:

Marketing (including research, writing queries, cold calls)	10%
Research/interviews for current assignments	20–25%
Writing for pay (primarily book and magazine work)	35–45%
Business management tasks	5–10%
Speaking/teaching	10–15%

Books take more time to write than magazine articles, so I'm spending more time writing and less time marketing myself. I also do more speaking, which requires time out of my office, so I look for projects like books that I can work on while I'm traveling. (Magazine articles tend to be more interview-intensive, and I almost always conduct interviews from my office at home.)

Get the idea? Once you know how you're spending your time, you can determine your own percentages and whether you need to make some changes. That's the first step to better time management. If you have no idea how long projects take you to complete, I suggest you think like a lawyer and keep a timesheet for each project. Keep it in your story file and simply make entries on it whenever you work on that assignment. You may be amazed that you're not working as efficiently as you thought. Here's an example:

Assignment: Beat Belly Bloat (1,500 words—due March 24)

Date	Task	Time
March 1	Background research	1.5
March 3	Research/line up interviews	1.5
March 8	Interview Shanta/transcribe notes	1.25
March 10	Interview Surawicz/transcribe notes	1.0
March 12	Follow-up w/ Shanta/start draft	3.5
March 16	Work on draft	2.50
March 19	Finish draft/proof and turn in	1.25

In this example, I spent a total of 12.5 hours on the story (not including any research time I spent to pitch the story before I got the assignment). If I'm asked to do revisions, I'll add that time to my assignment sheet. In this case, I was being paid $1,125 for this 1,500-word story. At 12.5 hours, I'm averaging $90/hour for my work—not bad for a straightforward service article. If I have to go back and contact my experts again, conduct additional research, and spend time revising the piece, and I put another three hours into the story (a total of 15.5), my hourly rate drops to about $72/hour. If the story turns out to be a nightmare, with even more revisions required, and I spend a total of twenty hours on it, my hourly rate plummets to $56.25/hour.

If you're not sure where your time is going, I suggest you use these methods to track yours for a month or two. You'll have a clear picture of where your hours are going—and hopefully discover some ways to better manage your time as well.

Make the Most of Your Time

Even if you're not as anal as I am and don't bother tracking your time (hey, I know despite my good advice, a lot of people will read that and think, "no thanks!"), there are a number of ways you can make the most of yours every day.

Shoot High

As I mentioned at the beginning of the chapter, some markets pay more than others. Of course, the amount of time you spend on these assignments affects your overall income, but if a story takes you ten hours to pitch, research, and write—and one market will pay $400 for it and another $1,000—that's a no-brainer. You sell it to the higher market, right? Yet, I see many writers—talented, smart, prolific writers—who get comfortable, or rather stuck, writing for markets that don't pay so well. They're making a decent living writing for trades or regional publications, but they're not confident enough to pursue the "big" magazines. Yes, markets that pay more tend to want a bit more for their money. But don't ignore markets that pay $1, $2, or even $3/word because you're afraid you can't cut it. Aim high, at least occasionally. The worst that can happen is you'll be turned down, and you can always schlep the story to your "regular" market afterward.

The corollary to this is to cut back on the markets that aren't really worth your while. I wrote for newspapers early on in my freelance career, but quit after about a year and a half. I just couldn't justify the time for the money I was making—a $50 story might take me six or eight hours to report and write.

Okay, I know there are some assignments that *aren't* just about the money. I occasionally write for less than I'd like to make. Maybe it's a subject I really want to cover, a market I've been wanting to crack, or it's good publicity for me. Sometimes, I'm slow work-wise and simply want to take on another assignment to keep some cash rolling in. But I don't write for low-paying markets very often—if I did, it would eat into my time and affect my bottom line. I'll occasionally take on lower-paying markets that offer steady work with few hassles, but I balance that out with bigger, more lucrative assignments.

Only you can decide whether a low-paying gig is worth keeping. If you're doing a regular column for your local paper that takes an hour or so to hammer out, pays $100, and gets you some free publicity, that's one thing. But if your $100 column requires interviewing and background research and eats up at least ten hours a month, consider how much marketing you could have done during that time—which would probably have paid for itself many times over with new assignments.

Consider the PIA Cost

In chapter 4, I included a list of factors to consider when deciding whether to accept an assignment. Not surprisingly, one of the biggest factors (in addition to how much you're being offered money-wise, of course) is how much time it will require. If you've worked with the editor before, you probably already have a sense for how much revising, reworking, and other hassles are involved. Yes, there's time involved, but there's something more amorphous at work as well—something I call the pain-in-the-ass (PIA) factor.

I've worked with editors who rarely ask for revisions (low PIA factor), and I've worked with some who I know will require edits as a matter of course (medium PIA factor), and some who just won't be satisfied until they've put me through the wringer (high PIA factor). That doesn't mean I won't work for the latter two (although I do try to avoid high PIAs). It *does* mean I'll make sure I'm paid enough to justify the time—and emotional drain—of spending several weeks, possibly more, going back and forth on an assignment. If it's a business project, nail down the scope of the assignment and what the client is expecting before you take it on. Don't forget to consider the deadline as well—if it's tight, you may have to put in overtime or pass up other gigs while you work on that project, which can boost the PIA factor as well.

Know Your Limits

First, determine how much time you have available for writing. If you're freelancing full time, that may mean forty hours a week or more, when necessary. (Of course, that doesn't mean that you *should* work fifty or sixty hours a week—just that you *can*, if you must.) If you're juggling another job, raising small humans, or have other responsibilities, however, your writing time may be limited to a few hours a day or less. If that's the case, planning ahead is even more important to make sure that you make the most of the few hours you do have.

Writing part time doesn't mean you can't be productive. When I started freelancing, I was still working full time as a lawyer, and I had to squeeze as much work as I could into my writing time. Guess what? Those were some of my most productive months. I only had an hour or two to write most days, and I knew how I'd spend that time before I even sat down. Now that I write full time, I've lost some of that sense of urgency. I'm still driven, but now my schedule's more flexible—I know I can work late or catch up on the weekend if I have to. While I have more time, I'm less productive. It's like that old business axiom about "a meeting will take as long as it's scheduled." The longer I have to work on a project, the more time I tend to put into it.

Organize Your Day

Freelancer Leah Ingram writes books and articles and does spokesperson work—and manages to juggle it all along with parenting and homemaking responsibilities. It just takes discipline—and organization, she says. "I put my children on the bus at 8:15. Between then and 3:45 is my time to work. If I don't use my time wisely, I'm screwed," says Ingram. She's found making lists at night for the tasks she must complete the following day helps her maximize her time.

Ingram also breaks her workday into thirty-minute sections and makes sure that she keeps on track as she's working. "I'll take my Palm out and check what I need to do next. If it's to research a story, I'll set my timer for fifteen minutes," she says. "When it goes off, I'll finish it up and then see what's next on my list. . . . Basically, it's first come first serve. Whatever deadline comes first, that's what I do first."

Like Ingram, I'm a list-making fan. I also prioritize my top three tasks for the day every morning and write them on my calendar in order—and then schedule them at specific times throughout the day. The best part? Crossing them off as I complete them.

Eliminate the Ugliest Tasks

Most days, I've got at least one thing I don't *want* to do. (Some bad days, many things I don't want to do!) Maybe it's revising an article, transcribing notes from interviews (ugh), or making cold calls to potential new clients (double ugh). I've learned that if I don't do these tasks first thing, I'll fret about them all day until I can finish them and check them off my list. That kind of anxiety makes me stressed and hurts my productivity. Now, I do my "ugliest" job first to give me the satisfaction of having finished it—and spare myself the mental anguish of worrying about it all day. It's surprising how much time you can expend worrying about something compared to how little it takes to actually complete the dreaded chore.

Invest Your Time

Some chores take time now but will pay off in the long run—like inputting data into a contact database. Investing a few minutes here and there may be worthwhile. For example, I record my income as I receive it and make a note of expenses as I incur them. I'd rather spend a minute doing it then instead of planning to do it later and forgetting about it—or losing a receipt. If I'm on hold on the phone, I'll use the time to do some background research for a story, or send follow-up e-mails to editors. In chapter 3, I talked about the importance of setting up an efficient filing system. Every week or so (usually on Friday afternoons), I take a few minutes to go through the pile of paper that's inevitably accumulated on my desk. Each piece of paper gets filed, responded to (if necessary), or tossed in the recycling bin. The time I spend then saves me hours later on.

Delete Distractions

Let me just say . . . no one *needs* to check her e-mail every five minutes. But hey, lots of times I do it anyway. If I need to get a draft of something written, though, I close my e-mail program, suffer e-mail withdrawal, and open it at the end of the morning and midafternoon—otherwise, I waste time reading, responding to, and deleting e-mails. This is easier said than done, I realize. I've learned to keep my e-mail program shut down when I'm working on something, and I'll often ignore the phone as well. If that doesn't work, sometimes I pack up my laptop and simply work at the library or Starbucks. When I'm away from my office, I have fewer distractions and am forced to write.

Take Breaks

Remember that old story about the two lumberjacks? They started off chopping down trees. One, we'll call him Anal Andy, worked steadily throughout the day, refusing to take a break. The other, Laidback Larry, stopped every hour or so. At the end of the day, it's Larry who winds up with a bigger pile of logs than his buddy, and Andy's amazed—and disgusted. "How could you possibly chop more than me?" Andy cries, "I've worked nonstop, and you've taken breaks all day long!" Larry's response? "I stopped to sharpen my saw."

Consider your breaks not as time-wasting but as saw-sharpening. Research shows that the average person can only listen for forty-five to fifty minutes before his attention begins to flag. I've found this is true for writing as well. Take frequent breaks throughout your work day, and you'll get more done. Even five or ten minutes away from the computer will help refresh you. I take unscheduled "puppy play breaks" every few hours, which makes both me and my dog happy. After turning in a big assignment, I'll also take an hour or two off before going back to work. I figure the larger the project, the bigger the break I deserve.

"I just finished a book a week ago, and I already have an idea for another one, but I'm not even going to start on it for a month or two," says Victoria Moran, who works on smaller projects like articles between book projects. "I wait until a few months to try to clear out my head . . . of course you don't want to say, 'I've written a book, now I'm going to wait for it to be a best seller.' That's a good way to starve, but on the other hand you don't want to just be pounding out stuff that's no good."

Harness Technology (or Not)

Some people swear by their PDAs, or use an electronic calendar like Outlook. With both, you can set alarms and reminders to keep you from wasting time or blowing a deadline, but I don't want to be pestered with more technology than I need. I prefer a paper calendar and would go bonkers having to enter all my tasks into Outlook Office. The key is to select what works for you.

Sam Greengard uses Info Select to help manage his assignments. "I keep detailed notes about who I've contacted, the date and time I left a message or sent an e-mail, and general notes about the project, including sources, Web links, et cetera," says Greengard. "I keep a separate document for each assignment. I organize them by client, and it's easy to check the status of each project at any given moment."

Keep Your Mornings (or Afternoons) Sacred

Are you a morning person or a night owl? I've found that I'm able to write more quickly in the morning—in fact, the first few hours in the day are my most productive. By early afternoon, my brain has slowed to a crawl and it's harder to focus and concentrate. As a result, I try to devote my morning hours to writing and save phone interviews, transcribing notes, researching, and other less-demanding tasks for after lunch. If you know you write better at night, on the other hand, plan your most demanding writing jobs then and protect that time. That may mean refusing to answer the phone, ignoring family members, and relying on TiVo to tape the latest episode of *CSI*.

Develop Time-Savers

In the previous chapter, I talked about the benefits of specializing. When you write about the same subject more than once, you needn't re-create the wheel with each story. Take a similar approach with other tasks you do more than once. For example, I have a set list of questions I ask at the outset of every interview (omitting certain questions as appropriate), including:

- Name
- Age (primarily for anecdotes)
- Mailing address (work/home)
- Telephone numbers (work/home/cell)
- E-mail address
- Job title
- Academic title (if applicable)
- Background/research area
- Book titles (including publishers and dates of publication)
- Association memberships (if applicable)

This simple list keeps me from forgetting anything basic; after I fill in these blanks, I go on to my substantive questions.

Farm Work Out

If you're too busy to handle the work on your desk, it may be time to hire some help. I use an assistant for basic research and other tasks. While Sam Greengard conducts his own interviews, he uses two assistants who schedule the interviews and transcribe the notes afterward.

"Most of us wait too long to spend money on subcontractors," says Bev Bachel. "Can you find a college student to make photocopies? Do you have a delivery service? I'm amazed at how many writers just don't have good infrastructure. If you

want to be professional, then your job is to be a writer. I could
make photocopies, but that doesn't make much sense."

Look for Repeat Business

Remember, it's easier to get work from clients you already
have than to get new clients. To maximize his time, Robert
McGarvey relies on relationship-building. "The essence of any
business is repeats and referrals. That's how you make
money," says McGarvey, who's based in Jersey City, New Jersey. "Cold calling and stuff like that you do to fill a pipeline.
You don't do it because you want to do it—you do it because
you have to do it. My business is about repeats and referrals. If
I can make $30,000 from one customer, I'd rather do that than
have thirty $1,000 customers. It's a lot less wear and tear on
me." I feel the same way—in fact, if I could find one client
who'd pay me $100,000 a year to freelance for him, I'd gladly
work for one boss again. Just as long as I didn't have to com-
mute to work or wear pantyhose.

Work for Money

It sounds obvious, but make sure that the lion's share of your
time is spent doing work for which you're paid. New book
authors often fall into the trap of spending so much time promoting their books that their income takes a hit. This happened to me when I was so busy promoting my first two
books, I didn't actively seek new assignments. A few months
later, I felt the fallout in my bank account.

Speaking and promoting your new title may result in bigger
royalty checks down the line, but there's no guarantee—which
means you have to keep doing paid work in the meantime.
"Once you have some kind of track record, look where your
money is coming from," says Victoria Moran. "Writing a book
makes money. Writing a proposal that will sell makes money.
Answering Profnet queries [as an expert] and trying to promote

yourself does not. I'm not saying you shouldn't do that, but if you work an eight-hour day, maybe four hours should be writing and the rest can be divided between research, promoting, and clerical stuff. It's really important to look at how much of your day is going to make you money."

Stock Your Office

You've got a package ready to send out to an editor. Problem is, you're out of big envelopes—or your last printer cartridge just ran out of ink. Stock up on basic office supplies and have the tools you need most—a good dictionary, thesaurus, and the phone number for your ISP—handy in your office. I've found that even a minor purchase like a postage scale can save tons of time—I weigh envelopes and then check out *www.usps.gov* for the appropriate postage amount. That's saved me both postage and countless trips to the post office over the years.

I also have dozens of books on health, nutrition, and fitness in my office for quickly accessible background information (in addition to the Internet, of course). "Because I specialize, I have all of the material I need to be prolific," says Jennifer Lawler. "I have whole bookshelves on the subject and I also know 12 billion martial-arts experts [we assume a slight exaggeration], so if I need a source, I know who to call."

While there are loads of tools out there to help you manage your time, the most important aspect is your mind-set. Make it your goal to be focused and accomplish more during your writing time. Once you do so, you'll become aware of your biggest time traps—and happily discover that many of them are easily overcome with some practice.

Research: The Big Time-Waster

Unless you're writing about a subject you're already intimately familiar with, you're going to have to do background research.

That's one of the perks of freelancing: You get to learn about all kinds of interesting (and not so interesting) subjects. It's all too easy to get sucked in to spending hours researching . . . and reading . . . and researching some more . . . and reading some more. As a writer, you must write to get paid. That means you want to minimize research time while still locating the information you need.

First stop, the Internet. Bookmark helpful Web sites that you use frequently. As a health and nutrition writer, for example, I often use sites like the National Center for Health Statistics (*www.cdc.gov/nchswww/default.htm*), PubMed (*www.ncbi.nlm. nih.gov/entrez/query.fcgi*), which allows me to search scientific and medical journals, and the U.S. Department of Agriculture's Nutrient Data Laboratory (*www.nal.usda.gov/fnic/ foodcomp/search/*) for research. Other helpful sites for freelancers include:

- *http://dictionary.reference.com/*. An online dictionary
- *http://thesaurus.reference.com/*. An online thesaurus
- *www.encyclopedia.com*. A free online encyclopedia with more than 57,000 entries
- *www.refdesk.com/*. An online reference desk with hundreds of resources
- *www.highbeam.com/library/index.asp*. This site, formerly known as *www.elibrary.com*, provides access for members to more than 28 million documents for a cost of $19.95/month or $99.95/year.
- *www.sree.net/stories/web.html*. This site includes an extensive list of online sources managed by journalist and technology expert Sreenath Sreenivasan.

Tracking your time will tell you how much you're devoting to research. If you want to reduce that, set a limit for how long you'll spend on background research for a story. Depending on the complexity of the subject, I'll spend anywhere from less than an hour to several getting up to speed, ordering journal articles, and lining up expert sources for a story. Remember, you can always do additional research as you work on the piece. You don't have to understand every facet of the subject as you start your interviews; just have a general understanding of what you're going to be writing about.

By the way, if you're stuck, consider calling on your local reference librarian for help. I've found reference librarians to be among the smartest, most helpful, most determined researchers on the face of the planet. When I'm about to give up, I'll give my local library a call, and the women and men at the reference desk can almost always track down the obscure fact or reference or citation I'm looking for. They've saved me time and innumerable headaches in the past, and I suggest you take advantage of the ones in your area as well.

How much research is enough? It depends both on the subject matter and the depth of your story. For a simple nutrition piece, I may spend an hour pulling recent studies and double-checking recent health statistics. When I recently wrote a more complicated piece on how technology has changed the way college students socialize, I spent the better part of a morning educating myself about the most popular technologies among students (instant messaging, or IMing, is huge on campus), media richness theory (which determines how people choose which media to use), and how colleges throughout the country are using technology to help students learn. That gave me the background I needed to line up my sources.

Interviews—both in person and by phone—can quickly eat up time. As a freelancer, I'll conduct as many as six or eight interviews in a day. That means I need to be able to interview efficiently, without sacrificing the quality of the resulting material.

Save Time Finding Experts

First, you need to find your experts. Your background research may reveal good potential sources, and online databases like *www.profnet.com* offer thousands of experts in every discipline. Profnet can be used two ways: you can search its database of experts or submit a query specifying what type of expertise you're looking for. Profnet will then send your query to hundreds of universities, hospitals, and public-relations (PR) firms, which will then contact you with relevant experts.

Of course, before web-based resources like Profnet, writers had to find experts the old-fashioned way—with lots of legwork. The starting point for me was, and sometimes still is, the *Encyclopedia of Associations*, a three-volume set that's updated annually. It includes more than 22,000 associations, organizations, and groups and is arranged and indexed by subject category. To use it, look for an association that matches the type of expertise you're seeking. Then call the association, ask for its public-affairs or public-relations department, and request a referral to an association member. The PR person will know who the media-friendly members are and usually will have background information on them as well—it's a huge time-saver.

For health experts, I'll often do a search on PubMed for authors of medical-journal articles on the subject I'm writing about. Books on the subject also provide qualified experts who actually *want* to be interviewed. If you can find a relevant title, especially a recent one, the author is almost always happy to talk to you to help sell her book. That's why so many "experts" in magazine articles also happen to be book authors. You can locate authors through their publishers; call and ask for the publicist who handles the book you're inquiring about.

Universities and colleges also offer a stable of qualified experts. Call the school, ask for its public-affairs or media-affairs office, and explain what type of expertise you're seeking. Like their counterparts at associations, they can also direct you to an appropriate professor or researcher in the area you're writing about. Usually, the bigger and more well known the school, the better.

Finally, in a pinch, don't forget about magazine and newspaper articles. When you find articles on a similar subject that quote appropriate experts, you can track them down as well. I've used a variety of web-based search engines like *www.google.com* and Internet directories to locate experts. The advantage is you know they've been quoted before, so they're probably media-friendly.

Make the Connection

Okay, you've located your experts. What's the next step? Making contact. I call, introduce myself, and explain how I got the person's name. Then I describe the story I'm working on and ask if she's available for a brief telephone interview in the near future. For example, "Mr. Lesyk, I got your name from the American Running Association. I know you're a sports psychologist and I think you'd be a great source for the story I'm doing on workout motivation for *Oxygen*, a women's fitness magazine. Do you have fifteen minutes during the next week when we could conduct a phone interview for this story?" I've found I can conduct most interviews in fifteen to twenty minutes. If I need more time, I tell the source that up front so he or she can plan accordingly.

Usually, I use the first call to arrange an interview time instead of conducting it right then. This gives your expert time to think about the story you're working on, gather any necessary information, and prepare to speak with you. It also ensures that you're calling at a convenient time. I double-check the time and date, paying attention to time zones, and tell the source I'll be in touch. "Okay, so I'll call you Monday the 6th, at 3:30 Eastern time, 2:30 central time at this number." I then make a note of the interview time, the person's name, and his telephone number in my calendar.

A quick comment on e-mail interviews. Occasionally, I will do an interview via e-mail, but I prefer phone. It's more immediate and easier on the person you're interviewing. He or she can simply answer your questions orally without having to type up responses. Of course, if a source prefers an e-mail interview, you can always accommodate this request.

Streamline Your Interview

If you're new to conducting interviews, write down the questions to cover. Don't forget basics such as name (and double-check the correct spelling!), address, phone number, e-mail, job title, academic title if applicable, and book title(s) if applicable. The template of questions earlier in this chapter is a great starting point. Having a list of questions will keep you from forgetting anything important (but if you do, don't worry—I'll cover that in a bit). You'll get better answers and more detailed information when you ask open-ended questions and avoid ones that can be answered with a flat "yes" or "no." Try to ask lots of "why" and "how" questions—like "Why did the results of your study surprise you?" or "How will this affect small business owners?" or "Why is this issue so important for parents today?"

Part of preparing for the interview is acquainting yourself with the subject you'll be asking about. That's where your background reporting comes in handy. If you're interviewing a doctor about a new medical procedure, read up on it so you have a better understanding of what it's designed to do. Your sources shouldn't be expected to spoon-feed you. By doing your homework in advance, you'll save time and be able to ask more probing questions.

Pick up the phone and make the call. When your expert answers, identify yourself and ask if this is still a good time for him to talk. Often, experts will ask me to call back in a little bit so they can attend to something else first. You'll set a positive tone for the interview when you first make sure that it's still a convenient time. Remember, they're doing you the favor, so accommodate their schedules.

Another thing: If you're going to tape-record the interview, ask permission. State laws vary, and you don't want to run into trouble with any wiretapping laws. I usually tape and tran-scribe as I go along, but a tape helps me go back and fill in any missing information if the subject turns out to be a "fast talker." When I explain that the tape recorder helps me quote them accurately, experts almost always agree to be taped.

I like to give the expert an overview of what I'm going to ask, and then proceed with the questions one by one. For example, I might say, "This story is about the benefits of eating more fiber to help you lose weight. I'll ask what fiber is, why it's important to eat it, good sources of fiber, and how it helps people with weight loss." Then I begin with my specific ques-tions.

As you ask questions, *listen* to the answers. Sometimes, the response will provoke a follow-up question that you hadn't anticipated. "When I do an interview, they're often very open-ended," says Erik Sherman. "I'm trying to understand things, not trying to fill out a checklist. I may have a checklist set of questions, but I'm not looking for short, snappy answers—I'm looking to understand and that's what drives the interview."

When you're finished with your questions, ask if the expert wants to add anything. I usually say something like, "Is there anything important I haven't asked you that you'd like to mention?" You might also ask if your source knows of anyone else you might talk to for the story. You can get great leads this way. I usually close the interview by telling the source I'll be in touch with any follow-up questions or if my editor needs any additional information.

Finally, I always send my experts personal thank-you notes to express my appreciation for their time. I include my busi-ness card and let the source know that I'll be in touch when the article is published so he or she can find it on the newsstand. (If it's a small-circulation magazine or a trade publication, I'll usually offer to send a photocopy of the story—not the magazine itself—to the source.) While this takes a little extra time, people appreciate it. They're also likely to remember you the *next* time you need an interview, which helps build your Rolodex and makes your job easier in the long run.

Using E-mail to Save Time

Technology has forever changed the way writers work. We can now research stories on the Internet in minutes rather than spending hours at the library, and submit queries, articles, and even book manuscripts via e-mail instead of relying on the postal service. In fact, e-mail can be one of your most effective and time-saving tools as a writer. Use it improperly, however, and it can harm your reputation, annoy editors, waste time, and even hurt your chances of getting assignments in the future. To make the most of it, follow these basic e-mail strategies:

State Your Subject

Use the subject line of your e-mail message to catch the recipient's attention and provide a preview of your e-mail contents. If you're querying a magazine editor, you might write something like "Women and weight-lifting query" in the subject. If you know the editor, include your name—"Query from Kelly James-Enger." If you've been referred to the person, you may want to include the person who referred you—"Contacting you per Elfrieda Abbe," for example.

Using the subject line appropriately will help draw attention to your e-mail and keep you out of the "deleted items" folder. Also, remember to avoid spam buzzwords like "lose weight now," "save," "breakthrough discovery," "opportunity," "friend," and other words (such as parts of the human anatomy) that may snag your e-mail in a spam filter.

Ask about Attachments

In most cases, don't attach documents to e-mail. The exception is if your editor has *requested* an attachment. (Always ask if she prefers an attachment or including the story in the body of the e-mail.) Most editors and agents won't open attachments from writers unknown to them, because the attachments can carry viruses that can corrupt their machines.

If you do include an attachment, ask the editor what program she'd like it saved in—for example, a .doc extension signifies a Word document and .txt signifies a text-only format. The same goes for graphic attachments or photos—does your editor prefer a .jpeg, .tif, .bmp, or .tif file? Finally, make sure you have a good antivirus program that scans attachments for viruses, like Symantec Norton Antivirus or McAfee's Virus-Scan, and keep it updated.

Take Your Time!

It used to be when you'd write an editor or client, you'd spend some time writing, revising, and double-checking before you mailed the query. E-mail has made this process quicker, but there's also a tendency to hit "send" too quickly—before you've really had a chance to edit, or possibly even reread, your work. Break yourself of that habit: Your e-mail makes an impression, and a badly spelled, grammatically incorrect note reflects poorly on you. Don't sacrifice quality for speed.

Be Patient

You compose your e-mail and hit "send." Then you wait. It's been an hour! It's been two! Why haven't you heard anything back yet? Remember, e-mail produces a sense of immediacy, but just because it's immediate for you doesn't mean it is for the recipient. Give the person a chance to respond. Sending follow-up messages before the person's even had a chance to read your original message wastes both of your time.

Watch Your Tone

E-mail messages tend to be more casual in tone than formal letters, but that doesn't mean you can let it all hang out. There is such a thing as too casual—remember, you're a professional and want to be treated and perceived as one. When in doubt, err on the side of caution and be a little more formal rather than a little too laid-back. Watch the emoticons and lingo— most of us now know that "BTW" is "by the way," but don't assume anything.

It's also smart to hold off sending an e-mail if you're upset, angry, or frustrated about something. Take some time to cool off before you compose and hit "send." Don't use all uppercase letters—which means that you're yelling—and remember that e-mails can be forwarded to anyone. Be very careful about putting anything negative about an editor, client, or agent in an e-mail—it may wind up in his or her inbox.

Remember Snail Mail

While e-mail is fast and convenient, remember that some editors and agents still prefer (gasp!) old-fashioned snail mail pitches. Check the guidelines before you submit to a new market. If you're contacting a market via regular mail, the question arises whether you should send a self-addressed stamped envelope (SASE) for a reply. This relatively minor issue is hotly debated among writers—some believe that if a market specifically requests a SASE and you don't include one, you may alienate the editor. Others claim that including a SASE is a sign of an amateur and simply a good way to waste an extra 37 cents every time you mail in a submission. If an editor wants to assign or buy a piece, she'll call or e-mail, the reasoning goes, so why bother with a SASE?

When I started freelancing full time in 1997, I always included SASEs with submissions. Most of the magazines I was targeting specifically requested them, and I wanted to ensure as speedy a response time as possible. Even if the SASE only came back with a bong, or rejection, that bong might contain encouraging words or a note about what kind of stories the editor was currently looking for. Would she have bothered to send those kinds of rejections in the absence of a SASE? Hard to say, but for me, getting a response was worth the postage. In several instances, editors used my SASEs to offer to look at articles on spec.

Today, I don't bother with SASEs. When I query a new market via snail mail, I include a package of clips. I then call to follow up on the query within the next month or so because I believe a phone call is more effective than a SASE. After I speak with the editor, I'll know whether he's interested in the story idea.

As far as requesting guidelines via snail or e-mail, it depends on the market. If a market has guidelines that you can request via e-mail, great. If they're only available by snail mail, to save time, I simply enclose a SASE, folded in thirds, with a Post-it note that says, "Please send a copy of your writers' guidelines in the SASE enclosed." Then on the outside envelope to the magazine, I write "Writers' guidelines request" to speed things up. I usually get them in a week or so. With trade magazines or custom publications, however, I'll sometimes call first to see if they have guidelines; if not, I'll send a cover letter introducing myself and expressing my interest in working for that publication.

Writing Faster, Writing Better

I admit it—I still experience pangs of anxiety when I'm working on a new assignment. Am I doing enough research? Does the lead work? Does the story flow well? Are the transitions strong? Do the quotes "pop"? It's only when the piece is accepted (and the check is on its way!) that I completely relax—only to start obsessing over my next project.

And I'm not alone. Call it writer's block, performance anxiety, or plain old-fashioned self-doubt—every writer I know suffers from it at one time or another. Anxiety is a common, normal part of the creative process no matter where you are in your writing career, but it can derail your productivity if you let it. If you're a full-time freelancer and rely on your writing to pay your bills, it can be even worse.

Just as every writer is a little bit neurotic, all successful freelancers have developed their own methods for fighting anxiety. Forget about how silly a technique may sound—if it works for you, use it:

- Keep a regular schedule. Humans are creatures of habit. If you often have trouble getting started when you try to work, set a strict writing schedule for yourself. Note when you'll start on a project and then do it. If your creative side resists, get in the habit of performing a few simple rituals before you begin. In the morning, I like to grab a can of Diet Mountain Dew, take a swig, stretch in my chair a little, and take a couple of deep breaths before I start writing. In effect, I'm saying to my creative self, "Time to wake up! Get your butt in gear!" These kinds of simple rituals accustom your subconscious to kicking in as soon as you begin writing—and even when you're churning out a corporate brochure or a quick roundup of tips, your creativity is involved.
- Screw the muse. When my brain feels dead and the words won't come, sometimes I just force myself to hammer out a draft—no matter how bad it seems like it is. "I think what stops a lot of people is the idea that they'll be a hack if they write too much, or their prose can't be good enough if they write too quickly," says Jennifer Lawler. "I

try to have the first draft be as good as [it] can be, but I don't look at every sentence. I get the words down, and get the ideas down. I usually will do another draft after that and *then* I'll polish it up. For nonfiction, people are looking for information presented in a friendly, accessible way . . . it's really not rocket science. You need to just get it down."

- Switch gears. Sometimes, the problem isn't writing per se, but what you're working on. If I'm struggling with the draft of an article, I'll sometimes quit and work on something else—for example, researching a story, transcribing notes, or following up on some pending queries. I'm still getting work done, so when I come back to the manuscript, I'm ready to tackle it. "Feeling stuck is part of the rhythm of writing, and I am used to the fact that it happens," agrees Sarah Wernick, who's based in Brookline, Massachusetts. "I try to stop working on whatever is stuck and do something else that needs to be done. Often, when I come back to it (usually in a day or so), either it goes more easily or I'm able to give it a fresh look and realize that I need to take a different approach."
- Break it up. I couldn't write a book for years. Why? Because a book was too long. It wasn't until I was mentally able to divide the book into smaller pieces—chapters—and then subdivide those into still-smaller pieces that I could overcome my book-writing anxiety. When you feel overwhelmed, step back and figure out how to break the work down into smaller steps—conducting research, doing interviews, transcribing notes, writing a draft, and so on—and focus on one step at a time. Try a different approach. If you're stuck, it may be a sign there's a problem with the overall structure of the piece. Taking time away from the piece for a day or two may give you a new idea of how to approach it. Wernick found this to be the case on a recent book-doctoring gig.

"We started by coming up with an outline, and there was one chapter—chapter 5—that wound up as a kind of catch-all. When I started to write chapter 5, I got completely stuck," she says. "So I put it aside for a couple of days and worked on a different chapter and caught up on personal chores. When I came back, I realized that the different elements of the chapter simply didn't hang together and needed to be separated and put into different chapters. So that's what we did. In this case, being stuck was a symptom of problems with content."

- Move your body. Yes, once again, I'm encouraging you to get off your butt. Nothing conquers writer's block like physical exercise. Research shows that both cardiovascular exercise and weight lifting reduce anxiety, and they increase blood flow to your gray matter as well. Take brief movement breaks away from the computer, even if it's only five minutes to get up, stretch, and take some deep breaths. You'll feel calmer and more able to focus on your work.

- Cut yourself some slack. Writers are often their own harshest critics and agonize over how stories sound before they're even completed. That's counterproductive. If you let yourself get sidetracked with these kinds of worries, your productivity will nose-dive. "Recognize that your natural voice—the one you use like you're talking to a friend—is probably going to be very appealing to people," says Lawler. "Get the first draft down. You can always go back and change and fix things."

The Big Picture

Most of this chapter has focused on all of the small things you can do to maximize your time. But don't overlook a bigger consideration: the type of writing you're doing. As someone who primarily writes service journalism stories, I can crank out work more quickly than a freelancer who specializes in investigative journalism or creative nonfiction pieces. Each of the latter takes significantly more time to research and/or write than simpler how-to pieces.

I realize I'm not likely to win the Pulitzer for writing about the weight-loss-benefits of a high-fiber diet. But I enjoy writing what I do, and I occasionally write fiction and essays when I want to be more creative. For me, the trade-off in terms of the type of writing I do is worth it in terms of productivity. "Focus on what works for you," agrees Jennifer Lawler. "For some people that might be a certain kind of media, or it might be a certain kind of writing. I have always felt like I should be able to write articles, but I don't have nearly as much luck writing articles in terms of getting people to purchase them." Realizing that, Lawler decided to focus on books and write articles primarily as a way to promote her books and her name.

Lisa Collier Cool has written both award-winning magazine articles and books for more than twenty years. Early on, she wrote about a variety of subjects but then chose to specialize in health subjects before narrowing her focus even further. "A couple of years ago, along with the regular writing about health—like stories about osteoporosis—I decided I would particularly focus on writing about medical dramas," says Cool. "It's an interest of mine and it's much less research-intensive where I could still make the same money. When doing a medical drama, I may interview the person, maybe her husband, and maybe her doctor. That's three people, whereas if you write an article about diabetes, you have to look at all different studies, interview different doctors, check out the latest research, and so on." Another advantage is it helps boost her chance of getting an assignment. "I'm not the only one in the world who knows about osteoporosis, but when you do medical drama, only *you* have that story," she adds.

Freelancer Jim Thornton discovered a time-saving technique for writing profile pieces several decades ago that still
works today. "When I first got started, a Midwest art magazine hired me to write a ton of profiles of 'duck artists'—those
guys who do limited-edition prints of birds on the wing, so I
came up with my own 'duck-art profile formula' to help crank
these out," says Thornton. "Interestingly, I later found that this
same approach works well when you're writing a profile of
almost anyone. I also found that my editor never suspected I
was using a 'formula.' There are obviously drawbacks to any
formulaic approach, but for a rookie, this is a good way to start
corralling info about a person—and present it in a logical, compelling way most readers will find enjoyable." He gave me
permission to include it here, and it's a great model to adapt to
your own profile-writing needs:

Jim Thornton's Duck Art-Inspired Profile Formula

The Hook

1. Introductory anecdote or scene showing profile subject
   in action—reveal essence of character by showing, not
   telling; if possible, pick an incident that has some conflict
   or paradox associated with it.
2. Description—age, appearance, size, fashion, speech,
   mannerisms—include what Tom Wolfe calls "status
   life."
3. Accomplishments—why this person is a Big Deal
   (awards and honors, massive amounts of money, glory,
   munificence, heroism, dastardliness, notoriety, whatever.)
4. The "Wart"—an intimation of the subject's less flattering side, perhaps bolstered by a few quotes from ene-
   mies or detractors (if the person being profiled is
   notorious, the "wart" should probably be a "reverse
   wart"—i.e., something good about him or her you
   might not expect).

Once you have the reader intrigued by the subject as Worthy of Attention in the here and now, you can then go back and talk about how the subject got to this point . . .

Chronology

1. What did the person's parents do, and what lessons did they impart?
2. What kind of childhood did the person have? Any inklings that he or she would end up doing what he or she is doing today?
3. Education, mentors, heroes, role models.
4. Obstacles overcome—what makes writing interesting is conflict. The easiest way to "humanize" a subject, to make the reader empathize and relate, is to show the troubles the subject has had to overcome. Conversely, nothing is duller and more obnoxious to read than a smooth, uninterrupted glide to glory. Always keep an eye out for rough times—and how the subject eventually triumphs over them. This is a good time to add a few more "warts" that humanize the subject and make him or her a more rounded and compelling character.
5. Epiphanies—moments of pivotal, defining change in the subject's life. These are often dramatic moments: life's big decisions. When did you decide to quit your job and pursue duck art full time? How did the death of that gallbladder patient affect your future surgical career? What made you decide to use poodle sled dogs in the Iditarod?
6. Current family data that may apply to the story—spouse, kids, pets, hobbies, sports, etc.
7. Future—what goals does the person have? Where does he or she hope to be in the short and longer-term future?

Chronology #2

Apply the same kind of inquiry to the person's project—i.e., the chronology of his or her company, book, idea, enterprise, etc.

Nuts & Bolts

Find out what the person does in the course of the work-day. If the person's a plastic surgeon, try to sit in on a nose job and take notes. If he or she is a politician, attend a rancorous session. Try to arrange to be a fly on the wall at a moment of drama and action. If this isn't possible, ask enough questions of the person (and others who have observed him or her in action) so that you can write about it as if you were there. [Note: feel free to put the "Nuts & Bolts" section before the "Chronology" section if it seems to make more sense to your subject.]

Philosophy

What does the person's life and work mean to him or her? Where does his or her passion come from? What keeps him or her going?

Ending

What often works well is something about the person's philosophy or future, or, best of all, an anecdote/scene/image that suggests these.

Note that you could apply Thornton's approach to any type of profile without ever writing the same story twice. This isn't sloppy journalism—it's working more efficiently without sacrificing quality. Adopting techniques like these will help you make the most of your time, whether you're working on a simple service piece, a corporate white paper, a speech, or even a longer narrative feature. Remember, your most valuable asset as a writer is your time. Track it, protect it, and make the most of it.

Section 3
Connections

CHAPTER 9
The Low-Maintenance Writer: Make Editors and Clients Love You

I f you write to produce income—or make a living—you need more than the ability to string words together in a pleasing fashion. You need people who will buy your work—and better yet, pay you handsomely for it. Yet, I'm amazed at the number of writers who ignore the importance of developing and sustaining relationships with editors and other clients. They mistakenly believe if they write well, they'll be successful. Sure, it helps, but it's no guarantee.

To make six figures or anywhere near it, you must be able to market yourself, obtain assignments, and develop long-term relationships with clients. This is where confident, extraverted writers have a leg up on more reticent ones, but even introverts can—and do—learn people skills to help them navigate in the real world.

The Hunt for Clients

I admit it. In my fantasy freelance career, I'd never have to write another query letter. Cold calls would be a thing of the past. I'd no longer have to send samples of my work to potential clients, or pass out business cards at conferences and networking events. I'd have retainer arrangements with a handful of high-paying markets, my phone would ring constantly with lucrative, interesting assignments, and I'd sit back and select only those projects that appealed to me—and get paid lots of money, of course.

Alas, that's not the case—at least not early in your freelance career. The less established you are and the fewer steady clients you have, the more time you're going to have to spend marketing yourself. "If you're starting out, you've got to do a lot of querying," says Robert McGarvey. "When I started freelancing, I worked eight hours a day, six days a week, and mainly I was sending out queries."

I took a similar approach when I started freelancing full time. My goal was to send out a minimum of one query a day, but I usually managed to crank out more than that. I knew the more queries I wrote, the more likely I was to get an assignment—as long as the ideas themselves were targeted to the markets. In that sense, marketing is a numbers game. No writer seems to enjoy it, but we all accept that it's part of freelancing.

Over the years, Jim Thornton has constantly had to hustle for new work. He improved his ability to market himself by doing lots of it. "No matter what your nature is, if you force yourself to do this, you can get better at this," he says. "Even if you're not a huckster-type guy or . . . woman, you can get better at selling yourself by practice alone. If you're going to be successful as a freelancer, you're going to have to do it or get a steadier job."

As your reputation grows and you begin to develop relationships with clients, your name will get passed along and you will have editors coming to you. But to reach that level, you must market yourself—often constantly. Establishing yourself as a successful freelancer doesn't mean the marketing machine grinds to a halt, either—even the busiest writers must occasionally look for new clients.

"I spend 20 percent of my time marketing," says Erik Sherman. "You need to be constantly looking for new markets and putting out new ideas and trying to close business. You can't just be sitting there with the markets you have."

Of course, the type of work you do may affect the amount of time you spend marketing. For example, corporate writer Bev Bachel usually works with only a handful of clients at any one time, so her marketing time is minimal. On the other hand, magazine journalists like Sherman spend a significant amount of time pitching new ideas and scouting for new markets. I spend about 10 percent of my time doing marketing, which is significantly less than when I started freelancing. Plan to spend between 10 to 50 percent of your time going after work, depending on where you are in your writing career.

While marketing is a necessary evil, you want to make the most of it. After all, it doesn't pay off until you receive an assignment. To maximize your marketing time, give these techniques a try:

- Schedule marketing days. Many writers find it easier to devote a particular day of the week to sending out queries and contacting new markets. I use this method and send queries in batches—once or twice a month, I'll sit down with my research folder, write up a list of possible story ideas, and then work on query letters. I'd rather take a day every week or two to focus solely on marketing than to try to fit it in throughout the week.
- Use a standard marketing letter. McGarvey no longer sends queries; instead, he contacts new editors with a brief introductory letter. Sam Greengard uses a similar approach. "I've found sending a marketing letter with my bio, a description of the type of work I do, and what I'm interested in is a very effective way of getting clients," says Greengard. "Obviously, I modify the message and credits slightly to fit the market I'm aiming

for. . . . The advantage is that it gets me in the back door while everyone else is trying to fit through the over-crowded front door." In fact, his marketing letter gets assignments about 50 percent of the time, which is an exceptionally high response rate. (A sample of Green-gard's marketing letter is included in chapter 6.)

- Pitch your regulars. One of the simplest ways to generate more work is to pitch to the clients and editors you're already working with. When you turn in an article, offer a new story idea. If it's been a while, look for excuses to make contact with past clients. Freelance speechwriter Karen Frankel of New York City sends copies of her magazine articles to corporate clients several times a year. "I write mainly speeches and videos, but I also write for two art magazines," says Frankel. "The magazines don't pay very much, but aside from the fact that I like art and I'm a painter, I use those articles and send them to my clients because they're impressed by things in print." It also lets her keep in touch without overtly pestering them for work.

- Focus on closing. It's not enough to send out the query or call the potential client. You have to follow up and "close" business, as they say in the world of sales. "You need to actively go out and solicit business, and you need to go out and bring the business to a close," says Sherman. "Get them to sign off. If you don't know how to do it, learn. If you're not willing to do that, go work on staff. The point is you have to keep on top of these people." I usually follow up on a new query in a week or two and give the editor a deadline to respond if he or she is inter-ested in the idea; otherwise, I'll market it elsewhere. If I send an introductory letter with clips, I call within a week to touch base with the person, which often results in an assignment. At the least, the editor knows I'm a proactive kind of person. Many writers send queries or letters but then drop the ball. Always follow up on any submission you make.

- Cast your net wide. Some writers prefer to work with a smaller number of clients, but most find that a more diverse group helps even out their workload and cash flow. "You have to have a lot of irons in the fire," says Sherman. I learned this lesson the hard way last year— two publications, owned by the same company, were responsible for more than $40,000 of my income. My editor was a source of steady work, and I got lazy about sending out queries. Guess what? The company decided to fold both publications—and I was left scrambling for markets to replace that regular work.

- Look for long-term prospects. Scout for markets that you can develop ongoing relationships with—you'll spend less time trying to obtain writing assignments and more time actually doing them. "I pursue markets that pay well, treat writers with respect, and mesh with my knowledge, expertise, and writing skills," says Sam Greengard. "I do not look for one-shot sales. I look for clients that I can build a long-term relationship with. That way, I get assignments from them, I don't have to query, and I utilize my time far more efficiently." McGarvey agrees with this approach. "Basically, I'm not going to pursue a magazine unless I think it's good for a minimum of $5,000 a year," says McGarvey. "It's not worth my time or trouble to do a $350 article three times a year. . . . I look at the publication and determine if there's much upside potential." How do you determine that? First, look at the amount of copy the publication runs; then check the publication's guidelines for the percentage of freelance material it uses; and finally, read the bylines. Are a lot of names listed on the masthead or is a wider variety of writers represented? Also pay attention to what you hear from other writers. Some markets are notorious for taking months to respond to queries or for putting writers through the wringer.

- Cross-market yourself. Don't let clients pigeonhole you. Just because you write magazine articles doesn't mean you can't write books or speeches as well. Your background in a particular subject can also lead to lucrative corporate gigs if you look for those kinds of opportunities. Andrea King Collier does health-care consulting and speaking in addition to writing. At first glance, these areas may seem diverse, but they actually complement each other. "It all works together in ways that I hadn't imagined. The work I do in magazines gives me credibility with my health-care clients," says Collier. "The work I do in health-care marketing gives me great access to top experts. They even call me. It all just keeps building the network." Just one example: After Collier profiled a physician who recently became a state's surgeon general, the doctor called to ask if she'd be interested in working on some outreach projects.

- Figure out where you belong. One of the reasons I look for markets that publish service articles about health, fitness, and nutrition is because I have more than seven years' experience doing these kinds of stories. I'd have a much harder time nailing a long, narrative piece for a market like the *Atlantic Monthly* or the *New Yorker* because that's not the type of writing I usually do. Sure, I could pitch these markets—and I might, if I have an idea I'm wild about writing for them—but in the meantime, I look for markets where I'm a natural fit.

- Offer the editor something unique. If you've got a dream market, don't pitch the same old idea. Come up with something special and you'll boost your chance of success. That's one of the ways Jim Morrison has nailed assignments from high-profile markets like the *Smithsonian*, *New York Times*, and *Wall Street Journal*. "Unless

you're brilliant—and I'm not—you can't always shoot
for the big boys like *Smithsonian*," he says. "So I'm
always weighing an idea's chances at a big market versus
the much-better chances I can sell it instantly to an in-
flight or smaller market with less hassle. It's a balancing
act. But I also think magazines have become so competitive that you really need special ideas to break into great
places."

- Strike fast when necessary. While I devote certain days to
  sending queries, I'm quick to respond when I hear of an
  editor or company looking for a writer with my experience. It only takes a few minutes to tweak my cover letter
  and mail or e-mail clips, and a speedy response often
  pays off with new work. I take a similar approach when
  I find out another editor or writer has passed my name
  along to a potential new client.

Make Clients Love You

So, your marketing has paid off, and you've got a client. Or
hopefully a whole lot of clients. The next step is developing
positive relationships with those clients. That's what I did
wrong the first few years of my freelance career. I was more
worried about getting assignments and building my portfolio
than developing long-term relationships. It's true that as a new
freelancer with no journalism experience, I needed clips. But
clips come from editors, after all.

The funny thing was that even though I wasn't consciously
trying to build relationships with clients, the fact that I did a
good job on assignments, turned stories in on time (well, actually I've only turned in stories on time twice—every other
story has been turned in *early*), and was easy to work with
meant I got repeat business. Over time, I began to realize
(finally) that it was much easier—and less stressful—to work

more for a smaller group of editors than to try to work for several dozen publications. That's been my focus since.

Like McGarvey, I no longer pitch a market that I think I can write for only once. Instead, I look for markets that I can have long-term relationships with—which usually translates into less time pitching and more work. And I always try to be, in the words of one of my editors, a "low-maintenance writer." The most successful freelancers have figured out that it's not just the quality of your writing that determines whether you'll get assignments. Other factors—like how easy you are to work with, how quickly you respond to requests for revisions, and how reliable you are—all play a role as well.

Remember that, while your work appears in a particular publication, you're actually working for a human being, not a company. Publications come and go. Magazines fold with little or no warning. Formerly flush corporations decide to cut back on freelancers, or reduce the amount of custom publishing they do. In the meantime, editors change chairs constantly, switching positions and jumping from magazine to magazine. Some freelance off and on before returning to editorial gigs. A strong relationship with an editor or client is your best protection against the ups and downs of the market. If he or she leaves for a new publication, you can go with the editor. In the best-case scenario, you can continue to write for the first market by pitching other editors there while maintaining your relationship with your original contact. Worst-case scenario, if the publication folds, you can follow your editor to a new market.

Make the Editor's Life Easier

Put yourself in your editor's shoes for a moment. Would you rather work with a demanding prima donna or a personable professional? That's why editors love low-maintenance writers. They have enough stress in their lives. You don't want to add to it. "Try to think from the editor's point of view. They get a constant salary, so no matter what you do, they're not going to make any less or more money," says Jim Thornton. "Figure out the way to make their lives easier. The three things are: (a) make sure you get the stories in on time; (b) do a good job; and (c) try as best you can to be pleasant when they change their minds."

Yes, editors and other clients change their minds. But often that's because someone higher on the food chain changed his or her mind. Now it's up to your editor to fix things—which means calling on you. Will you step in and save the day? Or will you make a stressful situation even worse? I'm not saying you have to bend over for an editor when you're on the third go-round of a story. But some things are not within your editor's control, so why carp about it?

"I think because I was on the other side of the desk, I know what it's like," says Sondra Forsyth, who was an editor before she began freelancing. "I don't whine, I don't fuss, and I don't think it's horrible that they edit by committee. I'm very professional about that . . . that's one of the reasons they trust me and find me reliable." Forsyth, currently a contributing editor at *Ladies' Home Journal*, recently received an assignment on top of her regular contributing-editor work. She knows why her editor came to her for this tight-turnaround story. "They need it fast, they need it done, and they know I won't complain," she says.

Make Yourself Available

Karen Frankel's workload as a speechwriter is sporadic, but when she gets an assignment, it often means two to four weeks of overtime to provide her corporate client with what it needs. The fact that she's willing to do that makes her invaluable. "Eighty to 90 percent of the speechwriting I do is for new-product launches. I will do speeches for six to ten people at one of these meetings, and they're done in a very fast turnaround," she says. "It could be as little as two weeks to as much as a month."

McGarvey knows his willingness to make himself available is one of the reasons he gets so much repeat business. Recently, an editor contacted him to assign a piece—then called back a few hours later. Another writer's story had fallen through and she asked if McGarvey could turn around his piece in a much tighter time frame. McGarvey agreed.

"She's going to generate $20,000 to $25,000 this year. And one of the reasons she's going to do that is because I said yes," says McGarvey. He admits he's not always in a position where he can take on such a short deadline, but if he can, he will. "If that would have hurt some other customers, I would have had to wait, but I had enough flexibility in my schedule that I could accommodate this customer with a pressing need," says McGarvey. "To me, that's what the business is about—helping people solve their problems. The more the editorial problems I help them solve, the more work they're going to give me."

Be Friendly

It's important to build relationships, not only on a professional level, but on a personal one as well, says Lisa Collier Cool. She calls editors to give them the heads-up on a new query, but touches base at other times as well. "If something positive happens in an editor's life—if they get promoted, or get married, or have a baby—I like to send them a card or a small gift," says Cool. She also sends holiday gifts. "Every year I send all the editors who gave me work the year before a modest Christmas present, and every year I find I get a lot of assignments in January. If you're before them in a positive light, they will think of you for work," she says.

Cool got the idea for holiday gifts when she was an agent. "I had a client who sent me this great lemon cake every year," she says with a laugh. "Even though she wasn't my biggest client, I actually liked her more than some of the other clients because of this lemon cake. So I figure if she can buy my love and affection with this lemon cake, maybe others are like me!"

Like Cool, I like to send my biggest clients holiday gifts. Not all writers do this, but most successful freelancers enjoy more than strictly business relationships with their clients. "To be a six-figure freelancer, you have to find clients who will rehire you back. Anybody in sales or marketing will tell you it's much easier to keep a client than it is to go out and find new ones," says Brian O'Connell. "You have to do the little things that keep clients happy like getting your work done a couple days before deadline. I always personalize my notes; even when sending a hard-copy snail mail, I'll write, 'I hope this finds you well,' and try to build a relationship. I think it's worth it. Of course, they have to depend on you to deliver copy on time and clean, but they're human and it doesn't hurt to build a relationship as well."

Serve the Client

When I query an editor with an idea, I have a specific angle and approach in mind for the piece. If the editor wants something different, though, I accept that my original idea may not be what I wind up writing. But what about when I write a piece I'm particularly proud of—and the editor decides he wants to change the story, for the worse? Sure, I can argue my case, but in the end, it will probably be the editor's decision that prevails (even if he's wrong). The same kind of logic applies when you're working for a business client. Sometimes, you need to set your ego aside and give the client what he wants.

Frankel works with a lot of high-ranking executives, and she's learned this lesson firsthand. "The thing that I think is most important: You have to listen to your client," says

Frankel. "I've found that young writers often want to say, 'let me add something really creative to the mix,' and your client doesn't want that. They want what they said they want." There's a fine line between thinking proactively and overstepping boundaries—as a writer, you should offer suggestions when appropriate but always honor your client's vision and desire in the end.

Honor the Deadline!

It boggles my mind that any writer would miss a deadline, but it happens all the time. In a word—don't. (And if you must, we'll discuss that in a bit.) Frankel wouldn't be in business long if she failed to meet a deadline for a high-profile speech. "I write for a few magazines, and if the article doesn't make it into an issue, it can always get in next month," she says. "When you're giving a speech, if you're not there ready to give the speech when the audience is there, that's it."

Remember, your deadline is tied to the editor's deadline and may affect the production schedule as well. I've never missed a deadline as a lawyer, or as a writer, but the reason is simple—I've never taken a deadline I couldn't meet. I have, however, turned down work that would be impossible for me to complete by the time the client needs it. I'd rather say no at the outset and save myself the stress of trying to do something I simply can't—and potentially burn a bridge with that editor.

Keep the Quality High

I admit I tend to work harder on assignments that pay me more. That makes sense from a cost-benefit-analysis perspective, but that doesn't excuse me from turning in shoddy work because I'm making less than I'd like. "I always try to do a great job on the project. Sometimes I'm making $0.50/word and sometimes I'm making $4/word, but I do the same quality of work on each," says Greengard. "You never know when an editor will refer you to someone else."

It's so basic I hate to say it, but keeping the quality of your work high includes:

- Giving the editor a piece that provides what he or she asked for in terms of subject, slant/angle, sources, sidebars, and other resources
- Writing to word count—within 10 percent of what was assigned (unless there's been a change along the way that you've discussed with your editor)
- Keeping the audience for your work—and the point of the piece—in mind so that it meets the client's expectations
- Turning in "clean copy" that's free from spelling errors, grammatical mistakes, factual errors, and the like

Basic stuff, isn't it? Yet plenty of writers fail to meet these elementary standards. Don't be one of them.

Stay on Their Radar

Earlier in this chapter, I mentioned the benefits of pitching new ideas to current clients. I'll let this slide when I'm busy, but when I'm slow work-wise, I make a point of touching base with my regular editors. I don't beg them for work (though sometimes I want to). Usually, I'll send an e-mail along the lines of "just wanted to check in—I'm working on some new ideas, so let me know if you're looking for anything in particular." Or I'll call editors I know well to give the heads-up that I'm actively looking for work. It doesn't always pay off immediately, but sometimes all it takes is a call to get an assignment.

Lisa Collier Cool, who congratulates editors on happy events, is quick to share news of her own successes as well. Recently, she was profiled by FreelanceSuccess.com, a popular

Web site and weekly newsletter for serious freelance writers. She forwarded the profile to her editors. "It resulted in several assignments," she says. "More recently, my college alumni magazine did a profile which was very flattering, so I photo-copied it and sent it to all my editors and again was rewarded with assignments. Every time something positive happens to me, whether it's receiving an award or whatever, I let editors know. I feel the more my name is in front of them, the more they'll think of me for work."

What to Do When Handling Sticky Situations

Regardless of how professional you are and how wonderful your clients are, at some point, you'll encounter a hassle or two. Whether it's a blown deadline, an editor sitting on a story for months, or a client who owes you money, expect these kinds of setbacks as part of the cost of running your freelance business. I've run into them all (except for missing a deadline due to my compulsive nature), and have survived. Don't let these challenges throw you. Deal with them, and move on.

Missing a Deadline

Okay. It hasn't happened to me yet, and I hope it won't, but it does happen to most writers. Despite your best intentions, you're not going to make your deadline. You got sick. Your kid got sick. Your dog got sick. You overbooked yourself. What-ever the reason, don't ignore the problem. Let the editor know as soon as you know that you've got a problem with the assignment.

"I try to tell someone at least a week in advance if I feel like I'm going to miss a deadline," says Margaret Littman. "I feel like that is enough time for them to readjust their schedule if they need to. I tell them in advance, and I tell them why. If I'm working on the kind of a story where there are specific sources I have to talk to and the editor wants a particular person, or a particular kind of person, there aren't that many options . . . and if my source is in Spain, he's in Spain."

The worst thing you can do is fail to notify the editor and simply miss your deadline. Worse yet is to then dodge calls and e-mails from your editor who wonders what happened to the story, and now, what's happened to you. That's a good way to ensure that you never work with this editor again—and probably not anyone at his or her publication, either. Editors realize that unforeseen problems do arise. Make the best of a not-so-great situation, contact the editor, and go from there. It may turn out that it's no problem to grant an extension or that the editor can suggest another approach for you to take with the story.

Trouble with the Story

Several years ago, I was working on a big story on oral contraceptives for a women's magazine. My editor wanted an angle along the lines of "what pill's right for you?" (For example, overweight women should opt for this particular pill; women with migraines, this pill; vegetarian women, this pill.) Sounds like a great setup for a story. Problem was that oral contraceptives don't work this way. You can make some general recommendations (like the lower-dose pills are less likely to produce side effects than higher-dose pills), but every woman is different. You simply can't make these kinds of blanket recommendations in a magazine article.

Instead of trying to write a 2,000-word story around that fact, I called my editor and explained this. After some discussion, we agreed to go with the general recommendations and include a sidebar of the different types of pills and their chemical formulations to show readers what their options were.

If the story isn't working out or you're having trouble with the research—tracking down a particular expert or finding the right sources—let your editor know. When I was writing a sex story, I spent six weeks searching for "real people" to provide me with anecdotes about how they'd improved their formerly lackluster sex lives. Um . . . gee, no one wanted to talk to me! I wonder why. Finally, after weeks and weeks of searching, I managed to locate three people who agreed to be interviewed—with pseudonyms. If that happened now, after a week or so of digging, I'd call the editor, and say, "here's what I've done so far and I'm having trouble lining people up. Any suggestions?" Don't be afraid to talk to your editor or client about the project while you're working on it. Better to do it then than to try to guess what she wants—and have to rewrite it afterward.

Your Story Is Killed

You slaved over your piece, turned it in on time, and your editor got back to you with the words, "You've got a great start, but . . ." You revised the piece to the editor's specifications, but now it's being killed. Or the story was assigned by an editor who's no longer at the magazine—and your piece has been "orphaned," the end result being that the remaining editors have decided not to publish it. Chances are, you'll have a story killed at some time—that's inevitable. It doesn't mean the end of the piece, though.

Several years ago, I had two stories—$2,800 worth of work—killed during a regime change at a national fitness magazine. The editor who had assigned the pieces had left along with other staffers. Now, the new editor in chief seemed determined to destroy anything that had been assigned by her predecessor, and my stories got caught in the middle. I argued that I should be paid the full fee, not the 25 percent kill fee the contract called for. After all, there was nothing wrong with the stories themselves. The magazine refused, opting for the kill-fee provision. I was ticked.

After I cooled off, I called an editor I'd worked with at another fitness magazine. "Are you busy? I've got two great ideas to pitch to you," I said, and sold both of them in five minutes. (I wish all my pitches sold so quickly.) Did I tell her that they'd just been killed by one of her competitors? Nope. When she asked how long of a deadline I needed, did I say "Um, two minutes?" Absolutely not. I turned in one piece two weeks later, the next piece the week after that. My editor loved both and accepted them. She paid me $1,750 for the stories—which, combined with the $700 kill fee, left me only $350 in the hole on the deal. Much better than if I would have simply accepted the kill fee and let the stories languish.

Like me, Margaret Littman doesn't reveal that a story's been killed when she shops it to a new market. "I try to take a day or two where I'm not mad anymore," says Littman. "Then I start thinking about where else I can sell it."

Problems with Fact-Checking

Most big magazines are notoriously careful to check the veracity of what they publish. That means you're expected to provide "backup," or fact-checking materials, like names and contact information of interviewees, journal articles, and sources for statistics you cite. Sometimes, editors request transcripts of interviews, although I've found that most are satisfied with contact information. (I don't want to turn over my transcripts unless I have to—besides, many of my notes are written in shorthand that I understand but a fact-checker may not.)

To avoid errors, do careful research before you turn in a story. Even a minor misspelling (and I have to admit, I have turned in a few) looks like sloppy journalism to your client. I'm careful to double-check anything I'm not sure about, and I have only had a fact-checking issue come up once. I had a physician recant something he had told me on the record during an interview. (It wasn't anything scandalous, but I'd quoted him in a women's-health story about oral contraceptives, and apparently he'd decided he didn't want his quote in the piece.) The fact-checker called me. She was getting close to deadline and was worried. "He says he never said that," she told me. I double-checked my transcript. Yes, he did, and I had the transcript and the tape to back it up. End of problem—but if I wouldn't have had the transcript, and the tape, it would have been my word versus his. (In the end, the editor decided it wasn't worth the hassle anyway, and let him modify his quote more to his liking.)

Losing a Client

Every long-term freelancer has had a number of steady clients over the years. He or she has also lost a number of steady clients. The response? Bounce back, return to marketing yourself, and replace the work you lost. "You kind of keep going with the flow," says McGarvey. "When you lose a client, you do the obvious—ask yourself, 'is there I anything I did I shouldn't have done?'" The next question? "'What have I learned from this that I can sell to someone else?'" That kind of response keeps you moving and prevents you from marinating in the loss of your client.

What about the clients you've decided you don't want to work for anymore? Let them down easy. "I don't fire clients, but I have told editors I am too busy if they're impossible to work with or don't pay enough. After a few times, they find someone else and I don't hear from them again," says Sam Greengard. "However, I never say anything nasty and I thank them for the opportunity to have written for them. Losing good clients is painful, but part of freelance writing. I try to focus on the positive. Losing a client is an opportunity to push myself and grow. Ultimately, I will find another publication or client to replace it."

Greengard's got the right approach. You can choose not to work with someone again. You don't have to tell the person why. "I try really hard not to burn any bridges. Even if I know with every fiber of my being that I don't want to work with someone again, I never say so," says Littman. "I just say, 'I'm too busy right now.' If there's something more specific, I'll tell them. I'll say, 'I just can't afford to work for this pay rate anymore—if you guys raise your rates or change your contracts, call me.' I just try to leave it open."

Yes, losing clients hurts—both financially and personally. But it's part of the business. "I think it's really important to realize that losing a client doesn't necessarily reflect on you," says Littman. "I wish I hadn't spent so much time in the beginning worrying about why someone wasn't calling me in the beginning. . . . You may lose a client not because the work sucks, but because it's not what they wanted or it's not a good fit [for the market]."

Slow Payment—or Worse, No Payment

Last, but certainly not least, one of my biggest peeves about freelancing: Being forced to chase down money. When you're an employee, you have the luxury of expecting that nice paycheck at the end of every week or two. You needn't harass the accounting department or pester your boss for the money that's owed to you for work performed. As a freelancer, however, sometimes you must do that—and more—to collect your money. It's not only an annoyance and a drain on your time, but working for clients who don't pay—or pay only after months of phone calls, letter, pleas, and threats—can also seriously threaten your day-to-day existence as a freelancer.

First, start with a good offense. Make sure that you receive a signed written contract specifying the details of your assignment—word count, due date, price, rights purchased, and the like—for your records and in case you ever have to pursue the publication for payment. I've found that most big magazines pay within about four weeks of acceptance. Businesses and associations tend to pay more quickly than magazines—usually you can expect a check within a week or two of sending an invoice. (Those speedy payments are another good reason to add some business writing to your repertoire.)

To avoid getting stiffed, keep your ears open and stay on top of what's happening in the publishing world. Sometimes, you'll hear about "slow-pay," or worse yet, "no-pay" publications from other writers. This doesn't always spell disaster, but it may mean that you should be cautious—I'd advise against taking on a 2,000-word feature for a magazine that seems to be having financial problems. Some writers' organizations such as the American Society of Journalists and Authors (ASJA) maintain "warning lists" of publications that have been slow to pay writers.

If you've turned in work and haven't been paid, call or e-mail your editor to follow up. If you still don't receive your check, call again. You might also contact the accounts payable (AP) department directly to see if your check has been cut. If you still don't receive payment, contact your editor again. It may not be your editor's fault that you're not being paid, but often he or she can set the wheels in motion. At that point, I'll often ask the editor whether I should pester the AP department again (as opposed to pestering my editor). Usually, another persistent but polite call is all it takes to get paid.

That being said, if you are owed money by a publisher, don't give up. It took me more than eight months to collect $1,000 from a publisher in New York. In the meantime, I called, wrote, faxed, threatened, and was told no less than four times by two different people in the company's AP department that my check had in fact been sent. I never received it. My editor promised she'd make sure that I was paid, but did little to help.

It's worth noting that even though I was and am a lawyer, that fact didn't do anything to help me collect. Part of the reason was that under the terms of the contract, I would have had to file suit in New York, and the chance that I would fly to New York to file a case or hire a local lawyer to represent me were slim. As the months went on, I'm sure the company figured I would just give up. Wrong! After ASJA got involved on my behalf, I *finally* got my check—and vowed to never write for the magazine again. (The National Writers Union also assists members in collecting money owed them.)

The thing is, I'd written for this particular magazine for several years before the payment trouble began. Over time, it took longer . . . and longer . . . and longer to get paid. The signs of financial problems were there, but I ignored them. I won't let that happen again. Remember, you don't have to take every assignment that's offered to you. Too many writers accept any work that comes their way, especially early in their careers, reasoning that they've got to make enough to pay their monthly bills. But if that little voice inside you is warning you that something doesn't seem right, listen to it.

One more thing: If you've written for a publication or client before and it owes you money, *don't* do any more work for it until you're paid. Duh, right? But I know writers who have wound up with unpaid invoices totaling in the thousands because they continued to write for magazines that never paid them. Sometimes, you have to cut bait and move on. Finding clients, getting clients, and alas, losing clients is all part of the freelancing game.

CHAPTER 10
The Members of Your Team: Working with Agents, Experts, and Other Writers

Writing is often thought of as a solitary business, and it's true that as a freelancer, you're likely to spend most of your time working alone. However, in addition to the clients that you work for, there are others who can significantly impact your career both now and in the future—people like agents, public-relations professionals, expert sources, and other freelancers can make the difference between eking out a living and being financially comfortable as a writer.

Forget about going it alone. Instead, think of yourself as a talent scout and always be on the lookout for potential valuable members of your personal writing "team."

Do You Need an Agent? And How to Get One

After your clients, the person who may have the biggest effect on your career is your agent. Even inexperienced freelancers understand the potential power of an agent—at least the right agent. When I speak at writers' conferences, I'm asked more questions about agents than about anything else. "Do I need an agent?" "Can you recommend an agent?" "How do I get an agent?" "How do I know if my agent's any good?" "How much do you pay an agent?" "Is it worth it to have an agent?" And the often-heard, "Can you get me an agent?" To the uninitiated, agents appear to be magical beings blessed with the power to make deals, sell books, and command big advances. And that's true—some are. Some are not. But regardless, not every writer needs an agent at every stage of his or her career.

Magazine journalists and business writers—those who do the majority of their work for corporations—usually don't need to worry about getting an agent. But if you write books— or want to—an agent may be worthwhile. Not every freelancer uses an agent or wants to, but I've found that the majority of six-figure book writers do use agents. Sure, some prefer to sell their books on their own, figuring that they'd rather keep the 15 percent commission most agents charge. But like me, other writers would rather let their agents handle the task of selling books to publishers.

Here's how I see it. First of all, a good agent is likely to know more—much more—about the publishing biz than I do. She knows editors at different houses, their individual quirks, likes, and dislikes. She's familiar with their lists and is up on new imprints and lines of books. She knows what's selling now and what's not—and what's likely to sell in the future. She knows what kinds of advances authors are getting—and whether those books have been successful. She's more connected to the publishing industry as a whole than I am.

In addition to this market knowledge, a good agent also has experience negotiating and working with editors. As a result, she can almost certainly get a better deal than I can on my own. Sure, I was a lawyer in my former life, and I can read and understand what the language in a book contract means from a legal standpoint. But that doesn't mean I understand the significance or impact of that language—like if the publisher is requesting a certain type of foreign language rights. What are those rights usually worth? Is the contract reasonable for the industry or should it be changed? Is the royalty percentage standard? Is it better to be paid a smaller percentage on gross sales or a larger percentage on net sales? I don't know the answers to these kinds of questions, so I want an agent to represent me in this all-important negotiation to make sure I get the best deal possible.

As a magazine journalist, I knew nothing about the world of agents, and I didn't need to know—at least not for the first four years of my freelancing career. But when I decided I wanted to enter the world of book publishing, I realized I needed an agent. Sure, I could try to sell a book on my own. Big publishers may request agented-only material, but small publishing houses are always willing to work directly with authors, and there are thousands of them to choose from.

But I wanted an agent. I didn't want to sell this book on my own, and I didn't want to write just one book. I wanted to launch my book-writing career and felt (rightly so) that having an agent would increase my chance of selling my book. I also wanted to spend my time writing, not marketing my book to publishers, and I was willing to share the proceeds of a book contract with someone who could make that happen. I had a good idea and believed that it would sell. Now, I just needed to find an agent who also believed in it.

But who should I choose? There are thousands of agents out there, after all, and I didn't know any of them personally. I started with *Jeff Herman's Guide to Book Publishers, Editors, and Literary Agents*, which is updated annually, and made a master list of possibilities, keeping the following factors in mind:

- Did the agent represent the type of book I was writing? My book idea was about how to sustain long-distance romantic relationships, so I looked for agents who represented other relationship, popular psychology, and self-help titles.

- How long had the agent been in business? I didn't want an inexperienced agent, so I looked for ones who had been agents for at least ten years.
- Was the agent located in New York? No, an agent doesn't have to live in New York, but I figure it's a plus when it comes to face-to-face meetings and keeping tabs on the publishing industry.
- Was the agent a member of the Association of Authors' Representatives (AAR)? Members of AAR are expected to adhere to its Canon of Ethics, which provides, among other things, that agents will not charge reading fees for potential clients. (Many writers have been duped by less than reputable "agents" who agree to evaluate and/or market a manuscript—for a fee of hundreds, even thousands, of dollars.)
- How many clients did the agent represent? I didn't want an agent who only had a handful of clients, but I didn't want a huge agency either. I thought between twenty and fifty would be a good number.
- What was the agent's philosophy toward his or her business? Did the agent sound like someone I'd like to work with?
- Had I heard anything else about this agent? I'd seen several agents present at conferences, for example, and knew a few book authors who had agents. Several seemed like they might be the kind of person I'd like to work with; others didn't sound like a good fit, at least not for me.

Considering these factors, I made a list of about forty agents. Then I headed to the bookstore, where I checked out the relationship/self-help books. I'd looked at the current titles before, when I was working on the competition analysis section of my book proposal. Now, I checked the Acknowledgments sections of books similar to mine—authors almost always thank their agents, and book editors, by name. (That's a great way to find potential agents for fiction as well.)

After my bookstore search, I added a few names to my master list, then went through it and selected my top eight choices. I sent letters out to this group. (The letter I used is reprinted in chapter 6.) Within several weeks, four passed and three asked to see the proposal. One letter came back to me—the agent had moved, so I sent her a letter at her new address. Out of those three who responded, one agent wanted me to radically rework the proposal, one thought it was too narrow in scope to sell, and one never got back to me. I was about to send letters to my next batch of possibilities when I heard from Laurie Harper, the agent who had relocated. She asked to see the proposal. I sent it to her and she called me within a week to tell me she loved it and wanted to represent me.

In the meantime, I'd talked to several authors who had worked with Laurie and heard positive things about her. We seemed to connect when we spoke by phone. I asked her about her current clients, how much contact she liked to have with her authors, and how she planned to sell my book idea. In turn, she asked me about my overall career plans and what I was considering for my second book. Her interest in my long-term goals (something I hadn't given much thought to at the time) was one of the reasons I decided to sign with her, and I've never regretted my decision.

But here's the thing: that book didn't sell. Publishers thought the book was either too narrow in scope ("better suited to a magazine article") or that the potential book audience wasn't big enough. In the meantime, though, I started working on some other book ideas. This time, instead of working in the dark, I could bounce my ideas off of Laurie. She encouraged me to consider the big picture and to think of how each book would further my career. That kind of guidance, in addition to market knowledge and negotiating abilities, is what you may want to look for in terms of the agent you choose.

While Leah Ingram knows a lot about contracts and negoti-
ates her own magazine-writing agreements, she prefers to
work with an agent on books. "I believe that an agent will do
better to get you a better advance," says Ingram, who has
authored six books on weddings and gift giving. "And for
things like this gay-wedding book [the new book Ingram's
working on], I would never know what publishers have gay
niches."

Ingram has worked with three agents throughout the
course of her career. "When you're looking for an agent, one of
the things I've learned is to ask, 'How are you going to sell my
book?'" says Ingram. "The most important thing is how is the
agent going to sell the book, and does it jibe with the way you
do business." Ingram saw her current agent speak at a conference and thought they'd work well together after she heard the
woman describe some of the techniques she uses to sell a manuscript. For example, her agent calls editors to determine their
level of interest in a project *before* sending out a proposal.
Impressed with that approach, Ingram decided to contact her.
That's why attending writers' conferences where you can hear
agents speak—or even meet with them in person—can be a
wise investment when you're looking for an agent.

Remember, marketing books yourself takes a lot of time—
time that could be better spent writing. Freelancer Terry
Whalin is no newcomer to the publishing world and has
worked on both sides of the desk, as an editor and an author.
He's somewhat unusual in that rather than working exclusively with one agent, he uses several to represent him on book
projects, depending on the subject matter.

"I work with a number of different agents. I don't have an
exclusive arrangement with any of them," says Whalin. When
he finds a project that he's interested in, he chooses an agent
who handles that type of book to sell it for him. "I'm better off
having someone else negotiate for me. I know that about
myself," says Whalin. "I think in the long run, for the higher

advances, the agents are worth their weight in gold. And then if there's ever a problem, they can go to bat for you."

Once you have a book deal, your agent functions as your intermediary between you and the publisher. He or she will negotiate the contract, taking a hard line when necessary, and you can focus on writing the book—and maintaining a friendly relationship with your editor. With my first book, a small publisher was already interested in the idea, so I didn't have to formally pitch a proposal through my agent. I sold my first novel on my own as well, but I still had Harper negotiate those contracts. She got me better terms, and in one case, a 50 percent larger advance, which more than made up for her 15 percent commission.

The right agent—one who believes in you and your work and who has the contacts and experience to sell your books—can be one of the most valuable members of your team. You may luck out and stumble onto the perfect agent your first time out, but many writers go through several agents over the course of a career—or, like Whalin, they choose to work with more than one. If you outgrow your agent or decide he or she is no longer the best person to pitch your work, look for someone who better fits your needs and end your relationship with the first one. While your personal feelings may affect who you choose to work with, at heart this is a business decision—an important one. Don't let misguided loyalty keep you chained to a substandard agent or one who isn't right for your career.

Making the Most of Your Contacts

In the previous chapter, I stressed the importance of developing and maintaining relationships with your clients. I take a similar approach with experts, public-relations (PR) representatives, and other sources as well. My Rolodex is filled with experts I've interviewed on dozens of subjects, names and contact information of media people at different associations and universities, and PR professionals who have helped me find sources. When I need to track down a source, especially when I have a tight deadline, I can usually reach that person with one phone call, maybe two. While PR people can be a bit too persistent in pitching their clients of the moment, they can often drop story ideas into your lap—and help you find sources as well.

"I'm amazed when I hear writers say that they have antagonistic relationships with PR people or they don't take tips from PR people. I don't know how I'd do my job without PR people," says Margaret Littman, who writes for both consumer and trade magazines. "It doesn't mean I get a tip from a PR person and don't check it out, or that I don't write a balanced story, but once you start getting relationships with PR people, they tell you things before they're public. That's how I get 'insider information' or a tip on a new restaurant before there's a press release or before it opens."

Littman also uses PR people to help her locate sources, especially when she needs a particular type of anecdote or example for a story. "I have a network of PR people, so I'll send a mass e-mail or make a bunch of calls and say, 'This is what I'm working on—do you have anyone who's right for this?" she says. "And if I build a relationship, when an editor needs another source at 4 P.M. on the Friday of a long weekend, they'll give me the cell phone number of someone on vacation."

Littman appreciates story tips, but she's quick to tell someone she's not interested in an idea. She also lets PR sources know when a client is quoted in a story or if they've been cut out of the piece for some reason. "I don't talk about my editors behind their back, but sometimes something gets cut or the story didn't really go the way you thought it would," she says. "I try to give them a heads-up so there are no surprises."

Lisa Collier Cool suggests that writers get on the mailing lists of PR people and organizations. Like Littman, she often turns down pitched subjects as possible stories, but always keeps her options open. "They'll come to me with story ideas and studies and other items they hope I'll write about. Although a lot of stuff unfortunately isn't helpful, I have people beating the bushes to find me stories," says Cool. "I would advise anyone who wants to specialize in any topic to identify the relevant organizations and get on their mailing lists and keep up with what's going on."

Like Littman, she cultivates PR sources. "Yes, they can be annoying, but they can send you good stories," adds Cool. "The more you can tell them exactly what you want, the more they will actually help you. I've gotten stories I've sold for thousands of dollars from PR people."

To find anecdotes and "real-people" sources, Cool also maintains a personal e-mail network of about 300 contacts. "Every time I need an anecdote for something, I send out a query to my own mailing list," she says. "It's not that these people are special—it's just people who for whatever reason I know all over the country. I ask them to pass it on to their friends. I think it's like Six Degrees of Separation. Between them passing things on and getting new names and so forth, I hear about information that I can never find another way."

PR professionals can often hook you up with qualified experts, or you may uncover them during the course of researching a story. Here's another place where most writers go wrong. The writer contacts the expert, conducts the interview, gets what she needs, and moves on. The expert never hears from her again—unless she has follow-up questions.

As I mentioned in chapter 8, I always do two things when I work with experts. First, I send personal notes post-interview thanking them for their time. Second, I *let them know* when they're quoted in a story. It only takes me a minute or two to call my sources and give a heads-up; if it's a market they don't have easy access to, I'll send them a photocopy of the story.

This minimal effort has made an enormous difference in my

writing career. Experts remember me and when I need a quick quote, they're always willing to talk with me. This makes for less time researching and lining up interviews and has led to work as well—for example, I've done corporate projects for a high-profile fitness expert. And when a media relations person at an association or university helps me out with a story, I do the same thing—send a thank-you note and give the person a call when the story runs. I also ask to be included on their mailing lists, and I find out about new research findings, programs, and other announcements ahead of many other writers as a result.

Two Names, One Byline: Pros and Cons of Collaborations

As you develop relationships with experts and other sources, you may want to consider the possibility of collaborating on books and other projects. I was introduced to the idea of collaborating several years ago, when a nutrition expert I'd interviewed several times contacted me. She was interested in working with me on a book.

We met in person, discussed the project, agreed to a split of the advance and royalties (80/20 in my favor on the advance, 50/50 on the royalties), and shook hands on the deal. I then spent two months researching and writing a book proposal designed to secure a sizable advance and a great book deal. Foolish me, I agreed to do the proposal for nothing, because I was so sure this book would sell for some serious money. (I wouldn't do that now—most writers charge at least $5,000 to $10,000 for a book proposal.)

Oh, did I mention that we didn't actually *sign* anything? But we'd agreed to terms and shook hands, so I wasn't worried.

You probably can guess the rest of the story. The short version is that she backed out of the deal, and I was left with no collaborator and nothing to show for several months' worth of work. But I learned my lesson. The next time I was approached to collaborate, I stepped more carefully and insisted on a written collaboration agreement. Happily, this time around the collaboration has gone swimmingly, and I've enjoyed working with my coauthor, nutrition expert Ellie Krieger, R.D. I have another collaboration book deal in the works now.

Collaborating—either with another writer or with an expert—can offer you a lucrative opportunity to expand your writing career, but can also present a new host of writing challenges. Carefully weigh the most common pair-writing pitfalls before you take the leap into shared byline territory.

Should You Collaborate?

It's common for writers to join up with experts to produce books, articles, scripts, and other pieces, but it takes more than a shared interest to go forward. "Ideally, the collaborators have complementary skills and information—their two (or more) heads are better than one," says frequent collaborator Sarah Wernick, coauthor of books including *Lung Cancer: Myths, Facts, Choices—and Hope* and *Strong Women Stay Young*. "I work with experts who have specialized knowledge and the talent to speak effectively, but who haven't written popular books, as I have. Together, we can do more for our readers than either of us could on our own."

Working with a collaborator can offer you access to book deals you might not otherwise have. If you want to write a book about parenting, for example, but aren't a recognized expert with a "platform" or an established name, sharing the byline with a well-known child care expert can help sell your book proposal and command a higher advance as well. In return, the expert gets to publish a book that he or she wouldn't have been able to write independently. That's one of the reasons Whalin collaborates with experts on books—he does the writing, while the "personality" is responsible for marketing the title. In the meantime, Whalin has moved on to the next project and doesn't have to spend his time selling the book.

However, some writers simply aren't cut out for a collaborative relationship. If you have a hard time with anyone changing or editing your work, you may want to rethink this option. "Some writers and experts prefer the freedom to work on their own, or they don't want to share the limelight. Even people who willingly collaborate bring different viewpoints to the project. Because of that, they don't always see things the same way," says Wernick. That fact can be an advantage, though, because the two of you can bring fresh perspectives and ideas to the material. Keep in mind, though, that if you're a writer working with a nonwriter, you'll probably wear an editor's hat as well.

Before You Sign

It's wise to hash out the terms of your collaboration before you invest a lot of time in the project. Wernick suggests that writers first do some preliminary research to learn about the potential collaborator, whether it's another writer or an expert. Then, meet in person to learn something about each other and to discuss the book. "If the meeting goes well, you might want to intensify the preliminary research efforts—for example, speak with people who have worked with the potential collaborator," says Wernick. This will give you an idea of what you can expect when working with the person.

Third, and most important, don't make the mistake I did. Get it in writing! A collaboration agreement should be in place *before* starting work on the project. "It's always sad to hear about a situation where people invest time and thoughts, things don't go as hoped—and then, because there's no written agreement, there's a messy battle," says Wernick. "The writer may wind up without compensation; the expert may lose control of material based on his or her expertise. A good collaboration agreement has provisions for the unexpected and the unpleasant."

Collaboration agreements should address the following issues:

- How will work be divided up? Will each of you write parts, for example, or will one write and the other edit?
- Who has the final say if a conflict arises in how the piece should be structured or written?
- Will you have deadlines for turning in sections of the work to each other? What will the turnaround time be? Will you set regular times to touch base via phone, e-mail, or in person? (It's a good idea to set some deadlines to keep your work on track, especially if you're working with a busy expert.)
- Who is responsible for selling or marketing the work, if applicable? If you're writing a book with a known "expert," it's generally accepted that he or she will do the lion's share of promotion. That's one of the things Wernick likes about collaborating—she's a writer, not a promoter. By the time a title hits the bookstore, she's already working on a new project. Her coauthor is the person responsible for handling promotion and publicity. In other cases, the two of you may agree to share the responsibility.
- How will proceeds from the work be divided? How will you split the advance and royalties? (Remember, less than 10 percent of books earn out and produce royalties. Best to assume that the advance is all you'll see.) Will you be equal partners or will you use another ratio to divide up the advance and royalty income? If other rights are sold (e.g., licensing and merchandising), how will they be divided?
- How will expenses like publicity and marketing be divided between the two of you? How much time and

money will each of you spend on publicity and promotion? Is one person responsible for this or are both?
- What happens if one of you dies or decides not to pursue
the project further? Who has rights to the work that's
already been written?
- What happens if one of you bails before the book is completed? Who owns the rights to what?

Having a detailed collaboration agreement should help you
avoid most problems that can arise. "For example, a colleague
wrote a book with an expert. After it was published, the expert
hired a publicist—without consulting the writer—and then
demanded that the writer share the bill, which came to $25,000
because publicists are very expensive," says Wernick. "This
kind of problem is easily avoided by including a list of acceptable joint expenses in the collaboration agreement, with a cap
on the amount that can be spent without preliminary discussion."

While you may share the proceeds of the advance, working
with a big-name expert can make the difference between a
small and sizeable advance. That's why Sondra Forsyth
decided to start working with experts on books. "I figured out
that a book collaboration with an expert on the *Today* show
paid more than my own little breaking-into-article-writing
book," says Forsyth. "Collaborating is lucrative and fascinating. You team up with a doctor and you practically have a
medical degree by the time you finish the book." Forsyth tends
to do one book a year and often receives the whole advance to
write the manuscript, with a share of the royalties as well. She
explains to collaborators that while they're still able to pursue
their professions, she needs to be compensated for the time
she'll spend writing their books. "The doctor gets to continue
being a doctor. That's how I see it," she says. Her approach
usually works.

If the idea of collaborating appeals to you, let agents and

editors know you're interested in these kinds of deals and keep your eyes open for potential coauthors. For more information on collaboration agreements, check out Brad Bunnin and Peter Beren's *The Writer's Legal Companion: The Complete Handbook for the Working Writer*, Third Edition, and Tad Crawford and Kay Murray's *The Writer's Legal Guide: An Authors Guild Desk Reference*, Third Edition. And check out Wernick's Web site, *www.sarahwernick.com*, for more information on collaborations.

Think Comrades, Not Competition

Depending on your goals and the type of writing you do, agents, experts, and PR professionals may all play a role in your career. But don't overlook the value of creating and maintaining relationships with other freelancers—you know, the competition.

Surprised? Don't be. Most six-figure freelancers have extensive networks of writers and other contacts they rely on. "You have to be good at your skill and your craft and practice that over and over, but publishing is like a lot of other businesses. It's not so much *what* you know, but *who* you know," says Whalin, who's always building his network. "I realize that information is power. A lot of writers blow that. They don't seem to understand the value of their Rolodex, but I'm always working on mine. I have about 2,500 names in my Rolodex. . . . I think it gives me a huge edge that I can pick up the phone and call almost anyone I want to get a hold of." While I can only wish my contact list is as extensive as Whalin's, I do maintain a database of about 1,000 contacts, and I keep notes on each person so I can remember when and where I met or spoke with him or her (e.g., "Met at Willamette Writers, August, 2003—marathoner, talked about running and mystery novels").

It's not just easy access that makes hooking up with other writers such a smart idea. If you've been holed up in your garret, consider these compelling reasons to network with your peers:

- More market info. Most writers find it difficult to find time to market themselves, and trying to keep up on all the new publications or companies looking for writers is next to impossible. Sure, I keep tabs on new magazines in my subject area, but I get leads from other writers, too. Just this week, a corporate writer sent me an e-mail to tell me she'd met a foundation director who was looking for freelancers. I contacted the director, sent clips, and nailed a lucrative assignment. I would have never even known of the foundation had it not been for the writer thinking of me. (And yes, I sent her a thank-you note!) One of the reasons I'm a member of ASJA and FreelanceSuccess.com, a newsletter and bulletin board for writers, is because it gives me access to market information I wouldn't have otherwise. I also attend writers' conferences, where I'm likely to hear about markets looking for work. Several years ago, at the Magazine Writers & Editors/One on One, a conference in Chicago, I was talking to another freelancer about writing for bridal magazines. We swapped contact information, which led to me writing for one of her regular markets. A five-minute conversation turned out to be worth about $5,000 over the next eighteen months.
- Better contract negotiation skills. When writers share experiences with each other, it helps them determine what's fair—and what's not—when accepting their first assignments. Many magazines have more than one contract, for example—the nasty all-rights agreement, and the more writer-friendly version. In many cases, you learn about that kind of thing from other writers. "When I first joined ASJA, I learned how other writers were functioning as professionals, and it changed the way I

functioned," says Wernick. "For just one example, I learned how much more money some of them were making writing for the same magazines, and immediately began negotiating better contracts." I found out from another writer that a certain magazine routinely paid its writers $1.50/word and up—a week *after* I accepted a big assignment for $1/word. If I would have known the publication regularly paid more, I probably could have gotten more for my story as well. "Knowing other writers helps me figure out which magazines to target and which ones not to bother with," agrees Littman. "Now I know before I even get into anything what someone's rates and rights are and whether to bother."

- Goal-setting inspiration. Too often, freelancers, especially new ones, stumble around in the dark when it comes to setting financial goals, and it's (incorrectly) assumed that writers can't make a good living. Knowing what others are making can be a powerful motivator, and knowing *how* they are doing it can boost your bottom line. For example, several years ago, when I was making about $60,000 a year, a magazine writer who was grossing more than $100,000 annually mentioned she turned down most short pieces because they weren't worth her time. I adopted her approach and began focusing on doing fewer, but longer, stories. The result? Less stress and more income—in fact, I broke the six-figure mark myself the next year.

- Realistic rate data. Magazines, newspapers, and Web sites often have set rates they pay for articles. But if you're a business writer or bidding on a type of project that's new to you, knowing what other writers charge helps you determine how high to set your own rates. For a recent ghost-writing project, I had no idea of what to charge, so I polled several freelancing friends to get an idea of what they would bid on the project. That gave me the market knowledge—and the confidence—to ask for much more than I would have otherwise.

- Help improving your craft. Don't overlook the impact that working with other writers can have on your writing itself. I don't belong to a formal critique group, but I have a handful of writers I can call on if I'm struggling with a particularly tricky lead or want advice on how to word something. "My writing group has improved my writing enormously, which has also increased my income. When I showed the fifth draft of the proposal for *Strong Women Stay Young* to a book proposal workshop leader, he said that he thought it was 'magazine-ish,' meaning possibly too slight for a book," says Wernick. "I pressed him to guess what kind of advance we might get, and he guessed $35,000. I brought this fifth draft to two writer friends, who pushed me to work on it some more—and they pushed me again and again through subsequent drafts. What finally went to publishers was draft twelve. The proposal was auctioned and we got over $300,000 for it."
- More confidence. When you're a new writer, you're likely to spend as much time agonizing over missteps, real and imagined, as you do writing. I know that when I started freelancing, I always assumed the worst when I didn't hear from an editor or get an assignment. Once I started meeting other writers, I realized it wasn't me. It was the nature of the business. "Having a network of writers has impacted my career in a lot of ways. It helped give me a lot more confidence when I realized a lot of little stuff I was running into—editors not calling me back or whatever—wasn't about me," says Littman. "People I really admired had the same situation!"
- Better karma. I can't take on all of the assignments that I'm offered, nor do I want to. For example, I usually don't write about subjects like technology or parenting—but I

know writers who do. When an editor contacted me last month to ask if I had child care stories available for reprint, instead of turning her down flat, I gave her the name of a friend who's written a slew of parenting articles. I helped the editor and my friend—and that kind of networking often comes back to benefit me in the long run. Sam Greengard often receives referrals from other writers who know he specializes in writing about business and technology and give his name to editors when they can't take on a particular story, and he'll refer editors to other writers as well. That willingness to share is good karma, and good business in the long run.

- Commiseration buddies. When I started freelancing full time, the most difficult aspect of the transition was going from being surrounded by people all day to working solo. While I was lucky to have a supportive partner and plenty of friends to call, I didn't know any other writers, and I felt isolated. I wasn't sure if I was taking the right approach with my career, if my queries were good enough, or if I should be pursuing a different type of writing, and I didn't have anyone to ask. It was nearly a year into my career when I made my first freelancing friend at a writers' conference. It marked a turning point in several ways. First, I met other writers who were successful freelancers, which gave me hope for myself. But I realized that having even one person to talk to about my writing career who "got" it helped tremendously. Kris and I stayed in touch through e-mail and phone calls, and I began seeking out other writers as well. It's taken me years to build my professional network, but I've benefited from some wonderful friendships along the way. I love my nonwriting friends, but no one understands how challenging—and rewarding—freelancing can be like another writer. Having a circle of friends who "get" the business—and will listen when you need to kvetch, celebrate, swap gossip, or simply connect with another writer—is essential for any freelancer, six-figure or not.

Early in my career, I was shy about looking for or reaching out to other writers. Don't let that be the case for you. Just keep in mind that there are unwritten rules of etiquette when networking with other writers:

- Ask permission before you use another writer's name with an editor or client. I've had writers ask me for the names of the editors I've worked with at publications, and I have no problem sharing them. But I don't want someone to use my name unless I'm familiar with the writer's work—and I tell people that.
- Share information, but don't give away the store. I recently got an e-mail from a writer I know from an online bulletin board about a publication I'd written for. She asked me about the market's pay rate and contract, and I gave her the information. That's different than e-mails I get from strangers saying something along the lines of, "I heard you're a successful writer. I have no writing experience but want to become a freelance writer—can you help me get started?" I used to compose long, thoughtful responses to these kinds of solicitations; now, I recommend several books and Web sites and suggest that the person get in touch with me "with any specific question not answered therein." Guess what? I've never heard back from any of them. I like to be helpful, and considerate, but I'm not going to spoon-feed someone.
- Don't expect another writer to give you the store. See above. It's one thing to ask about a particular market. It's another to ask for another freelancer's client list.
- Be willing to help when you can. Freelancing, like life, is a two-way street. I've had writers ask me for contact information, sample queries to use when teaching,

advice about publishing a novel, and direction on writing for certain publications. If I can offer something helpful, I will. I know how hard it is for me to ask someone else for help, and I'm happy to lend assistance when I can. After all, it feels good to help out another writer. Just watch out for the leeches—those writers who always ask *you* for help, contact info, or market suggestions and rarely say thank you, let alone return the favor. (Don't worry—you'll figure out who they are.)

- Don't be a gossip. And if you do gossip (okay, we all do), don't put it in writing! If you ask a writer about his experience working with an editor, and he tells you about it in confidence, respect that. But you can't be too careful. That's why I advise against putting anything negative about a client, editor, or agent in writing—you never know where it will end up. I recently had a writer e-mail me about my experience working with a particular publication. I'd had a horrible time with the editor I worked with, and it sounded like she was having a similar experience, but I told her if she wanted details, to call me. She did, and I told her the whole sordid experience—but I will never do that in an e-mail.

- Don't be negative. I'm a positive person by nature, but I'm amazed at the number of writers who whine endlessly. They whine about the state of contracts today, how hard it is to get work, editors not responding to queries, small advances, and how publishers don't help promote their books. Guess what? I'm facing all of the same issues, but I'd rather focus on the factors that I *can* control than all the obstacles that stand in my path. Search out positive people and cull the "glass-half-empties" from your writing life. Even if you have to work with some pessimistic clients because they pay you well and *you* decide it's worth it, you needn't fill the rest of your writing life with them.

Face-to-Face Networking

So, how do you find these kinds of writers? Depending on where you are in your career, you can join organizations like ASJA, the National Writers Union, and the Authors Guild. If you're a newer or less-experienced writer, you may want to consider attending a writers' conference for the networking and marketing opportunities. With hundreds of conferences throughout the country, you'll get the most for your time and money by deciding in advance what your goals are, choosing a conference that fits your needs, and making the most of your time at the event.

Before you select a conference, consider your writing goals. What do you hope to get out of attending? Are you looking to meet editors who may be interested in your work? Is your goal to improve your writing skills or simply to make more contacts with agents, editors, and other writers? If you're looking to improve your skills, a workshop that focuses on craft may be a better fit. If you want to hook up with editors, though, a conference like Magazine Writers & Editors/One on One (held each July in Chicago) or ASJA's annual writers' conference (held in April or May in Manhattan) is a better bet.

The location and the price of the conference are two more factors to consider. While you can write off the cost of attending as a business expense, your budget may dictate an event closer to home than Maui or New York. You may want to consider attending with a friend to help keep your costs down.

The next step is to select a conference that fits your writing needs, your budget, and your schedule. ShawGuides lists hundreds of conferences at *http://writing.shawguides.com*. On ShawGuides, you can search by date, location, and topic; the listings also include links to conference Web sites and contact information.

As you research different conferences, check what each offers. Does it include panels of editors, agents, and publishers, or is the focus more on hands-on workshops? Do you have the opportunity to sign up for one-on-one sessions with editors or agents? Who are the featured speakers and presenters? Are there many sessions that interest you? Does the conference offer tapes of sessions that you can purchase if you're unable to attend all of the sessions you want? Some workshops require that you apply with samples of your writing; others are open to all writers. Check the details and confirm the dates and locations with the organizers before registering.

Give yourself plenty of time to travel to the event, and once you get there, register and pick up your materials. Check to see if the schedule has changed. Circle or highlight the sessions you want to attend and make a special note of any one-on-one meetings with agents or editors. If you're going to be pitching a project, practice what you'll say in advance. You'll only have a small amount of time—ten to fifteen minutes—to make a favorable impression and get the editor or agent excited about your work.

I suggest leaving the T-shirts and jeans at home. Dress up a bit. You needn't wear a three-piece suit, but you may be meeting editors, agents, and other writers who will influence your career. Opt for a polished, professional look. You'll make a better first impression and feel more confident as well.

At the conference, make an effort to meet other writers. Many people there will be first-time attendees. Simply asking, "Have you come to this conference before?" or "What kinds of writing do you do?" are great ways to break the ice. "Why did you decide to come to the conference?" or "What do you hope to get out of being here?" are other good questions to ask. Many writers are shy, but don't let your introversion prevent you from being friendly. I've made lots of valuable contacts at writers' conferences, and Terry Whalin's latest editorial job was the direct result of a brief conversation he had with another writer at a conference.

When attending panels, don't be afraid to ask questions

during the question-and-answer period or introduce yourself to the presenters afterward. However, there's a fine line between being assertive and pushy. It's frowned on to monopolize an editor's or agent's time. Limit your questions, especially when there are other writers who want to ask questions as well. Do ask if you can follow up after the conference.

Take notes during sessions and obtain copies of handouts to read later. If you have time, try attending panels outside of your usual genre—if you're working on a nonfiction book, you may want to explore the idea of writing magazine articles to help publicize your title. Agent and editor panels where panelists share what they're looking for are always a good source of insider information.

When you get home, you'll probably be both energized and mentally exhausted by the experience. Put into practice what you've learned, before your excitement wears off. If an agent or editor expressed interest in your work, follow up with him or her immediately. Send e-mails to writers you met, suggesting that you keep in touch. And don't forget to save your receipts to take them as tax deductions. The travel expenses you incurred and the cost of the conference itself are legitimate expenses if you're operating as a business.

The Pros of Speaking Up

If you want to expand your network, don't limit yourself to *attending* conferences. You also want to consider being a presenter yourself. Introverted types may rate the idea of speaking to a group up there with dental work in terms of stress, but many writers find that speaking and writing are natural complements. If you crave attention, like teaching people new skills, or enjoy making people laugh, speaking can offer a lucrative sideline.

Speaking boosts your visibility and helps strengthen your position as an expert in a particular field. If you're insecure about your knowledge, remember that if you're already writing about a subject, you're usually perceived as an "expert." Speaking also gets you away from your desk and out of your house, giving you the chance to network and make connections you wouldn't have otherwise. And finally, it can lead to writing business—and give you an opportunity to promote and sell your books as well.

Yet, speaking involves a different skill set than writing. You can be a fabulous writer and a terrible speaker—or you may be a mediocre writer but wonderful at sharing your knowledge and expertise with an audience. If you haven't done a lot of public speaking, consider joining Toastmasters, which helps people in different professions hone their speaking skills. I also like watching *Book TV,* which runs every weekend on CSPAN2—it broadcasts nonfiction authors at book signings, panels, and other events, and you can see firsthand what works and what doesn't.

What Will You Say?

First things first. What will you talk about? What do you know? What have you written about? What are you passionate about? I launched my speaking career by teaching classes on magazine writing. While I was a relatively new freelancer, I knew more about writing for magazines than the average person, and there were no local classes being offered. I called the closest community college and pitched the idea. From there, I began speaking at libraries, writers' conferences, and other venues, and when my first book came out, I looked for more speaking gigs. Now, I'm branching out to cover fitness and nutrition topics in addition to talking about writing-related subjects—a natural outgrowth of my specialty.

Realize that unless you're doing high-paying corporate gigs, you're probably not going to get rich from a speaking career. But income may be a secondary goal to selling books or developing a name for yourself. "For authors, there are two kinds of speaking," says Victoria Moran. "One is where you speak for money. The other is that as an author, when you have a brand-new book, you speak at anything that will let you show up—book signings, your cousin's luncheon, whatever you can do within the first three months." Because speaking is so time-intensive, however, Moran focuses on engagements to help promote a new book for the first ninety days after its release. After that, she continues to promote the book in other ways, but looks for paying speaking gigs rather than freebies.

If you have a book coming out, it's natural that you speak about the topic. But keep in mind that it's not enough that you find a particular subject fascinating—you need an audience, too. Who will you talk to? People interested in your subject, of course. When you're starting out, local libraries, bookstores, service groups like Rotary, and writers' groups all offer speaking possibilities. You won't be paid, but the idea is to gain experience and confidence and build that all-important platform.

Simple Speaking Tips

So, you've decided what you want to speak about, and you've lined up your first gig. Feeling nervous? Or rather, petrified? That's normal. While some new speakers like to write out their speeches word for word, I think it works better to make a basic outline of what you want to cover and rely on that instead. Have three to five major points to share, and run through your speech a few times on your own before you give it. Preparing ahead of time will help you deliver a good speech and reduce your anxiety.

If you're riddled with anxiety, keep these tips in mind:

- Practice ahead of time. You'll know how long the speech will take and become more familiar with the material.
- Have your opening down pat. You don't have to memorize your entire presentation, but I find that knowing my

opening cold helps me feel more comfortable. I usually determine what I'll close with ahead of time, too.

- Arrive early at the location you'll be speaking at. You don't need the anxiety of worrying about running late. That also gives you a chance to scope out the setting, visit the bathroom, and get a bottle or glass of water to keep nearby.

- Don't read from a prewritten speech. Look at your audience frequently and make eye contact with people. I make a point to look at different members of the audience throughout the room as I speak.

- Include plenty of real-life examples to illustrate your main points. Audiences love war stories.

- Demonstrate your familiarity with the audience. Arrive early and introduce yourself to attendees and ask what they're hoping to get out of your session. Then, you can incorporate their comments into your speech and make sure that you're answering their questions.

- Focus on an attention-getting opening, three to five major points, and an inspiring or motivational closing. (Think of the "call to action" copywriters use at the close of a pitch.) Research shows that audiences tend to remember the first and last things that you say.

- Leave time for questions and answers, when appropriate. If people are shy about asking questions, suggest some of your own. "I'm often asked about how to sell an article when you don't have any writing experience. In that case, I suggest . . ." Answering a question or two usually provokes some queries from the audience. Or "seed" the audience ahead of time by asking one of the organizers to toss you a question at the beginning of the question-and-answer period.

An easy way to break into speaking is to start small, by teaching a writing class or talking to a writers' group at a local library. Offer to talk about a subject you have experience with or about how you make a living as a freelancer. These events help get your name out, not just to other writers, but to potential clients as well.

Most days, I love being a freelancer, but this career sometimes has more downs than ups. One of the reasons I've managed to sustain a career in this business is because I've built relationships with people—not just clients who pay me—over the years. The thing is, I didn't set out to create a huge network of people. I just tried to be considerate, polite, and nice, and those relationships got built along the way. The bonus is that I've made a number of wonderful freelancing friends who have enriched my life not only professionally, but personally. Build relationships with professionals who you respect and admire, and you can create your own successful writing "team" as well.

CHAPTER 11
Where Do You Want to Go? Your Writing Career Now—and in the Future

I have to admit that when I started my freelance career, my long-term goals were murky at best. The only thing I knew for sure was that I absolutely did not want to return to practicing law. My biggest hope was that I would be able to eke out some sort of existence as a full-time writer, but I didn't expect to ever make more than $30,000 or $40,000 a year. (That in itself seemed too much to hope for.)

In the beginning, it was impossible for me to formulate any long-term plans because I didn't know enough about the writing business. Over the years, when I'd pictured "being a writer," I'd fantasized about sitting around in a black turtleneck drinking coffee and producing angst-ridden poetry and compelling short stories. I never expected to have to learn how to market myself, locate and interview sources, write hospital ads, or chase down money as a full-time freelancer.

During my first few years, I focused almost exclusively on making money—as much of it as possible—and I tended to be more reactive than proactive when it came to my career. Sure, I set income goals for myself, but most of the work I did was driven more by what the market appeared to need and what I was able to write quickly than what I wanted to do long term.

Even when I decided to start specializing in health, fitness, and nutrition, it was primarily because there were many high-paying markets for stories about these subjects, and I knew I could make significantly more money if I narrowed my focus to a handful of subjects.

Along the way, I set annual income goals, but I found that I wasn't really thinking of the big picture. When I decided I wanted to start writing books, it was because I saw other magazine writers going on to become book authors. Why not me? When I heard about other freelancers making good money doing corporate work, I pursued those kinds of projects. I was easily influenced by other writers without having a clear idea of what I wanted to do writing-wise—besides make more money each year.

I certainly didn't mind making more money, but a higher income in itself wasn't that satisfying. I thought the answer might be to start writing fiction again to try to recapture some of the joy of writing I'd misplaced along the way. That did help, but fiction writing was something I did in my spare time, not my Career (with a capital "C"). By the time I hit the six-figure mark, I discovered I wasn't that excited about my writing career anymore. Yes, I was making a good living. Yes, I'd been published in more than fifty magazines. Yes, I'd sold my first novel and was working on my second nonfiction book. But was that it? What was next? To keep setting higher and higher income goals? I knew writers who made more than $200,000 a year, but continually raising the bar didn't appeal to me.

I hit a place that all successful writers encounter eventually. When you're starting out as a writer, you may dream of getting published, or of making enough to live on to quit your day job. Then when you do it, you set a new goal for yourself: to make a six-figure living, to write your first nonfiction book, or to publish an essay in one of your favorite markets. But eventually you realize you've met your initial goals—and probably even exceeded your expectations. And the question is: What's next? How do you sustain this career for the rest of your life—without getting burned out?

Surviving in Stage Three

To new writers, this may seem ridiculous. Come on—you're making a great living! What do you have to complain about? But freelancing is a lot like acting. You're only as good as your last role. A true actor never thinks, "That's it—I'm done." He or she is always looking for a new role, a new challenge, a new opportunity to stretch and grow. And what no one tells you early in your career is that success carries with it its own challenges.

When I speak at writers' conferences, I often talk about the three basic stages of a writing career. Stage one is when you write simply because you want to. You write for the satisfaction of expressing yourself, of getting your words and thoughts down on paper. You may fantasize about being published, but your focus is pure. You write for the love of it.

Stage two kicks in when you decide you want to be published—and possibly paid for your work. Now it's no longer just about the act of writing. Now you have to begin thinking about things like potential markets, word count, sources, style, angle, tone, audience, and submission guidelines. This kind of market analysis and basic business knowledge—for example, how to write a query—is critical if you want to be published. Stage two is not only about the writing—it's about the publishing as well.

Most writers will never progress to stage three, when you begin writing for a living. Now the stakes have risen considerably. Your writing ability, marketing savvy, time management skills, and productivity must do more than get your work into print or provide a nice second income. Your mastery of these

skills will determine whether you'll be able to pay your mortgage, afford health insurance, save for your kid's college education, put some money away for retirement, and occasionally
even take a much-needed vacation. Not only that, but you also
can't afford to get burned out or lose clients you're unable to
replace. You have to be able to maintain your drive and motivation for years on end—or look for a different career. Welcome to stage three.

In my teens and twenties, I was entrenched in stage one—
writing because I wanted to. When I was ready to send work
out for publication, I spent a couple of years making the transition from the first stage to the second. Then when I quit my
job as a lawyer to write full time, I focused on making a living
as a full-time freelancer. I thought in terms of daily, monthly,
and annual goals, not considering what I might do in the years
to come, and I didn't realize that at some point, I'd have to figure out how to sustain my career over the long haul. I alone
would determine not only how to spend every hour of the day,
how many hours a day to work, and how much money to
make, but the overall direction of my long-term writing career
if I wanted to write for a lifetime.

Making a good living from writing full time is a dream
shared by many freelancers. But the reality is that to maintain
a career for years takes fortitude, drive, and resiliency. You discover that there's no finish line. You never hit the mark, and
think, "That's it—the end of the road." You re-create yourself
and your career along the way. I think that one of the biggest
misconceptions about writing full time is that it gets easier
after a while. Sure, as you learn how to market yourself and
improve your writing skills, you may spend less time chasing
work. Building a network means clients will begin coming to
you. Developing expertise in a certain area enables you to
charge more for your work. But you still have to be able to
avoid burnout, stay productive, and cope with the ups and
downs of daily life as you maintain your writing business.

Writing over the Long Haul

Successful writers aren't created overnight, and they usually don't intend to make six-figure incomes from the outset. Maybe they wanted the freedom of freelancing, or the flexibility of setting their own hours. Maybe they saw an opportunity to become their own bosses or wanted to use the knowledge they'd gained in another career to launch a successful writing business. Or maybe they were simply pursuing a dream to write full time.

Regardless, all of them expected to work hard from the outset. They realized that during the first months—or, more likely, years—they might have to struggle to build their businesses. Eventually, they realized they'd have to figure out how to keep going over the long haul. For most writers, that means adapting to the changing market and learning new skills—and often following their own passions as well.

That may mean writing in a new genre, covering different topics, teaching, or switching forms—say, writing books instead of magazine articles. Freelancer Margaret Littman had been writing for magazines and newspapers for years. She hadn't aspired to be a book author, but when she heard about a book that would be perfect for her, she took the plunge. "To be honest, I was kind of scared of doing a book," says Littman of her book, *The Dog Lover's Companion to Chicago*. "But it was a fit for me and I thought it would be a good starter book because it was a lot of little articles . . . and I thought it would let me find out if I like books." The biggest challenge was overcoming her fear that she wouldn't be able to produce a book-length manuscript, but Littman loved the challenge of working on a bigger project. The book did well, and now she's working on her second, *VegOut! Vegetarian Guide to Chicago*.

To stay fresh, Littman also makes an effort to vary the types of writing work she does. "Honestly, I don't know anyone in the world who can do the exactly same thing every day for ten years, and if there are people like that, don't introduce me!" says Littman. "What I do every day is not exactly the same. Even though it's still journalism, writing a one-day story on deadline for a newspaper is completely different than writing a book or a magazine feature. Not just the pace, but everything about it is different."

Littman recently began adding more editing work to her repertoire as well. "I started doing more editing, which is what I did when I started with my career, and I'm really enjoying it. I think that writing and editing kind of feed each other," she adds. "It's made me a better writer and made me think about ways that I pitch story ideas. . . . I think it helps me a little more with the big picture."

Robert McGarvey, who's been freelancing for more than thirty years, says he reinvents himself as a writer every few years by learning about new subjects that interest him. That's kept him marketable and helped prevent him from becoming bored. For example, several years ago, an editor at *Midwest Express* asked him to write a couple of stories on biotech. The money was minimal, but McGarvey was interested in the topic—and suspected that biotech might be big news down the line.

"I thought, I'll make the $900 and it will be an education, and that's what it turned out to be," says McGarvey. "Flash forward a couple of years and *Harvard Business Review* asks if I have any experience with biotech. I send them these two stories, and now they think I'm a bona fide biotech expert." Last year, he wrote several major stories on biotechnology for the *Harvard Business Review*, *New York Times*, and *Boston Globe*, which totaled more than $30,000. "I'm basically following my own interests to a large extent, but my interests have been shaped by commercial realities over twenty years," he adds.

Long-term freelancers have to remain flexible. Speechwriter Karen Frankel, who has freelanced for almost thirty years, has maintained her career by adapting to an ever-changing market. She left her job as a staff writer/producer at McGraw-Hill Films to freelance in 1976, originally doing educational films. A few years into her freelance career, the market for educational films disappeared and she decided to branch into corporate writing. It took months of cold calling before she started landing corporate writing gigs. "I had no work and I had to learn to sell," says Frankel. "I never knew you had to do that—I'd always had a staff job. Finally, some people recognized that writing educational films was certainly applicable to what they were doing, and so I moved over to corporate writing."

Years later, Frankel found a niche that was perfect for her experience and background: speech writing. Her first assignment grew out of the work she was doing for a new product launch. "One of the production houses that I was working for at the time had a client that needed a speechwriter, and they asked if I'd like to do some speeches for this company," she says. "I had never done speeches before, but since I'd written for people on camera, it was the same kind of thing. I started doing speeches, and found it was something that I really liked, because it was a one-to-one relationship and it was extremely lucrative. So I became a speechwriter."

While I specialize in a handful of subjects, I occasionally take on work that's outside my usual areas of expertise. The stories usually take more time to research and write, but I find that I enjoy tackling new subjects. I've also discovered that being willing to write about a wider variety of subjects makes me more marketable to a broader range of clients, which is good for me in the long term. The more experience and knowledge I have, the more valuable I am as a writer—and it helps prevent me from getting bored churning out the same articles day after day.

"I think the key is to find ways to renew oneself," agrees Sam Greengard. "I specialize but I also try to work on projects that don't fit into this narrow little niche too much, because I find myself getting bored after a while and I think it's important to find new challenges and new markets."

When you're writing for a particular client, you should be serving that client. But most writers must juggle more than one client to keep their businesses running. That may mean that you're working on a customer service story for a trade publication, writing an internal newsletter for a corporation, ghostwriting a book for an expert, finishing an essay, and researching several consumer magazine stories at the same time. You want to achieve a balance where you can keep your clients happy—and coming back—while keeping your options open.

Even when times are flush, it's smart to keep more than one or two clients in your stable, says Jim Thornton. "I've seen people become really wedded to one thing. . . . Don't get too comfortable with any given relationship," warns Thornton. "Some people will sort of affix themselves to the side of a corporation or other client like a remora to a shark, but if your shark gets killed, you're up the creek."

Make sure you always have more than enough markets, agrees Lisa Collier Cool. "If you rely on only one or two clients or magazines, if a catastrophe occurs, you're very vulnerable," she says. "Whereas if you have a number of different markets, you're more protected from magazines folding, et cetera. All of that has happened to me, but thanks to diversifying I haven't been seriously wounded by these things."

Get on the Masthead: Becoming a Contributing Editor

While diversifying can help you protect your cash flow, steady relationships with clients usually mean you have to spend less time marketing yourself, leaving you more time to write—and make money. Think about it. Perhaps you already have a steady relationship with a publication. Or you'd like a more formal arrangement with the magazine. Consider whether a contributing editor (CE) gig is right for you. While he or she is usually listed on the publication's masthead, a CE isn't a true editor, but rather a freelance writer with an ongoing relationship with the publication.

CE relationships vary. Some CEs have a contract to write a certain number of stories for a certain amount of money each month; some write as many pieces as the editor needs for that issue; and others receive a retainer regardless of what they produce that month. CE gigs offer steady income and the opportunity to develop long-lasting relationships with publications, and having your name on the masthead can lead to other writing assignments as well.

Margaret Littman has had a number of CE jobs, including jobs at *Crain's Chicago Business, Teen, Snack Food Magazine, Bakery Production,* and *Marketing* during her freelance career. How did she get them? She simply asked. "I make sure it is an editor I feel appreciates me and someone with whom I want to work on a more regular basis," says Littman, who's currently a CE at *Chain Leader.* "If I get a vibe that they're really appreciative of what I do . . . I've asked to make it more formal."

Littman agrees that there are several advantages to being a CE. They often make more money than "standard" freelancers—some magazines have paid her a flat monthly retainer in addition to what she gets for the stories she writes. As a CE with a retainer agreement, she knows that she'll be receiving a check at the same time every month, which makes managing her cash flow a little easier.

Another aspect of being a CE that Littman, a former magazine editor, enjoys is the chance to work more closely with the editors on stories. "It's not just querying and then waiting to see if they accept it," she says. "I feel like I have a little more say in shaping the stories, and shaping the section or direction they take. I like that—for me, it's a good compromise. I don't miss editing on a day-to-day basis, but as a freelancer I do sometimes miss the big-picture editing in terms of thinking and developing a whole package for a story."

Of course, editors are always looking for stellar writing talent. After Jim Thornton won a National Magazine Award in 1998 for personal-service articles published in *Men's Journal*, he got his first CE contract with *GQ*—to the tune of $80,000. That contract lasted two years, and since then, he's found other CE gigs with national magazines. "Maybe editors are influenced by that kind of thing," Thornton admits. "Since then I've been able to get contracts with magazines where basically they want me to do X number of stories and columns per year and they pay me every month. That's made life much more predictable and steady." Today, he has several CE gigs, including ones with *Men's Health*, *Field & Stream*, and *National Geographic Adventurer*, which comprise about $100,000 worth of work a year. His CE gigs also give him visibility—he's often contacted by other big-name magazines that want him to write for them as well.

If you're going to approach a market about becoming a CE, you should already have a good relationship with the publication. Consider the benefits to the magazine of making you a CE so that you can make a strong argument in your favor. Point out that as a CE, you'll always be available for assignments, which will save them time and hassle looking for other writers. If you'll come up with ideas for the editors, show how this will benefit them as well. "If you have an agreement where you're going to come up with the ideas or maybe 50 percent of the ideas that you're writing, that's another time-saver for them," says Littman. "Make the point of why it's good for them."

Whether you receive a retainer or are paid per story, there's another plus to becoming a CE. While there are no guarantees in the freelance world, CE gigs tend to be a little more stable than simply writing for a magazine. "You have some job security," says Littman. "If they have to cut back, they'll give me something before they give it to another freelancer."

One drawback? As CE, the magazine you work for may ask you not to write for any of its competitors. That's the possible tradeoff to the relationship, but for most writers, it's worth it. If you want the opportunity for steady work, a higher profile, and possibly extra cash, take a closer look at the markets you write for regularly—a CE gig may be waiting to be discovered.

Crack the Most Lucrative Writing Market

Many writers are drawn to freelancing because they want to write magazine articles and books. If you want to make more money as a freelancer, don't overlook one of the most lucrative writing niches there is: freelancing for businesses and corporations. Maybe you think you don't have enough experience, or you don't know anything about the world of commerce. But while good writing skills are essential, you don't have to have ten years' copywriting background to crack this promising market. You do, however, have to understand what good business writing consists of, know who your clients are, and be able to deliver what they want.

Getting Started

Writers who work for corporations (we'll call them "copywriters," although most write more than ad copy) often charge hourly rates of $50 to $100 and up, depending on their expertise, or they charge by the project. When you're starting out in this niche, you probably can't charge as much as more experienced copywriters, but be careful not to undersell yourself either. Depending on where you're located, $40 to $60/hour is a fair rate for new writers.

If you have a business background, that's great, but if not, educate yourself about sales writing techniques. When writing ad copy, for example, you should know the difference between features and benefits (for the record, features are aspects of a company's product or service, while benefits are how they impact the customers' lives). Robert W. Bly has some excellent books on copywriting, including *Secrets of a Freelance Writer: How to Make $85,000 a Year*, that address the basics of writing pieces like brochures, ads, and sales letters.

Making Your Approach

The next step is finding clients, which may be easier than you think. Make a list of area companies you can contact, and spread the word that you're available for copywriting projects. If you don't have any samples to show, offer to write brochures, newsletters, or ads for your favorite nonprofit organization to make contacts and develop your portfolio. That's what potential clients will want to see, says Peter Bowerman, author of *The Well-Fed Writer: Financial Self-Sufficiency as a Freelance Writer in Six Months or Less*, who built his successful corporate-freelancing career from scratch.

"For starters, you need to build up some sort of portfolio. Just having articles is definitely a good start, but corporations are going to want to see more samples like the stuff they'd hire you to do, like brochures and newsletters," says Bowerman. "Also, if you don't have a big portfolio, or it's mostly periodical stuff, then I would focus on smaller companies because smaller companies are going to be much more likely to give a writer without a lot of experience a chance." Smaller firms are also less likely to have writers on staff, meaning they may need freelancers like you.

While it may be nerve-wracking at first, cold calls are the most efficient way to contact companies about writing projects, says Bowerman. "The law of averages absolutely, categorically works," he says. "If you make enough calls, you will get the business." He reminds phone-shy freelancers that the people they're calling expect to hear from copywriters and don't consider you telemarketers. "You're a professional selling a needed professional service to other professionals," says Bowerman. "I tell people to focus on action as opposed to results. . . . If you make fifty phone calls, it will happen. You don't have to worry about how each call is going to turn out—just make them."

Introduce yourself and ask if the person hires freelancers. Try to make an appointment for a face-to-face meeting where you can bring your portfolio. If your contact asks for more information, send a letter along with a few samples of your work, and then follow up on the package a few weeks later.

What Corporations Want

Writing for businesses requires many of the same skills as writing for a magazine or book publisher. You're expected to turn in well-written work on deadline and to behave professionally. If you've been used to working with hands-on editors, however, writing for corporate clients can be an eye-opener. Most expect you to come in, gather the information you need, and produce clean, professional-looking copy the first time out. "Corporations want the same kinds of things they expect from any vendor. They expect you to be reliable; they expect you to be dependable; they expect you to be easy to work with; and they expect you to deliver a product on time within the budget that you said you would," says Bowerman.

Being able to grasp the nature of the company, the motive behind the project you're working on, and the corporate culture is an essential part of copywriting. "They don't want to hold your hand through the process," says Bowerman. "They want someone who can come in and in the course of a meeting or an initial phone call get a sense of what the client wants, and ask the right questions to get all the information that they need right then, so you're not bothering them. It all comes down to that the client is hiring you to make their life easier, not to make it more complicated."

Just as you'd keep a publication's readership in mind when writing a magazine article, you must also keep the customers or corporate audience in mind while writing for a business. For example, I freelanced for several years for a small company that sells and installs technology modules to schools. The owner wanted me to write newsy stories about different school projects he could then use as part of his overall marketing materials. Each article, while written in a journalistic style, was an advertorial of sorts, designed to demonstrate to potential clients (in this case, teachers, administrators, and school board members), the advantages of installing modular technology. And when I was hired to write newsletters for "The Pampered Chef," I asked about the typical kitchen consultants who would be reading them, so I had a good feel for the audience. That kind of understanding is what makes you invaluable to corporations and can help ensure a steady flow of work. As your portfolio and experience grow, you can step up to the next level, working for larger corporations and raising your fees.

When I started writing for businesses, I had no copywriting background, but I did have experience writing for different editors, audiences, and types of markets. When you meet with a new client, ask the following questions to help you come up with writing that will produce the desired results:

- Who is your audience for the piece? For example, is it current customers or new customers?
- Who are your customers? Are they men or women? How old are they? Where do they live? What are their demographics? What do they care about? (Answering these questions will help you hone in on the audience for the piece.)
- How will the piece be used? What's the primary purpose for it? (For example, to let customers know about a new product?)

- Is the company selling a product or a service? What makes it better than and/or different from the competition? (The latter question helps you identify the features of the product or service that you may want to highlight.)
- How does the product or service improve the lives of the people who purchase it? (For example, does it save the customer money, improve physical appearance, reduce stress, protect health, or make the customer's home safer?) This question helps you identify the benefits of the product or service—and those will often be the strongest selling points. Usually, you lead with benefits and follow with additional information about features.
- What kind of "call to action" or special offer can you make? The call to action is the request that asks the customer to do something—"call us today to learn how we can save you money on life insurance," for example.
- What message do you want customers to remember?

When writing for businesses, keep the answers to the questions in mind. Use everyday language and avoid clichés and jargon. Remind your client that the customer is more interested in how this product or service benefits him or her than in the fact that the company has been in business for seventy-one years or just won a local award. Use specific examples, when appropriate, and avoid overly wordy copy. Show how this client surpasses the competition and remember to include a call to action or an incentive offer in every sales-writing piece you produce.

Even in today's economy, the market for good copywriters is promising. Another advantage is that once you're working with a company, it's likely to use you for a variety of writing projects. Bev Bachel works primarily for Fortune 500 companies, working in the areas of employee communications, total quality management, investor relations, and marketing communications. She also writes video scripts and speeches for CEOs and other senior-level executives. She typically works for a small number of clients, spending a lot of time working for each one.

"I primarily work for a small group of clients—maybe between three and six or eight clients a year," says Bachel. Her ideal client is what she calls an "open checkbook" client— where it wants her to work as many hours as she can. Her expertise has made her a valuable asset to the corporations she works for, which means she can charge higher rates. "My work has allowed me to be an expert in certain areas. Clients are paying me to develop an expertise that allows me to charge a higher hourly rate than if I were a freelance writer coming in without this expertise," she says. "Even just having a general good sense of business overall helps, so my client feels really comfortable with me meeting with a senior-level executive."

Balancing Work and Life

Whether you write for corporations or magazine editors, one of the most challenging things about being self-employed is that it's all too easy to spend eight, ten, twelve, or more hours a day working. That's fine when you need to make a deadline, but I've learned I can't work these kinds of hours without getting sick, exhausted, or extremely cranky.

Most successful writers don't work seventy-hour weeks. They balance their work lives with the rest of their lives. Karen Frankel plays squash and paints watercolors in her free time. She's also developed a thick skin and plenty of perspective when it comes to working with her often-demanding clients. "You can't take any of it personally when a client says, 'I didn't like it or you didn't do what I wanted or I'm not 100 percent happy with it.' You have to let it bounce off you," she says. "You can't stay in the career if clients say that to you often, but you can't let them put you in a funk. It *isn't* the most important thing in your life. While it seems that way for the two or three weeks that you're involved in it, it just isn't."

Becoming less sensitive to criticism helps, but you also have to draw the line in terms of protecting your "free" time. You want to be accessible and available to clients, but that doesn't mean you're expected to be on call 24-7. I don't answer my business line at night (unless I'm expecting a call), and I don't work evenings or weekends anymore unless a pressing deadline requires it.

Margaret Littman refuses to give out her cell phone number to clients and maintains separate personal and business telephone lines. "Even if I'm sitting there working, I don't answer the phone at 9 P.M. at night," says Littman. "I feel like I have to set the boundaries. Even if they're sort of artificial boundaries, doing that makes me feel like I can control this."

Building some "downtime" into even the busiest day can also make a big difference in your overall productivity and mood. If I don't run first thing in the morning, I'll sometimes take a long lunch and go to the gym and work out. It cuts into my official "work time," but I find I'm much more productive in the afternoon than if I sit at my desk all day. "It's important to have some downtime if possible," says Sam Greengard. "I try to maintain work-life balance by running, having breakfast or lunch with my kids (whenever possible), and taking occasional breaks to read magazines or browse the Internet for a few minutes. I try to spend a fair amount of time with my family, though when I get really busy it's tough. However, I always make it a point to have dinner with everyone and visit for a few minutes afterwards." Greengard, like many freelancers, also plans a long vacation at least once a year.

Leah Ingram balances her writing work with nonprofit activities and finds that it enhances her overall satisfaction with her chosen career. "Another way to be thankful for what you do is to give your time to give back like volunteering," says Ingram. "If you can balance doing good for others with doing good for yourself, I think you're a better, happier person."

Simply taking the time to determine your writing priorities can breathe new life into your writing career. Ingram recently decided she needed to take a new approach to her freelance career. "For the longest time, I've felt like I've been machine-gunning it. I knew what I liked to write about and I knew where to look for story ideas, but I felt like everything was cart before the horse," says Ingram, who writes books and articles and does spokesperson work for corporations. "I didn't feel like there was a focus on what I was doing and there was no way to measure my investment on my time or on anything."

She took several weeks to write a business plan that included writing a personal mission statement. That forced her to consider her experience and expertise and to hone in on where she wants to go long term, and it's changed the way she approaches her business. Instead of scattering different ideas to a variety of markets, she's positioning herself as a wedding, gift-giving, and celebrations expert. "It's almost like I'm back to square one but with a very different focus," says Ingram. "The whole idea is that everything has got to feed into everything else. The books lead to spokesperson work, the spokesperson work leads to books, the spokesperson work leads to articles, and so on." She has another long-term goal when her children are older: to start a foundation or nonprofit organization.

It's natural to become a bit disenchanted when you've finally reached the point of success. "I think it's true for all businesses. For us solo people, there's something in that. You have to say, 'what would get me excited again?'" says Bev Bachel. "I've been writing since I graduated from college and more and more I think that one of the great things about writing is that I can do it forever, but that's also one of the bad things about it." In addition to working for corporate clients, Bachel began pursuing projects she was interested in personally. In writing her first book on goal-setting for teens, *What Do You Really Want? How to Set a Goal and Go for It*, she discovered that she enjoyed writing about goal-setting. Now, she's working on a series of "Idea Girl Guides" designed to help women achieve their own goals. "I love what I do and I get paid to say what my corporate clients want to say, but I have things that *I* want to say," she says. "I think part of it is wanting to take control of my destiny."

Jennifer Lawler is an extremely productive writer, but she speaks frequently, appears at conferences, and keeps up her martial-arts training between deadlines. "People feel like that really gets them away from their writing, but I think it's all mutually reinforcing," she says. "If I'm teaching martial arts and going to professional development and attending classes, that makes me that much more of an expert and more able to write about new trends and issues that are coming up."

Listening to audiences to determine what they were looking for in martial arts made an impact on Lawler's writing career. Lawler began writing from a more personal standpoint instead of doing straight how-to books, and her readers responded. "All of a sudden things clicked for me. It really resonated with people," she says. "I wouldn't have gone that route if I hadn't been out there meeting my readers one and one, and finding out what they wanted from me."

Lawler says that flexibility has been her strongest asset in maintaining her career. "You have to be willing to go in different directions, to go where your career leads you," says Lawler. "I never really intended to be the queen of martial-arts writing, but that's what people wanted. People seemed to want more self-help and more personal experiences. I've gone through several transformations as a writer, and each time I feel refreshed."

The Rest of Your Life . . . Eek!

If you've reached the point in your career where writing full time is starting to feel like a drag (and it will happen—just wait), it may be time to set some new long-term goals. Even if you're newer to writing, it never hurts to have some kind of plan for the future. In chapter 1, I encouraged you to consider what subjects you were writing about, what markets you were writing for, and how much money you were making—and wanted to make. That's the first step. But now I encourage you to think more about your long-term writing career.

Do you want to freelance for the next two years? Five years? Ten years? The rest of your (gulp) life? For some reason, I find the idea of committing to anything—at least as far as my career goes—for the rest of my *life* terrifying. I like to plan on the fly. I'm not even sure what I want to do this weekend, let alone a few years from now.

As Bachel says, the great thing—and the bad thing—about writing is that you can do it for your entire life. But if you don't think about what you want from your writing career, you probably won't be satisfied with it over the long haul. Long-term freelancers have to have the physical and emotional fortitude and flexibility to adapt, grow, and change over the years. Sure, they adapt to the marketplace, but they also grow in terms of their personal and professional goals and learn to balance their work lives with the rest of their lives.

I lived this lesson firsthand as I worked on this book. Over the years, I'd gotten into a lucrative groove. I was churning out service articles like mad, but part of me was getting tired of covering the same subjects over and over. I'd thought I wanted to write fiction full time, but after trying that for a summer, I realized I don't have the stamina (at least not now) to devote my life to fiction writing. Then I debated whether I wanted to continue writing magazine articles or whether I should switch over to books completely.

Along the way, I started wondering if freelancing was still a good fit for me and began fantasizing about pursuing other careers. I thought about going back to school for my MFA, becoming a massage therapist, opening my own vegetarian restaurant, or becoming a full-time dog walker. I even went so far as to take a part-time job working at Trader Joe's, a sort of hippie grocery store known for its "Two-Buck Chuck" bottles of wine. I loved the physical exertion of the work and the constant customer contact, but I got tired of being on someone else's schedule and having to "ask off" to pursue my writing career. After several months, I decided that working for $9/hour wasn't for me. I needed to recast my career and figure out what I wanted to do long term and to stop simply responding and reacting to the market.

You can do the same by answering the following questions: What's the most satisfying part of your writing career?

_____

_____

_____

_____

What's the least satisfying part?

_____

_____

_____

_____

Picture your dream life as a writer. What are you doing? How are you spending your time? What kinds of projects are you working on? How does it differ from how you're spending your time today?

_____

_____

_____

_____

What aspects of your writing career would you change if you could, for example, market yourself less, write about more topics that interest you, or explore a broader range of types of writing?

_____

_____

_____

_____

Think about when you started your writing career. What were your goals then? Have you achieved them all? Did some goals fall by the wayside? What are your goals now? Are they meaningful to you?

_____

_____

_____

The most telling question of all: If you'd made enough money to never _have_ to write again, would you? What would you write? If you'd do something else, what would it be?

_____

_____

_____

_____

Once I went through that process, things got easier. When I'd started freelancing, my overriding goal was to make enough money so that I didn't have to practice law anymore.

That led to me taking a businesslike approach to my writing, developing relationships with clients, and specializing in several lucrative areas. Then, when I decided I wanted to crack the six-figure mark, I found it tremendously satisfying to meet that goal—at least at first. I was disappointed to discover that making money in and of itself wasn't enough to satisfy me. But it wasn't until I sat down and looked at the pros and cons of my writing career that I realized my current goals didn't mesh with the way I was spending my time.

I wanted to spend more time pursuing more projects that were of personal importance to me—like essays and fiction. Part of the reason was that I wanted to improve my writing skills, which meant taking on new challenges and branching away from the relatively simple service journalism articles I'd been writing for years. And I wanted to do more speaking, teaching, and consulting in the areas of fitness and nutrition. Switching gears meant taking some of the focus off of how much money I'd make and focusing more on my overall career satisfaction. In the short term, I'll make less money, but in the long term, I'll be happier and more satisfied as a writer.

Despite this book's title, I believe success as a writer *isn't* measured by the amount of money you make or whether you hit the six-figure mark. It's measured by the satisfaction you feel in pursuing this challenging career, regardless of your reasons for choosing it. Whether it's the freedom, the ability to reach and connect with people, the pleasure of making a living from your words, or simply the chance to pursue your dream of writing full time, I hope you, too, will take as much pleasure in freelancing as I have.

So go for it! Shoot for the six-figure mark—but make sure you enjoy a challenging, stimulating, and satisfying writing career along the way.

Get in Touch

Has this book made a difference in your bottom line? Helped you crack the six-figure mark? Or simply enabled you to become a more productive, successful writer? I welcome your feedback. You can reach me at *kelly@becomebodywise.com.* In the meantime, visit my Web site, *www.becomebodywise.com*, for more information about successful freelancing.

Appendix

If you're looking to make a living as a freelancer, there's no shortage of excellent resources out there. The following are some of my favorites:

Book Writing/Authorship

Damn! Why Didn't I Write That? How Ordinary People Are Raking in $100,000.00 . . . or More Writing Nonfiction Books & How You Can Too!
Mark McCutcheon (Quill Driver, 2001)
Includes some great advice on finding an underserved audience and catching editors' and readers' attention with your book

The Forest for the Trees: An Editor's Advice to Writers
Betsy Lerner (Riverhead, 2001)
Fascinating, funny, and full of anecdotes about the real world of book publishing

How to Write a Book Proposal, Third Edition
Michael Larsen (Writer's Digest, 2003)
Excellent how-to guide with plenty of practical advice

Jeff Herman's Guide to Book Publishers, Editors, and Literary Agents
Jeff Herman (Writer Books, 2004)
The scoop on hundreds of publishers, editors, and agents

Making the Perfect Pitch: Advice from 35 Top Book Agents
Katharine Sands (Kalmbach, 2004)
Advice on nabbing a great agent to represent your book ideas

Nonfiction Book Proposals Anybody Can Write: How to Get a Contract and Advance before Writing Your Book
Elizabeth Lyon (Perigree, 2002)

Another excellent book; I used both Larsen's and Lyon's books to write my first book proposal

Write the Perfect Book Proposal: 10 That Sold and Why Second Edition
Jeff Herman and Deborah Levine Herman (John Wiley & Sons, 2001)
Includes ten actual book proposals

Business Writing/Copywriting

Advertising Manager's Handbook, Second Edition
Robert W. Bly (Prentice Hall, 1998)
Excellent, *huge* resource; 793 pages covers everything from setting an ad budget to writing ads for a variety of media

The Copywriter's Handbook: A Step-by-Step Guide to Writing Copy That Sells
Robert W. Bly (Henry Holt, 1990)
Somewhat outdated but good basic info on getting ready to write, writing print ads and direct mail, and writing to communicate, to sell, and so on

Create the Perfect Sales Piece: A Complete Do-It-Yourself Guide to Creating Brochures, Catalogs, Fliers, and Pamphlets
Robert W. Bly (John Wiley & Sons, 1994)
Good resource; includes lots of suggestions for writing, planning, graphic design, and production issues

Persuading on Paper: The Complete Guide to Writing Copy That Pulls in Business
Marcia Yudkin (Plume, 1996)
Good overview; includes information on basic layout, different formats, and working with printers and graphic designers

The Well-Fed Writer: Financial Self-Sufficiency as a Freelance Writer in Six Months or Less
Peter Bowerman (Fanove, 2000)
Good overview of writing for corporations and businesses; lots of practical suggestions and samples; includes how to freelance full time, find clients, sell yourself, and the like

Words at Work: Business Writing in Half the Time with Twice the Power
Susan Benjamin (Addison-Wesley, 1997)
Excellent resource; covers the basics of business writing and avoiding common mistakes; includes models for reference

Inspiration/Motivation

Dojo Wisdom for Writers: 100 Simple Ways to Become a More Inspired, Successful, and Fearless Writer
Jennifer Lawler (Penguin Compass, 2004)
Feeling stuck? Insecure about your ability? Lawler's got 100 ways to maintain enthusiasm for your writing career.

Writer's Block and Other Problems of the Pen
Jenna Glatzer (Lyons, 2003)
Great advice for getting past writer's block

Magazine Writing

How to Write Irresistible Query Letters
Lisa Collier Cool (F & W, 2002)
Nuts and bolts on the all-important queries, with plenty of examples

Magazine Writing That Sells
Don McKinney (Writer's Digest, 1994)
Good overview of queries, interviewing, writing techniques, and so on

Ready, Aim, Specialize! Create Your Own Writing Specialty and Make More Money
Kelly James-Enger (Writer Books, 2003)
Covers magazine-writing basics and describes the ten hottest writing specialties and how to break into them

The Renegade Writer: A Totally Unconventional Guide to Freelance Writing Success
Linda Formichelli and Diana Burrell (Marion Street, 2003)

Helpful examination of the "rules" of magazine writing and when and why you should break them

You Can Write for Magazines
Greg Daugherty (Writer's Digest, 1999)
Pretty good guide for beginners; offers practical tips and suggestions

Market Resources

Bacon's Magazine Directory and *Bacon's Newspaper Directory*
(Primedia Information, 2004)
Published annually; includes 70,000 magazines and newspapers, divided into subject headings

Gale Directory of Publications and Broadcast Media, 138th Edition
(Gale Group, 2004)
This multivolume series is updated annually and includes over 54,500 newspapers, magazines, journals, and other periodicals, subdivided by city and state

The Standard Periodical Directory, 2004, Twenty-seventh Edition
(Oxbridge Communications, 2003)
Published annually; lists more than 75,000 U.S. and Canadian publications by subject

The Writer's Handbook (updated annually)
Elfrieda Abbe, editor (Writer Books, 2003)
Excellent market guide; includes articles about writing, marketing, and publishing

Writer's Market (updated annually)
Katie Struckel Brogan and Robert Brewer, editors (Writer's Digest, 2003)
Popular market guide; includes rate information and how-to pieces

Running Your Writing Business

The ASJA Guide to Freelance Writing: A Professional Guide to the Business, for Nonfiction Writers of All Experience Levels
Timothy Harper, editor (St. Martin's Griffin, 2003)

Excellent overview of issues facing full-time and part-time free-lancers

How to Open and Operate a Home-Based Writing Business, Second Edition
Lucy V. Parker (Globe Pequot, 1997)
Excellent resource; covers most nuts and bolts of starting a free-lance business

J. K. Lasser's Taxes Made Easy for Your Home-Based Business, Fifth Edition
Gary W. Carter (John Wiley & Sons, 2003)
Excellent "plain-English" guide to what you need to know about taxes, deductions, and the like

Secrets of a Freelance Writer: How to Make $85,000 a Year, Second Edition
Robert W. Bly (Henry Holt, 1997)
Good advice on getting started, marketing your services, and running your freelance business

Tax Tips for Freelance Writers, Photographers, and Artists, 2004
Julian Block (order by sending $9.95 for an e-mailed copy or $14.95 for a postpaid, printed copy to Julian Block, 3 Washington Sq., #1-G, Larchmont, NY 10538)
Good reference guide specifically for writers, with plenty of practical examples and advice

Too Lazy to Work, too Nervous to Steal: How to Have a Great Life as a Freelancer
John Clausen (Writer's Digest, 2001)
Interesting read on the freelance life; includes anecdotes from other freelancers and general advice on the pros and cons of free-lancing

Writer's Digest Handbook of Making Money Freelance Writing
Amanda Boyd et al., editors (Writer's Digest, 1997)
Excellent; covers nearly every type of writing opportunity and gives advice on setting up your office, staying motivated, and so on

The Writer's Legal Companion: The Complete Handbook for the Working Writer, Third Edition
Brad Bunnin and Peter Beren (Perseus, 1998)
Legal advice for freelancers

The Writer's Legal Guide: An Authors Guild Desk Reference, Third Edition
Tad Crawford and Kay Murray (Allworth, 2002)
More legal advice for freelancers

Organizations/Web Resources

American Society of Journalists and Authors
1501 Broadway, Suite 302
New York, NY 10036
Phone: 212-997-0947
Fax: 212-778-7414
Web: *www.asja.org*
This 1,100-member organization consists of nonfiction writers, most of whom are freelancers. $195/year; I've found it worth the money for the contract and rate info members can access.

Authors Guild
31 E. 28th St., 10th Floor
New York, NY 10016
Phone: 212-563-5904
Fax: 212-564-5363
Web: *www.authorsguild.org*
This 8,100-member organization consists of professional book and magazine writers. First-year dues: $90. Offers health, hospitalization, dental, and life insurance to members.

Cassell Network of Writers/Writers-Editors Network
PO Box A
North Stratford, NH 03590
Phone: 603-922-8338
Web: *www.writers-editors.com*
Members have access to market info, publishing updates, and other information; basic membership: $39/year.

Freelance Success
Web: *www.freelancesuccess.com*
Freelance Success includes a weekly e-mail newsletter with detailed market reports; members have access to an onsite bulletin board. $89/year; great resource.

National Writers Union
113 University Place, 6th Floor
New York, NY 10003-4527
Phone: 212-254-0279
Fax: 212-254-0673
Web: *www.nwu.org*
The NWU consists of freelance writers, journalists, authors, and other writers. $95–$260/year. Offers health insurance to New York–based members.

Index

A

Accounting, 63, 95–106
Agents, 87–88, 90, 237–243
American Society of Journalists and Authors (ASJA), 87, 93–94, 235, 236, 252–253, 258
Assignment types, 210–214
Assistants, 195–196
Attitude, 3–7, 9–14, 36–38, 67–68, 197, 207–210
Authors Guild, 40, 258

B

Bacon's Magazine Directory, 168
Bacon's Newspaper Directory, 168
Benefits, 40–41
Bidding, 145–149
Billing, 149–151
Bookkeeping. *See* Accounting
Books, 87–88, 134–139
    proposals, 134–139
Budgeting, 26–30
Business of writing. *See* Writing as a business

C

Career goals, 69–74, 265–287
Children, 16, 47, 64–67
Client base, 32–36, 70, 216–236
    closing the deal, 219–220
    diversity, 220, 221, 271–272
    identifying market, 221–222
    loss of client, 233–234, 272
    marketing, 216–222
    payment, 234–236
    regular clients, 219, 220–221, 222–223
    relationship with, 222–229
    specialization, 221, 271
Collaboration, 237–264
    agents, 237–243
    conferences, 258–260
    contracts, 248–251
    experts, 246–251
    other writers, 251–260
    professional organizations, 258
    sources, 243–246
    speaking, 260–264

Computer, 49–52, 56–57, 60,
     194
Conferences, 258–260
Contracts, 78–79, 84–94,
     167–168, 248–251,
     252–253
Contributing editor,
     272–275
Copyright, 74–77
Copywriting. *See* Corporate
     writing
Corporate writing, 34–35, 87,
     139–145, 168, 218,
     275–280
   marketing, 218
   pitches, 139–145,
     276–279
Cover letters, 131

D
Day care. *See* Children
Deadlines, 12–13, 227,
     229–230
Deductions. *See* Taxes
Depreciation. *See* Taxes

E
Editor & Publisher, 175
Electronic media, 91
E-mail, 52, 201–202, 204–207,
     257
Encyclopedia of Associations,
     200

Equipment, 48–63
   computer, 49–52, 56–57,
     60, 194
   fax machine, 55–56
   Internet, 51–52
   Personal Digital Assistant
     (PDA), 57–58
   recording devices, 56
   software, 50–51, 57,
     61–62
   stationery, 53–54
   telephone, 53, 56
   Web site, 54–55
Exercise, 42–43
Expenses, 29–30, 63,
     98–106
Experts. *See* Sources

F
Fact-checking, 232–233
Family, 16, 30, 47, 64–67
Fax machine, 55–56
Featurewell, 175
Fees, 69–94, 180–181,
     187–189, 252–254
   bidding, 145–149
   reprint, 174–175
Filing systems, 62–63
Finances. *See* Benefits;
     Budgeting; Income;
     Retirement; Taxes
Follow-up letters,
     130–131
Foreign rights, 89–90

FreelanceSuccess.com,
252
Full-time writing, 15–44,
265–287
Furniture, 58–61

G
*Gale Directory of Publications
and Broadcast Media,*
168
Goal-setting, 6–7, 69–74.
See also Career
goals

H
Health, 42–43
Health insurance, 29, 40

I
Image. *See* Attitude;
Professionalism
Income, 4–7, 15–17, 26–32,
38–41, 63, 69–94,
180–181, 234–236,
253
Indemnification, 91–92
Internal Revenue Service.
See Taxes
Internet, 51–52, 198,
199–201
Interviews, 195, 199–204,
212–214

finding experts,
199–201
preparation, 202–204
scheduling, 201–202
Invoices, 149–151

K
Kill fees, 92, 231–232

L
Leisure time, 41–42,
280–283

M
Magazines
contracts, 87, 90–91,
168
marketing, 33–34, 35,
110–134, 218
Marketing, 63–64, 69–72,
216–222, 276–277
closing the deal,
219–220
diversity, 220, 221
identifying market,
221–222
magazines, 33–34, 35,
110–134, 218
regular clients, 219,
220–221, 222–223
Municipal regulations,
47–48

N
National Writers Union, 87, 94, 236, 258
Negotiation, 77–94
  contracts, 78–79, 86–94, 252–253
  electronic rights, 91
  fees, 79, 81–86, 92–94
  foreign rights, 89–90
  kill fees, 92
  publication rights, 77–79, 84–85
  reprint rights, 77, 78, 84, 167–175
  resale rights, 89–90
Networking, 19, 24–25, 34, 63–64, 251–260
Newspapers, 34

O
Office, 45–68
  equipment, 48–63
  expenses, 29–30, 98–100, 105–106
  home, 45, 46–48
  location, 45–48
  renting, 46–47
  supplies, 197
Online discussion groups, 19, 24–25

P
Payment. *See* Income
Personal Digital Assistant (PDA), 57–58
Personality traits, 19–24
Pitch letters, 131–134. *See also* Query letters
Professionalism, 9–14, 223–236
  attitude, 223–224, 225–227
  availability, 224–225
  deadlines, 12–13, 227, 229–230
  problem situations, 229–236
  quality, 227–228
Professional organizations, 258
Profiles. *See* Interviews
Proposals, 145–149
  book, 134–139
  magazine, 33–34, 35, 110–134, 218
  See also Query letters
Publication rights. *See* Copyright
Publicity, 63–64, 249–250

Q
Query letters, 108–139
  books, 134–139
  magazines, 110–134
  See also Templates

R

Reasons to write, 3–6,
    24–26
Recording devices, 56
Record-keeping, 61–63
Reprint rights, 77–78, 84,
    167–175
    fees, 174–175
    markets, 168–174
    syndicates, 175
Resale rights, 89–90
Research, 152–167, 170–171,
    197–204
    Internet, 198, 199–200
    interviews, 199–204
Reslanting, 152–179
Retirement, 40–41
Rights. *See* Copyright

S

Scheduling. *See* Time
    management
Social contacts, 17–19
Software, 50–51, 57,
    61–62
Sources, 199–204,
    243–246
Speaking, 260–264
Specialization, 7–9, 33, 35,
    175–179, 210–211, 221
Standard Periodical Directory,
    168
Stationery, 53–54
Syndicates, 175

T

Taxes, 29, 95–106
    business vs. hobby,
        96–98
    deductions, 53, 98–106,
        258, 260
    depreciation, 105–106
Telephone, 53, 56
Templates, 108–151, 218–219,
    276–279
    book proposals,
        134–139
    corporate pitches,
        139–145, 276–279
    cover letters, 131
    follow-up letters,
        130–131
    interviews, 195,
        212–214
    invoices, 149–151
    magazine proposals,
        110–134
    marketing, 131–134,
        218–219
    proposals, 145–149
    query letters, 108–139
Time management,
    180–214
    assignment types,
        210–214
    assistants, 195–196
    e-mail, 204–207
    interviews, 195,
        199–204
    office supplies, 197

Time management, (*cont.*)
   paid vs. unpaid work,
      196–197
   prioritizing, 191–193
   profiles, 212–214
   repeat clients, 196
   research, 197–204
   scheduling, 182–188,
      190–191, 194, 218
   tracking hours, 182–188
   work habits, 193–194,
      207–210
   working hours, 190–191
Topics, 7–9, 152–179, 261. *See
   also* Specialization
Travel expenses, 100–101,
   258, 260

W
Web site, 54–55
Work habits, 207–210
Working hours, 190–191
Workload, 38–40
Writer's Handbook, 168
Writer's Market, 168,
   175
Writers' organizations, 19,
   24–25. *See also*
   American Society of
   Journalists and Authors;
   Authors Guild;
   National Writers
   Union
Writing as a business,
   2–106